A Guide to Cleveland's Sacred Landmarks

A Guide to Cleveland's Sacred Landmarks

Foster Armstrong

Richard Klein

Cara Armstrong

Photographs by

Thomas L. Lewis

With a Foreword by

The Reverend Thomas F. Pike

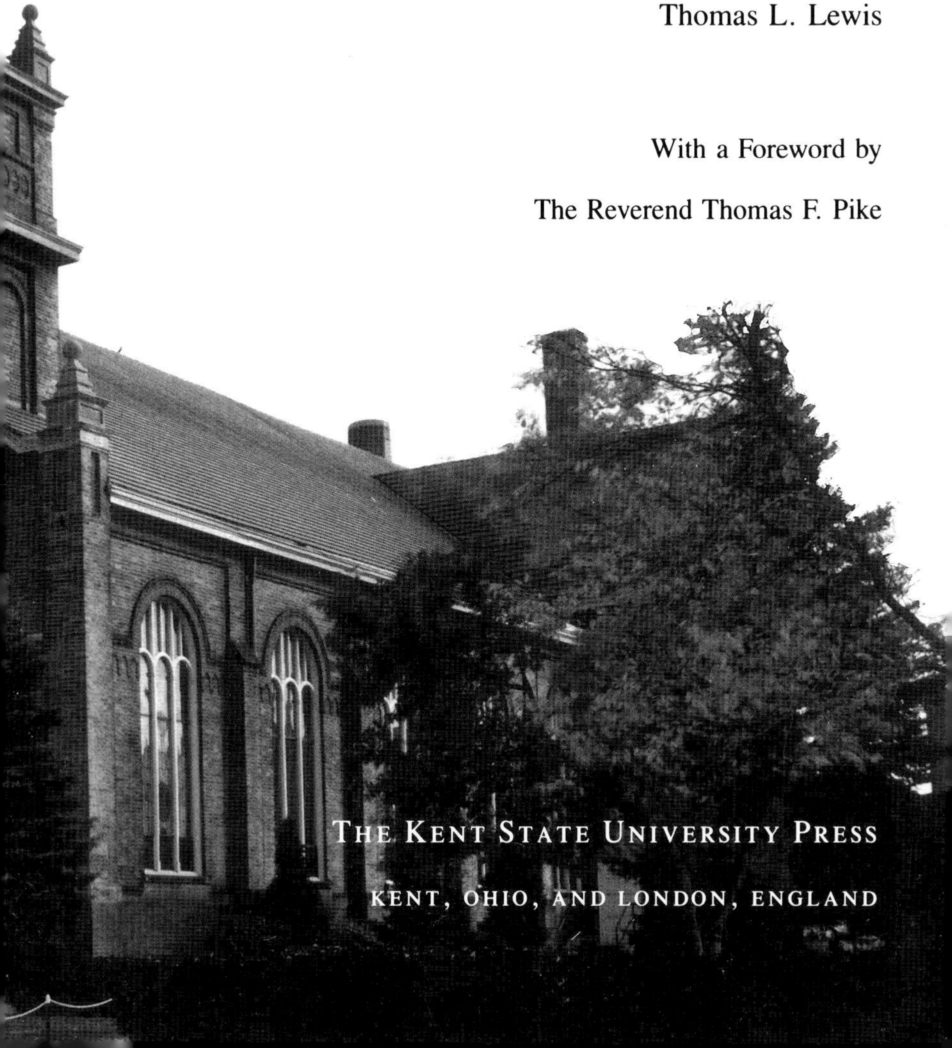

THE KENT STATE UNIVERSITY PRESS

KENT, OHIO, AND LONDON, ENGLAND

© 1992 by The Kent State University Press,

Kent, Ohio 44242

ALL RIGHTS RESERVED

Library of Congress Catalog Card Number 91-30918

ISBN 0-87338-454-7

Manufactured in the United States of America

This project was made possible in part by the OAC/OHC Joint Program,

a program of the Ohio Arts Council and the Ohio Humanities Council,

65 Jefferson Avenue, Columbus, Ohio 43215,

and the John P. Murphy Foundation, 100 Public Square,

Cleveland, Ohio 44113.

Library of Congress Cataloging-in-Publication Data

Armstrong, Foster, 1936–

A guide to Cleveland's sacred landmarks / Foster Armstrong,

Richard Klein, and Cara Armstrong ; photographs by Thomas L. Lewis ;

with a foreword by Thomas F. Pike.

p.   cm.

Includes bibliographical references (p.   ) and index.

ISBN 0-87338-454-7 (paper : alk.) ∞

1. Cleveland (Ohio)—Description—Guide-books.   2. Churches—Ohio—
Cleveland—Guide-books.   3. Sacred space—Ohio—Cleveland—Guide-
books.   4. Architecture—Ohio—Cleveland—Guide-books.   I. Klein,

Richard, 1949–   .   II. Armstrong, Cara, 1969–   .   III. Title.

F499.CA76   1992   91-30918

917.71′320443—dc20

British Library Cataloging-in-Publication data are available.

Contents

Foreword

THE REVEREND THOMAS F. PIKE

It is often difficult within the religious community to convince members of the importance of maintaining landmark buildings. There is even a suspicion by some that a person concerned about the maintenance of buildings is somehow not faithful to the religious agenda. As a member of the clergy, I have always felt that people were more important than buildings, that the struggle for human dignity and justice in this society is of primary importance. I have never wanted to be a museum curator. And I have never felt that I would sacrifice the basic agenda of the Church for the preservation of a building. However, I have learned that you can't do very much without buildings. Buildings are critical for a community that seeks to serve and interact with society. And some religious communities are privileged to possess, as part of their resources, great sacred landmarks. Buildings say something about who we are and where we have been and that we are here to stay. Buildings express a view of human life that is deeply rooted in the biblical understanding of life. Therefore, we must raise money to preserve and maintain them.

The German philosopher Ernst Bloch (1885–1977) wrote a collection of books called *The Principles of Hope.* In one volume, he said that architecture is the external sign of hope. Likewise, Solzhenitsyn said that the churches in Moscow's Kremlin should not be torn down because they are part of the hard life of Russia. To tear them down would be to rip out the heart of the nation. Religious institutions are in many ways the heart of our communities, the heart of our neighborhoods, the heart of our cities. They are, in the best sense, landmarks.

We call them landmarks because they mark the land, not just in a geographical sense, but in a humanistic sense. Nowhere is the fabric and texture of our pluralistic American society better documented than in our religious architecture. Our sacred architecture shows how people from different parts of the world, in different times, have lived together, worked together, struggled, fought, compromised, and made their contributions. Across the face of this nation, our religious buildings give testimony to the possibility that people from different traditions, backgrounds, races, and ethnic groups can together forge a society that will promote justice and dignity.

In some neighborhoods religious buildings are all that is left. These neighborhoods have been decimated by crisis, conflict, and economic oppression. In

Thomas F. Pike, rector of Calvary and St. George's parish in New York City, is national chair of Partners for Sacred Places and of the advisory committee for *Common Bond,* a newsletter on church and synagogue maintenance and repair. In New York City he chairs Partnership for the Homeless and is a trustee in the Cathedral Church of St. John the Divine. On September 23, 1989, Dr. Pike presented these remarks at Trinity Cathedral, Cleveland, Ohio, at "Inspired Partnerships: A Conference on the Management and Restoration of Historic Religious Buildings," sponsored by the Cleveland Restoration Society and the Urban Design Center of Northeastern Ohio. Dr. Pike has graciously permitted us to use his remarks from that day as a foreword to this book.

community after community across this nation, the religious buildings stand out as the only statement of hope and continuity amidst burned-out automobiles, empty buildings, and battered streets. A raised spire in the middle of chaos and human tragedy is a landmark of possibility, a community center, a place to serve. What does this landmark building say? It says that a religious community is here to stay; others may turn their backs, but here is a place that will continue to welcome. A landmark religious building stands as an icon, a holy picture, a sign of hope.

Is it any wonder that political leaders often turn to religious leaders in desperation when confronted with the problems of the homeless and the hungry? There is no conflict between the stewardship of a landmark church or synagogue and a ministry serving the poor, oppressed, and the hungry. For example, St. George's Church is on the National Register of Historic Places, is a city and state landmark, and also has the longest history in New York City of providing shelter for the homeless, welcoming them every night into a quiet refuge. There is no issue as to whether the buildings are more important than people. People are always important, and our buildings can do much for them. They can be the context from which we reach out; they can be the places where the community is reshaped; they can be the loci where we celebrate the ebb and flow of life in cities and neighborhoods.

No one familiar with the challenge of maintaining and preserving important religious architecture will underestimate the task. The preservation of sacred landmarks taxes the imagination and stamina of even trained engineers and architects. Few clergy have ever had a course in real estate management or formally studied building issues. And yet clergy are sent forth to chair, administer, and coordinate maintenance programs worth millions of dollars. No one has easy answers on how a great building, an important architectural gem, should best be preserved. But, arm in arm, Jews and Christians, ordained and lay leaders, people who are concerned directly with the program and agenda of religious institutions must find ways to work together so that this nation will not lose its most important sacred landmarks.

As we seek to preserve these great sacred structures with integrity, we must do it in a way that does not jeopardize our basic religious agenda, burn out the clergy and lay leadership, or squander financial resources. How can we do this? We can do this by finding the people who may not wish to be part of the temple or the church but are willing to support this cause because they recognize that sacred landmarks are signs of hope. There are individuals willing to contribute to the maintenance of a spire, to the preservation of stained-glass windows, or to keeping a roof on. They may not want to be a part of the theological or spiritual agenda that may energize us, but we can develop partnerships with them.

If there is anything that is apparent to me as a religious person, as a person whose worldview has been shaped by scripture, prayer, and a life led within the community of faith, it is that there is nothing more authentic to the religious agenda than a concern for the environment in which people live. The air, the water, the food we eat, or the buildings we live in, these things comprise the landscape in which our life is lived and affect the way we think and act. Sacred landmarks are an important part of this landscape, for through these structures we symbolically interact with society. But we must also interact with society through the shaping of our environment, neighborhoods, and cities. The religious community everywhere should actively participate in the development of preservation laws so that they reflect the authentic and unique agenda of the religious community. I look for religious leaders who will enter the debate for the welfare of their city or neighborhood with courage and wisdom, with conviction, and with an admitted agenda shaped by scripture, prayer, and the experiences of community faith, but also with a point of view that the welfare of the city, the welfare of the total community, is an authentic part of the religious agenda.

Sacred landmarks communicate many things. They communicate grandeur; they communicate worship. They also communicate hope—hope to the people who may be unknown to us by name, even unseen to us in our busy lives. Therefore, preserve these sacred landmarks not only to serve God, but to serve countless people and future generations that you will probably never know but who will, nevertheless, thank you.

Acknowledgments

We have had a great deal of help and support during the time it has taken to conceive and create *A Guide to Cleveland's Sacred Landmarks,* and here we would like to express our feelings of gratitude to everyone who helped us.

Four organizations worked together in this effort: The Urban Design Center of Northeastern Ohio, based in Kent State University's School of Architecture and Environmental Design; the Sacred Landmarks Research Group, based in Cleveland State University's College of Arts and Sciences; the Cleveland Landmarks Commission, based in the Department of City Planning in Cleveland City Hall; and the Cleveland Restoration Society, a regional organization committed to preserving the best of Cleveland's past.

The Urban Design Center had a small group of people working part time on the project for most of 1990, with the group fluctuating in size from three to six according to the demands of the work. Ann Bryner Hedington was involved from beginning to end. She happily typed the original proposal for funding, suffered through several iterations of text, and helped in preparing the final report. Dr. Virginia Benson, as always, pointed us in the right direction, introduced us to very important people, and assisted in getting a grant from the John P. Murphy Foundation. Students in Ohio's public universities hired part time by the Center for this project have included Tina Araujo, Cara Armstrong, Amie Brown, Amy Doyle, Claudette Krause, Siew Hong Ong, Lee Phillips-Goodman, Melanie Porcella, Melanie Schwentz, Traci Thomas, and John Walkosak.

The Sacred Landmarks Research Group was helpful in many ways. They provided a Cleveland office for the project and put us in touch with Tom Lewis, who generously gave of his time and talent to photograph and print each and every picture in this *Guide.* Much of the research material for this *Guide* can be found in the files of the Sacred Landmarks Research Group, College of Arts and Sciences, Cleveland State University. Mike Wells helped us organize the format of the book and assisted in writing the introduction. Mike Tevesz was the most enthusiastic supporter of this project from its inception to its completion. He read each draft, made helpful suggestions, and provided encouragement when we needed to be reenergized.

John Cimperman, director of the Cleveland Landmarks Commission, permitted us to use the commission's files, helped prepare the introductory comments to the *Guide,* and assisted in the preparation of the Inspired Partnerships conference. Following his retirement, we were ably assisted by Bob Kaiser, secretary of the Landmarks Commission.

On two occasions the Cleveland Restoration Society provided us with the opportunity to showcase our work. In December 1988, eight churches included in the *Guide* were visited by about 100 local citizens on a bus tour. In September, seventeen additional churches in the *Guide* were included on a bus tour as part of "Inspired Partnerships: A Conference on the Management and Restoration of

Historic Religious Buildings.'' In both instances Kathleen Crowther, executive director of the Cleveland Restoration Society, did the lion's share of the organizational work. We also wish to thank Holly Fiala of the Midwest Office of the National Trust for Historic Preservation for encouraging our interest in this project.

The staffs of the Cleveland Public Library, the Western Reserve Historical Society, and the Catholic Diocese of Cleveland were all most helpful to us, as were people in the individual churches that we contacted. In particular we wish to thank Christine L. Krosel at the archives of the Catholic Diocese and Claudia Fechter of the Temple Library and Museum at Silver Park for their knowledgeable assistance and efforts.

We also wish to graciously acknowledge Patricia Moots of the OAC/OHC Joint Program and Herb Strawbridge of the John P. Murphy Foundation for their encouragement and financial assistance. And, of course, we extend our thanks to the Urban University Program of the Ohio Board of Regents and the General Assembly of the State of Ohio for their continuing support of The Urban Design Center of Northeastern Ohio.

Finally, we wish to thank our friends and families for their caring and understanding.

Foster Armstrong
Richard Klein
Cara Armstrong

Introduction

Since the Middle Ages in Europe and the eighteenth century in America, sacred landmarks have served as spiritual, civic, and cultural centers. They have also often become significant places in our daily lives. Among the most important architectural treasures in our neighborhoods, sacred landmarks also often contain exemplary works of art. They tell the story of the particular place in which they are located and how that place has changed over time. They bring back memories of important events in our lives: baptisms, marriages, deaths. They help to guide us and sustain us in the happy and trying times between.

In Cleveland, many of the sacred landmarks express the city's great ethnic diversity. Churches and synagogues, through their architecture, art, and craft, have enabled each ethnic group to express its most noble aspirations. Sacred landmarks are the anchors of neighborhoods, symbols for a group's desire to put down roots in Cleveland. The resulting ensemble of ethnic landmarks contributes much to the city's dynamic and visually interesting architecture. Whether seen from afar in the thirteen domes of St. Theodosius Russian Orthodox Cathedral or viewed up close in the Germanic wood carvings and stained glass of St. Stephen Roman Catholic Church, each structure contributes to a diversity of visual form that is unique to Cleveland.

While Cleveland's sacred landmarks exhibit a wide variety of ornamentation and style, they nevertheless evolve out of two standard geometric forms, the line and the circle. The line is used to emphasize procession and hierarchy while the circle is used to promote the concept of unity between clergy and laity and emphasize the preaching of the Word. A house of worship based on the procession is often laid out in the form of a Latin cross (with one axis longer than the other) or a simple rectangle preceded by a tower often capped with a steeple. A church or a temple that emphasizes unity often has a central focus and is laid out in the form of a Greek cross, a circle, or an octagon. Both forms were used early, became standard, and have served liturgical and symbolic purposes throughout the history of religious architecture.

Because of these liturgical differences, one might expect, therefore, that Roman Catholic churches, at least until Vatican II, would have taken a linear form and Protestant churches and Hebrew synagogues would have selected a form based on the circle. Nevertheless, there are a number of Protestant churches in Cleveland that belie this logic. For example, the Church of the Covenant on the East Side and Trinity Evangelical Lutheran Church on the West Side are examples of Protestant processional-aisle churches. Apparently these and many other Protestant congregations were more persuaded by the tradition of the built form than liturgical needs when designing and constructing these facilities. On the other hand, Pilgrim Congregational, East Mount Zion Baptist, Temple Tifereth Israel, and the First and Fifth Churches of Christ Scientist represent centrally focused preaching places. Still other sacred landmarks, notably the new St. Andrew's

Abbey, successfully incorporate both the tradition of procession (line) while encouraging participation among worshipers (circle).

Cleveland's sacred landmarks, like the city, have matured. There are few new structures, but change continues within the existing city fabric. The city's population diminished by almost one-third between 1930 and 1990, with many of the original ethnic groups departing and newer groups arriving. The population that moved in is poorer than the population that moved out, and the city's building stock is aging. Thus, it is not unusual to find a magnificent sacred structure towering over a neighborhood in the midst of decline.

This ironic juxtaposition of finely wrought art and architecture amid deteriorating surroundings is evident throughout the city. A growing concern is that some of these very fine buildings are becoming isolated from the population. The declining population and loss of the original immigrant groups combined with such problems as rising utility costs, increased labor expenses, changing transportation patterns, and delayed maintenance have greatly affected the conditions of the city's religious buildings, as well as many other older structures. City, state, and federal governments have developed programs of economic assistance to encourage the reuse of older and historic buildings as part of the Economic Recovery Act. However, these funds are not available for religious buildings, so churches have come to rely on their own resources, which are often inadequate. Today there is a need for assistance in preserving the buildings that have been entrusted to us. If we do not, within a decade we will lose many of our most historically and architecturally significant buildings.

Yet, there is no single successful formula to save buildings; we must make value judgments. Such judgments can only come from careful study. The first step in any preservation plan is to determine what structures are most significant to the city, then to the neighborhoods. That is the major purpose of this book: to better acquaint people with the architectural, aesthetic, and cultural resources represented in Cleveland's enormous stock of sacred landmarks. Hopefully, this will lead to an enlightened management of these important resources.

To encourage visits to these landmarks, all located within the city limits of Cleveland, ten driving tours have been organized. The tours are organized as follows:

1. *The Dual Hub Corridor:* Downtown, the Euclid Corridor, and University Circle
2. *North Central Cleveland:* Goodrich-Kirtland, Hough, and St. Clair–Superior
3. *Northeast Cleveland:* Glenville–Forest Hill, Collinwood, and Euclid Green
4. *South Central Cleveland:* Central, Fairfax, and Kinsman
5. *Southeast Cleveland:* Buckeye-Woodland, Shaker, Mt. Pleasant, Lee-Miles, Corlett, and Union
6. *The Broadway Corridor:* Broadway and Miles Park
7. *The Near West Side:* Ohio City and Tremont
8. *West Side South:* Old Brooklyn, Archwood-Denison, and Fulton Clark

9. *West Central Cleveland:* West Boulevard–Lorain, Edgewater-Cudell, and Detroit Shoreway

10. *West Park:* Jefferson, Kamms Corners, Riverside, and Puritas-Longmead

Directions for the tour are given at the beginning of each chapter. The tour description is accompanied by a map that identifies each landmark mentioned in the text. Sacred landmarks that appear in bold type in each tour are elaborated on in the pages following the tour. For each such sacred landmark there is a photo and a historical and architectural description. The current name of the landmark is listed first; the founding congregation, if different from the current congregation, is listed next. The date of construction and the name of the architect, if known, along with the building address are also provided.

CHAPTER ONE

Sacred Landmarks in the Dual Hub Corridor

Unlike the other communities described in the *Guide*, the Dual Hub Corridor is not made up of contiguous neighborhoods. Rather, it is defined on the west by Public Square—the city's office, retail, and government hub—and on the east by University Circle—the city's cultural, educational, and institutional hub. The two hubs are connected along the Euclid Corridor, which centers on Euclid Avenue but also encompasses all of the land area between Chester Avenue on the north and Carnegie Avenue on the south. The Dual Hub Corridor contains Cleveland's two most important centers of activity as well as its most important street. Thus, it is not surprising that this district also contains many of the city's most significant sacred landmarks.

TOUR

Begin this tour at Public Square on Superior Avenue traveling east. Look to the north and note the **FIRST PRESBYTERIAN CHURCH**, known locally as **THE OLD STONE CHURCH (1)**. Located on the northwest corner of the Square in the midst of skyscrapers, this is one of the oldest buildings in downtown Cleveland. Travel east for five blocks. At the northeast corner of Superior Avenue and East Ninth Street is **ST. JOHN ROMAN CATHOLIC CATHEDRAL (2)**, another old structure that was completely rebuilt after World War II. Continue to move east for four more blocks. At the corner of Superior and East 17th Street, turn south (right) and note **ST. PETER ROMAN CATHOLIC CHURCH (3)** on the southeast corner of the intersection. It is one of the oldest churches in the city and is now in the process of being restored. The cap on the central tower is temporary and will be replaced in the future with a tall spire.

Travel south on East 17th Street. At the end of the street turn east (left) onto Euclid Avenue. Euclid Avenue, called Buffalo Road until 1825 because it was a major route to Buffalo, follows what used to be the Native American Lake Shore Trail. By the mid–nineteenth century, many of Cleveland's elite built their mansions along Euclid Avenue, earning it the name Millionaires' Row. The growth of the city's commercial district to the east encouraged the abandonment of Euclid as a residential street, and today only seven of the forty Millionaires' Row mansions remain standing.[1]

Travel east on Euclid Avenue for four blocks. At East 22d Street note **TRINITY EPISCOPAL CATHEDRAL (4)** to the south. Designed by local architect Charles Schweinfurth, Trinity is one of Cleveland's finest sacred structures.

Continue east on Euclid over the Innerbelt until East 30th Street. Note **ZION EVANGELICAL LUTHERAN CHURCH (5)** at the southwest corner of the intersection of East 30th and Prospect, one block south. Also note at the southeast corner of East 30th and Euclid the **FIRST UNITED METHODIST CHURCH (6)**, designed by another important local architect, J. Milton Dyer. Travel east on Euclid for two blocks and notice the rather ornate **ST. PAUL SHRINE (7)** located at the

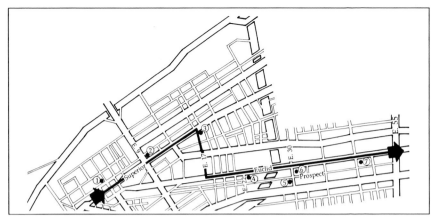

DOWNTOWN

1. First Presbyterian Church
   (the Old Stone Church)
2. St. John Roman Catholic Cathedral
3. St. Peter Roman Catholic Church

4. Trinity Episcopal Cathedral
5. Zion Evangelical Lutheran Church
6. First United Methodist Church
7. St. Paul Shrine

southeast corner of the East 40th Street–Euclid Avenue intersection. Originally built as a Protestant church, St. Paul's is now Catholic. Continue to move east on Euclid under the railroad at East 55th and onto East 71st Street. Then turn south (right).

Travel south on East 71st for one block. **ST. TIMOTHY MISSIONARY BAPTIST (8)** is located at the northeastern corner of East 71st Street's intersection with Carnegie Avenue. Now housing an African-American congregation, the church was founded as the First United Presbyterian Church by area residents of Scottish descent. Turn east (left) on Carnegie and travel for one block.

Turn north (left) onto East 77th Street and travel north for one block. Turn east (right) onto Euclid Avenue and note **TRUE HOLINESS TEMPLE (9)**, built as the Second Church of Christ Scientist; it later served as the Cleveland Playhouse. This is followed by **CALVARY PRESBYTERIAN CHURCH (10)**, another important church designed by Cleveland architect Charles Schweinfurth.

Move east on Euclid Avenue. At the southwest corner of Euclid and East 81st Street, note what was once **St. Agnes Roman Catholic Church**. The tower is the only architectural element left standing from this now-demolished but once-magnificent French Romanesque–style church designed by John T. Comes. Its presence is a reminder that Cleveland's sacred landmarks must be preserved.

Continue to travel east on Euclid. In quick succession on the south side are **LIBERTY HILL BAPTIST CHURCH (11)**, formerly the Euclid Avenue Temple, the new Cleveland Playhouse, and **EMMANUEL EPISCOPAL CHURCH (12)**, by noted Gothic revival architects Cram and Goodhue. Stay on Euclid Avenue. Immediately after passing the Cleveland Clinic, note **EUCLID AVENUE CONGREGATIONAL CHURCH OF THE UNITED CHURCH OF CHRIST (13)**, which serves the cultural needs of neighborhood residents and workers. Its rich, light, rough

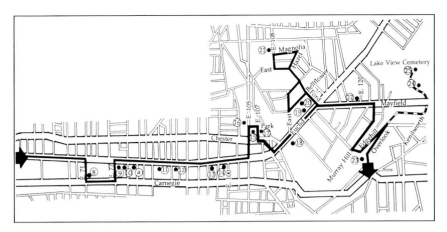

UNIVERSITY

8. St. Timothy Missionary Baptist
   Church
9. True Holiness Temple
10. Calvary Presbyterian Church
11. Liberty Hill Baptist Church
12. Emmanuel Episcopal Church
13. Euclid Avenue Congregational Church
    of the United Church of Christ
14. East Mt. Zion Baptist
15. Pentecostal Church of Christ
16. Temple Tifereth Israel (The Temple)

17. Epworth Euclid Methodist Church
18. Amasa Stone Chapel
19. Church of the Covenant
20. Florence Harkness Chapel
21. Mt. Zion Congregational Church
22. Holy Rosary Roman Catholic Church
23. First Church of Christ Scientist
24. Garfield Memorial Monument
25. Wade Memorial Chapel
a. St. Agnes Roman Catholic Church
   tower

stone contrasts with the smooth surfaces of Caesar Pelli's Cleveland Clinic Out-patient Building nearby, and the darker green stone of **EAST MT. ZION BAPTIST CHURCH (14)** at the southwestern corner of East 100th Street and Euclid Avenue.

Stay on Euclid until East 105th Street. At East 105th, turn north (left). Travel north for two blocks. At East 105th's intersection with Chester Avenue, note the **PENTECOSTAL CHURCH OF CHRIST (15)**, formerly the Fourth Church of Christ Scientist, on the northeast corner. Stay on 105th Street for one more block. Look to the northwest and see **TEMPLE TIFERETH ISRAEL (16)**, a Middle Eastern–style building that serves as a western gateway to the University Circle neighborhood.

Turn east onto Park Lane and enter the University Circle district. University Circle is home to many of Cleveland's cultural, educational, religious, and social service institutions and is the only parklike cluster of its kind in the world.[2]

Travel east on Park Lane for one block and then turn south (right) onto East 107th Street. On the left, facing the Fine Arts Garden, is **EPWORTH EUCLID METHODIST CHURCH (17)**. The shape of its spire has caused some to affectionately name it Church of the Holy Oil Can. Turn left on Chester then bear right to get over to Euclid Avenue.

Turn northeast (left) onto Euclid and drive in a northeastern direction. Opposite Severance Hall is the **AMASA STONE CHAPEL (18)** located on the Case Western Reserve University campus. It was designed by Boston architect Henry Vaughan.

Continue to move northeast on Euclid. Note the large late–English Gothic revival **CHURCH OF THE COVENANT (19)**, designed by Cram and Ferguson, on the left just east of the Case Western Reserve student center, Thwing Hall.

Turn northwest (left), after passing the Church of the Covenant, onto Ford Road. Stay on Ford for one block and then turn southwest (left) onto Bellflower Road. Follow the gentle curve of Bellflower and note the fortresslike building of the **FLORENCE HARKNESS CHAPEL (20)** located immediately behind the Church of the Covenant. At Bellflower's intersection with East Boulevard, turn north (right) and follow the curve until East 108th Street.

At East 108th Street turn north (right) and travel on it for one block to Magnolia Avenue. To the northwest, note **MT. ZION CONGREGATIONAL CHURCH (21)**. This simple contemporary structure is effectively scaled to reconcile the larger institutions of University Circle to the smaller mansions of the Wade Park neighborhood to the east. Turn east (right) onto Magnolia and travel on it for one block, and then turn south (right) onto Hazel.

At the end of Hazel, turn southeast (left) onto East Boulevard. Where East Boulevard forks, take the easternmost branch, Ford Road. Travel southeast on Ford until Euclid Avenue. Cross Euclid to travel east on Mayfield Road. Pass underneath the Rapid Transit tracks and enter Little Italy, a trendy, upscale center for art and dining from East 119th to East 125th streets on Murray Hill and Mayfield Road.[3]

At the northeast corner of the intersection of Mayfield and East 120th Street is **HOLY ROSARY ROMAN CATHOLIC CHURCH (22)**, an important neighborhood institution. Continue to move east on Mayfield until it intersects with Murray Hill. Turn south (right) onto Murray Hill and travel on this street until Edgehill. Turn east (left) onto Edgehill and then south (right) as soon as possible onto Overlook. Follow Overlook until you see the **FIRST CHURCH OF CHRIST SCIENTIST (23)**. Here, you may want to stop and look back down to the part of the city through which you have just traveled.

Though this ends the tour of the Dual Hub Corridor, you may wish to also visit the nearby Lake View Cemetery. Of special note here are the **GARFIELD MEMORIAL MONUMENT (24)** and the **WADE MEMORIAL CHAPEL (25)**. To reach Lake View Cemetery, backtrack (northeast) on Overlook until it intersects with Kenilworth. Then turn left and travel one block northeast on Kenilworth to its intersection with Mayfield Road. The main cemetery gate is directly in front on the north side of Mayfield Road. From here, follow the signs to the memorial and chapel.

1. FIRST PRESBYTERIAN CHURCH (THE OLD STONE CHURCH)
Architects: Heard and Porter (1853), Charles Schweinfurth (1884)
Location: 91 Public Square

The First Presbyterian Church commands the northwest corner of Public Square. Set adjacent to Cleveland's central open space, the First Presbyterian Church, commonly referred to as the Old Stone Church, has long been a city focal point. The church has witnessed such historic events as the passing of Lincoln's funeral bier in 1865 and the lighting of America's first streetlamps in 1879.

This church was an outgrowth of the First Presbyterian Society founded in 1827. The congregation's first church, built in 1834, was a Georgian-style gray sandstone edifice that soon became known as the Old Stone Church. The congregation's growth during the 1840s and 1850s necessitated the construction of a larger church in 1853. The present structure was completed in 1855 by the Cleveland-based architectural firm of Heard and Porter with the assistance of masterbuilder W. J. Warner. Heard, the son-in-law of Western Reserve builder Jonathan Goldsmith, was the most prolific local architect of his time and the designer of many early commercial blocks, public buildings, and private residences. Today, however, this is one of only three structures by Heard that remain.[4]

Romanesque designs were popular in the United States at the time of the church's construction, and the Old Stone Church is an example of this architectural trend. The massive coarsed-ashlar sandstone and rounded hoodmolds over the window and door openings are characteristics generally associated with nineteenth-century Romanesque detail. The use of geometrical medieval-style moldings above the base floor and the squared-off towers of differing heights and shapes are also reminiscent of Romanesque revival churches of the era.

The original facility was topped by a 228-foot steeple, which was destroyed along with the interior by a series of fires in 1857. Heard and Porter supervised the refurbishment of the interior completed in 1858; a spire was added to the southeast tower in 1868. However, in 1884 another fire destroyed the church's interior and the spire. In response to this emergency, the congregation hired architect Charles Schweinfurth to redesign the interior and reinforce the damaged exterior walls. This was the first important commission for Schweinfurth in Cleveland. Later he designed many significant local structures, including Calvary Presbyterian Church and Trinity Cathedral. Schweinfurth totally redesigned the interior of the church, making it much more elaborate than the original. The most interesting architectural feature of the remodeled interior is the roof structure. The church's roof rests on two longitudinal trusses that are partially supported by a series of arched braces springing from the side walls. The trusses are treated as false clerestories and admit no natural light; they are artificially lit from behind. The apparent model for the new interior was Trinity Church in Boston, designed by Henry Hobson Richardson in 1873. Indeed, Richardson even used a similar semicircular arch with wooden tie beams at the base.[5] The interior also contains a variety of stained glass by artists such as Louis Tiffany, John La Farge, and F. and S. Lamb; painted and frescoed walls by Julius Schweinfurth; and a pipe organ

by Walter Holtkamp, a local organ builder who sought to construct instruments to serve American congregations rather than to emulate instruments used in European churches.

The congregation of the Old Stone Church has long had a commitment to helping those in need. One hundred years ago it was instrumental in founding Goodrich House, a social service agency that has since developed many significant social service programs in Cleveland. Today the congregation employs a social services director who serves clients and provides counseling, financial aid, and help with food and clothing.[6]

2. CATHEDRAL OF ST. JOHN THE EVANGELIST
Architects: Patrick Keeley (1848), George W. Stickle (1945)
Location: 1007 Superior Avenue

Located two blocks south of Cleveland's new, modern shopping center, the Galleria, is architecture reflective of an earlier era—St. John Roman Catholic Cathedral. The cathedral originated in 1847 when the first Roman Catholic bishop of Cleveland, Amadeus Rappe, decided to establish a new church within the downtown area. Two years earlier, four parcels of land located at the corner of Superior Avenue and East Ninth Street had been purchased by Father Peter McLaughlin for a religious facility, and in 1848 five other adjacent lots were added. A small temporary church of 1,800 square feet, called the Chapel of the Nativity, was erected on the enlarged site that year.

The basic form of the present cathedral, named for St. John the Evangelist, was begun later that same year. Designed by Patrick Keeley, the most important American Catholic architect of the mid–nineteenth century, this brick structure measured 175 feet by 75 feet. Completed in 1852 and designed in what was then called the ornamental Gothic style, the church featured decorative interior columns, delicate stained-glass windows, and interior wall surfaces made of stucco.[7] A handcut wood altar and the statues of the Blessed Virgin were imported from France. The original exterior had decorative buttresses topped by crockets and pinnacles in the Gothic tradition. Later additions to the church included a Gothic-style steeple and spire in 1879 and a refurbished interior with an enlarged sanctuary in 1884. A chancery and a residence for the bishop were also added in the

1880s. In the same decade a new fifteen-room school containing a chapel and meeting room was erected next to the church.

The present edifice displays the major renovation efforts begun by Bishop Edward Hoban in 1946. Under the direction of George W. Stickle, the church's exterior was totally modernized. The original brick exterior was replaced with multicolored Tennessee crab-orchard sandstone. The old tower and other Gothic features were removed.[8] A new tower and transepts north and south of the nave were added. The Lady Chapel in the south transept contains an impressive marble altar that is lit by two small stained-glass windows. The original stained-glass windows, groined ceiling vaults, and ornate supporting columns were retained, but various colored marbles and dark oak woodwork were added to complement the interior. The walls of the cathedral are decorated with murals and frescoes depicting the lives of Jesus and the Apostles. Though the cathedral now has a seating capacity of over 1,500, greater than the original church, the overall effect of the renovation was destructive to the building's basic architectural character.

In response to the liturgical concerns expressed in the Second Vatican Council, a renovation project in 1977 moved the altar forward to the crossing. At the same time, confessionals were updated. In the 1980s the reredos curtains and Mortuary Chapel draperies were replaced and a new sound system was installed.

3. St. Peter Roman Catholic Church (1859)

Architect: Heard and Porter
Location: 1533 East 17th Street

In the emerging new urban residential district just east of downtown, St. Peter Roman Catholic Church is an old, familiar landmark at Superior Avenue and East 17th Street. The church and adjacent school serve downtown residents as well as those from outlying areas.

Founded in 1853 by Father John Luhr to serve recently arrived German immigrants, St. Peter Roman Catholic Church has the distinction of being the oldest continually operating Catholic parish in Cleveland.[9] About the same time, Catholic German settlers living on the West Side formed their own parish, St. Mary of the Assumption, and built a church at the corner of Carroll Avenue and West 30th Street (now demolished). Other Catholic Germans residing further east in the Woodland neighborhood established the St. Joseph parish and built their first church in 1857 at East 25th and Orange Avenue (now demolished).

The congregation of St. Peter's erected its first combination church-and-school in 1854. This was followed by the construction of the present sanctuary in 1859. Additions and improvements since that date have included a 250-foot bell tower

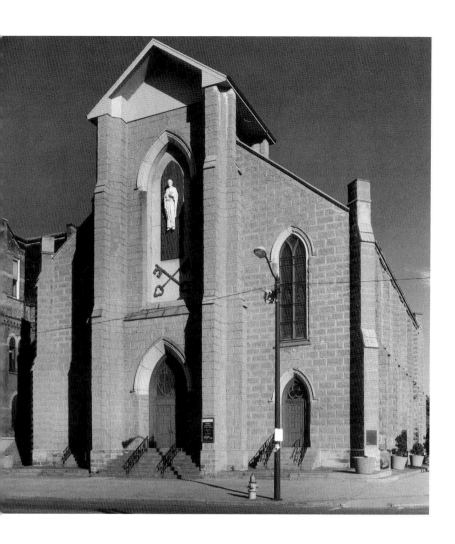

with spire in 1865 and revisions to the interior in 1885, 1929, 1943, and 1965. The tower was shortened and capped in 1984, but only as a temporary measure.[10] A more permanent tower and spire is anticipated to be completed by the mid-1990s. Recent renovation efforts are directed toward restoring the facility to its original late-nineteenth-century appearance.

Pointed arches above window and door openings and side wall buttresses suggest a Gothic influence. During the early Gothic revival period (1820–60), the use of one or two Gothic elements was deemed sufficient to indicate that the designer was attempting to create a Gothic image. The common church form was a simple basilica with a central steeple. St. Peter's on the East Side and St. John's on the West Side are, thus, typical churches of that era. In contrast, the details evident on the old school to the east of the church and the parish house south of the sanctuary show how Gothic revival changed during the High Victorian period (1860–90).

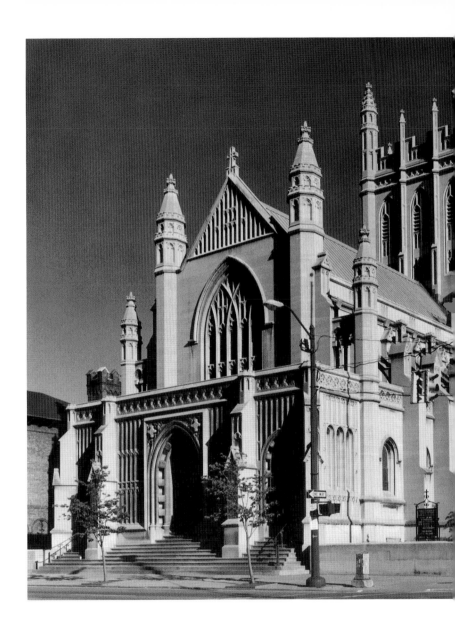

Although the Trinity parish originated in 1816 in a home in what was then known as the Village of Brooklyn, the congregation typically met in the Village of Cleveland from 1816 to 1820. The congregation then moved to Brooklyn; five years later it decided to relocate in Cleveland and erected a new frame Gothic-style church at the corner of St. Clair Avenue and Seneca Street, now West Third. The parishioners living on the West Side, however, soon left the congregation to establish St. John Episcopal Church in Ohio City in 1834, while East Side members remained at the St. Clair location.

The growth of the East Side congregation during the 1840s and 1850s and a disastrous fire in 1853 led, in 1855, to the building of a new Gothic-style edifice

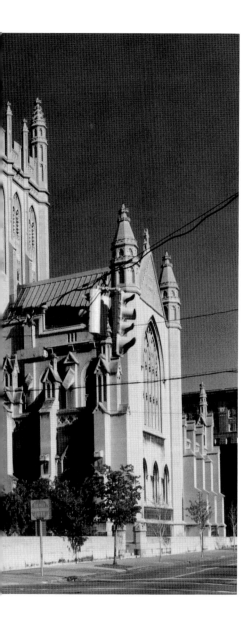

4. TRINITY EPISCOPAL CATHEDRAL (1901)
Architect: Charles Schweinfurth
Location: 2021 East 22d Street and Euclid Avenue

two blocks east of Public Square on Superior Avenue on the site of the present Leader building.[11] In 1865 a new brick chapel was erected south of this church.

In 1890, Bishop William A. Leonard authorized the establishment of an Episcopal cathedral in Cleveland and made the decision that Trinity parish was to maintain it. The Hills property on Prospect Avenue was acquired and adapted to the uses of a deanery and cloister hall, and the cathedral home was built. Cleveland architect Charles Schweinfurth, who redesigned the interior of the Old Stone Church and many of the mansions on Millionaires' Row, was commissioned to design the new adjacent cathedral on Euclid Avenue at East 22d Street. Schweinfurth responded by submitting plans for both Romanesque and Gothic structures.

After much discussion, the leaders of the congregation selected the English Gothic–style alternative. Construction commenced in 1901 and the finished cathedral was consecrated in 1907. Trinity Episcopal Cathedral and Trinity parish is the seat for the bishop of the Episcopal Diocese of Ohio.[12]

The cathedral is designed in perpendicular Gothic style adapted from fifteenth-century English models. Windows, doors, capitals, and gargoyles are cut in the conventional Gothic sculpture. The plan is cruciform, with the chapel at the right and the parish buildings at the left. The clergy room, sacristy, dean's room, chapter room, parish house, choir room, cathedral hall, and church home, all older than the cathedral, are connected to the newer structure along an aisle east of the choir.

The exterior of the building is constructed from Indiana limestone, cut and laid in courses. The clerestory, gable, baptistery, and tower windows are filled with cut-and-molded limestone tracery. Several of the stained-glass memorial windows are particularly noteworthy. The Louis Comfort Tiffany Studios in New York created the glass angel that is the focus of the window in the sacristy. Designed for an earlier church, the window is now located in a hallway near the dean's office. The aisle window portraying the adoration of the Magi demonstrates some of the technical features of stained glass. Its anonymous designer filled it with intense but subtly shaded colors; these are particularly apparent in Mary's robe. Carefully controlled color and shading permit the window to achieve a realistic, natural effect as worshipers view it in a range of light conditions from thirty or more feet away.[13]

A bell tower rises over the edifice at the crossing of the nave and transepts and is supported from the interior by four cruciform pillars with ornately carved capitals. The tower, 40-feet square, rising over the crossing 108 feet from the floor level, has octagonal angle pinnacles at the corners. The main entrance, from Euclid Avenue, is through three deeply recessed, molded, and carved arched openings. The total length of the sanctuary inside is 163 feet; the total width at the transepts is 107 feet.

The interior facings of the walls are of russet-colored, vitrified brick with cut-and-molded limestone pillars, arches, and trimmings. The spandrels of the arches of the nave and sanctuary are of heavily molded stone with panels formed by tracery moldings. This detail in the sanctuary is more elaborate in design than that in the nave, culminating at the chancel wall with a rich perpendicular, 18-foot-high reredos. The ceilings of the nave and transepts are plain, early Gothic barrel vaulting in English oak and are supported by heavily molded principal ribs springing from above each pillar and intersecting with the molded and carved ridge rib. The seating capacity of the cathedral is approximately 800.[14]

At the time it was built, Trinity was at the center of an elite neighborhood. After World War II, however, the neighborhood became rather poor and dilapidated; today it is undergoing renewal. Yet throughout its history Trinity has struggled to serve its community, consistent with the purpose of American Episcopal cathedrals:

The Cathedral is the Church for the masses of the population; it is intended to offer doors wide enough for the religious ingatherings of many who are even churchless and perhaps creedless. It should be large and spacious and architecturally imposing, so that the passerby and the stranger will realize that it is more capacious in its intention than the local needs.[15]

5. ZION EVANGELICAL LUTHERAN CHURCH (1902)
Architect: Frank R. Walker
Location: 2062 East 30th Street

Zion Evangelical Lutheran Church stands on the corner of Prospect Avenue and East 30th Street among the few remaining mansions and apartments that harken back to a more prosperous age. Although Zion Lutheran has been a neighborhood landmark since the beginning of the twentieth century, it can trace its history to earlier Cleveland locations.

Founded by the Reverend David Schuh in 1843, the congregation originally held services at the Cleveland Concert Hall on Superior Avenue. In 1846, the members built their first frame church on Hamilton Avenue just west of present-day East Ninth Street. Zion then moved this original church from Hamilton to Bolivar Avenue just east of East Ninth Street in 1865. A nearby school was built later that same year. This was quickly followed by the construction of a new church building located on the northeast corner of Bolivar Avenue and East Ninth Street. This religious facility served the congregation until 1900, when the group built the current church, which can seat 1,200.[16] The parish school erected next to the church in 1901 closed in 1974.

Architecturally, the basic proportions of the front facade, though slightly more vertical, are similar to those of the Old Stone Church. Details such as rounded arches above some of the windows, corbel tables below the roofline on the west tower and below the belfry on the east tower, and the squared-off bell towers with pyramidal roofs give the church a Romanesque flavor. However, the main perpendicular-style window with its tracery and the dormers at the top of the higher bell tower and pointed arches above the door are Gothic design features.

Zion Lutheran is important to Cleveland not only because of its architecture and history but also because through its growth and expansion Trinity Evangelical Lutheran Church (Ohio City) and St. John Lutheran Church (Newburgh) emerged. Nationally, Zion Lutheran also deserves some claim to fame, for under the leadership of the Reverend Henry C. Schwan the church introduced a candle-lit Christmas tree into their Christmas Eve service in 1851—one of the first congregations in the country to do so.[17]

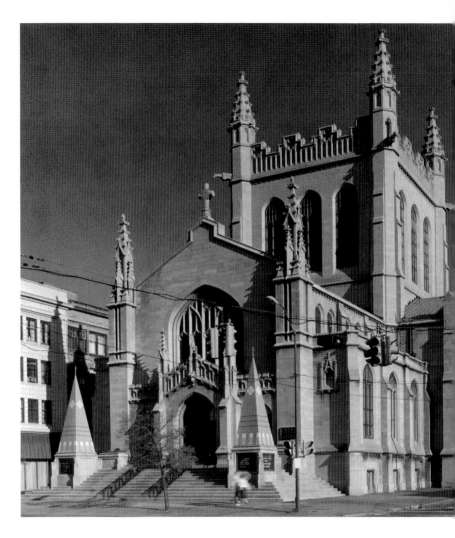

Anchoring the southeast corner of East 30th Street and Euclid Avenue, the early twentieth-century building of the First United Methodist Church contrasts with the surrounding office district that emerged a half-century later. However, one block to the south, near East 30th and Prospect Avenue, are several old mansions and apartment buildings reminiscent of the context in which First United Methodist was built.

Organized with nine members in 1827, the congregation of the First United Methodist Church built its first permanent home in 1841 at the corner of St. Clair Avenue and East Third Street. By the late 1850s the congregation had outgrown the earlier structure, so plans were made to construct a new building at the southeast corner of Euclid Avenue and East Ninth Street. Because of the high costs associated with their first plans, the members built a less-elaborate structure that served them until 1874, when they built a larger Gothic-style church on the same site. In 1900, the congregation decided to move away from downtown to East 30th Street and sold its building at Euclid and East Ninth to the Cleveland Trust Corporation (predecessor of Ameritrust), which built its main headquarters on the site.[18]

6. First United Methodist Church (1904)
Architect: J. Milton Dyer
Location: Euclid Avenue at East 30th Street

In March 1905, the First United Methodist Church congregation moved into the new church at the corner of Euclid and East 30th Street. Built of Indiana limestone, this structure can seat 1,200 worshipers. J. Milton Dyer designed the building to suit the neighborhood and complement other religious buildings found on Euclid Avenue, such as Trinity Cathedral and St. Paul Episcopal Church (now St. Paul Shrine).

Dyer was an important local architect who changed with the times. For example, it is difficult to believe that this was the same architect that designed City Hall and the Coast Guard station. In First Methodist a squared-off tower with lancets, crockets, and pinnacles and pointed widows with tracery indicate a Gothic precedent. However, the interior design reveals some surprises. For example, there are no aisles in the center of the nave leading to a communion table; instead, a curved auditorium with a slanting floor projects into the transepts. Stained-glass windows imported from Munich allow light to colorfully filter into this unique house of worship.[19]

7. ST. PAUL SHRINE

(Originally St. Paul Episcopal Church, 1875)
Architect: Gordon W. Lloyd
Location: 4120 Euclid Avenue

The delicate ornamentation of St. Paul Shrine contrasts with its surroundings and the bland architecture of the commercial and industrial strip near East 40th Street and Euclid. At the time the church was built, however, this was the center of the "most beautiful street in the world."[20]

St. Paul Episcopal Church was founded by Rector Gideon B. Perry in 1846 at the American House Hotel, located on Superior Avenue at the foot of West Sixth Street. The congregation held services in a number of different locations until 1848, when the group authorized construction of a new frame church at the southeast corner of Euclid Avenue and East Fourth Street. A fire destroyed this church before its completion.

Through funds partially donated by local Presbyterian and Baptist congregations, a Gothic-style brick building featuring a 161-foot spire was erected on the same site in 1851.[21] This structure was the home of the congregation until the late 1870s, when commercial expansion along that section of Euclid Avenue encouraged the group to move down the street. Prominent members of the congregation convinced church officials to build their new religious facility at the corner of Euclid Avenue and East 40th Street in what was then the center of Millionaires' Row.

The new Victorian Gothic structure, designed by Gordon W. Lloyd of Detroit, built of Berea sandstone, and designed to hold nearly 1,000 worshipers, opened in 1876. The church is cruciform in plan. The 120-foot tower with its four very exaggerated turrets and pinnacles and projecting porches add a Victorian Gothic flair to the exterior. Decorative supporting wood trusses in the nave and chancel bring a similar panache to the interior.

In the late 1920s the congregation decided to relocate to the corner of Coventry Road and Fairmount Boulevard in Cleveland Heights. The church at Euclid Avenue and East 40th was sold to the Catholic Diocese in 1931 and dedicated as St. Paul Shrine of the Blessed Sacrament and as a home for the Franciscan nuns. Renovations were done during the 1930s; a new convent was constructed and the rectory was remodeled.[22]

At the eastern end of the Midtown Corridor is St. Timothy Missionary Baptist Church. Built as the First United Presbyterian Church, it is a reminder of the grandeur once found in the old residential neighborhood.

Founded by the Reverend J. W. Logue in 1843 as part of the Northfield Association of Presbyterian Churches, the First United Presbyterian Church was a social and religious focal point for its twenty-three founding members, all of whom traced their ancestry to Scotland. Within fifty years of its founding, the congregation built two downtown churches, first on Michigan Avenue at Seneca Street (the site is now buried under Tower City Center) and then on what is now

8. ST. TIMOTHY MISSIONARY BAPTIST CHURCH
(Originally First United Presbyterian Church, 1891)
Architect: Sidney R. Badgley
Location: 7101 Carnegie Avenue

Prospect Avenue and East Ninth Street. A third church was constructed on Carnegie Avenue in 1891.[23] In 1948 the facility was sold to the congregation of St. Timothy Missionary Baptist Church.

Designed by the local architect Sidney Badgley, this church reveals Boston designer Henry Hobson Richardson's Romanesque influence.[24] Though not as robust as Pilgrim Congregational Church, also designed by Badgley, the coarsedashlar stonework, broad roof planes and gables, and deep-set window and door openings are consistent with the era. The towers and chimneys are also in the Richardson style.

Just west of Doan's Corners at 105th and Euclid is an institutional district that includes the Cleveland Clinic, the Cleveland Health Museum, and the Cleveland Playhouse. At the western end of this Euclid Avenue district is True Holiness Temple. This neoclassical building was originally constructed for the congregation of the Second Church of Christ Scientist.

Established in 1901 as an outgrowth of the First Church of Christ Scientist, the congregation of the Second Church of Christ Scientist erected the present structure in 1916 on the site of an earlier frame church. This facility served the group until it was purchased by a local development corporation in 1946. In the late 1940s, the Cleveland Playhouse bought the building from the developer and renovated it as the Euclid–77th Street Theater, a live theater. Later a combined supper club and theater occupied the building. In the early 1980s the Playhouse Association decided to sell the structure and consolidate operations into the ex-

9. TRUE HOLINESS TEMPLE
(Originally Second Church
of Christ Scientist, 1916)
Architect: Frederick W.
Striebinger
Location: 7710 Euclid
Avenue

panded, modernized Brooks Theater complex.[25] The True Holiness congregation bought the building in 1985 and began refurbishing it as a church.

The low-slung 86-foot central dome rests on a drum that originally flooded the main auditorium space with natural light. However, the clerestory windows in the drum wall were closed when the church became a theater. The dome rests on a square platform that is supported at the corners, and elliptical barrel vaults on each side of the square platform extend the central space in four directions, making an interesting spatial composition that was intentionally quite classical. In the design of Christian Science churches, classicism stands for the rationalism of a new faith that is based on a scientific system of reason and demonstration.[26] The extended front portico with Ionic fluted columns, the continuous balustrade of decorative ornaments, and the semicircular forms above the doors emphasize the neoclassical style.

10. CALVARY PRESBYTERIAN CHURCH (1887)
Architect: Charles Schweinfurth
Location: Euclid Avenue at East 79th Street

Located in a rapidly changing commercial district, Calvary Presbyterian Church reminds one that in spite of the presence of many new buildings the area has a long history. Calvary Presbyterian originated in the late 1870s when Dr. Hiram C. Haydn, pastor of the Old Stone Church, founded the Calvary Mission and Sunday school at East 75th Street and Euclid Avenue. Initially referred to as the Calvary Chapel of the Old Stone Church, the original frame chapel was moved to the East 79th Street site in 1880. Here the mission remained closely tied to the Old Stone Church until it was incorporated as the Calvary Presbyterian Church in 1892.[27] By the turn of the century, the church had grown to over 600 members, and many were deeply committed to foreign missionary work.

Changes in the Euclid Avenue neighborhood after World War I, partially caused by the movement of the wealthier residents to the suburbs, led to the creation of a strong working-class congregation devoted to serving the more immediate community. In 1923 the congregation merged with the Bolton Avenue Presbyterian congregation. This produced new vigor in the church, which continued to be active in serving the community during the 1930s and 1940s. Again, in the 1970s and 1980s the church was involved with endeavors designed to improve the greater Euclid Avenue neighborhood.[28]

Designed by Cleveland architect Charles Schweinfurth, the church was not far removed from Schweinfurth's own residence located at 1951 East 75th Street just north of Euclid Avenue. Calvary was built only a few years after the interior of the Old Stone Church was remodeled following the 1884 fire. Because founding minister and church architect were both formerly associated with the Old Stone Church on Public Square, it is not surprising that the churches' interiors are remarkably similar in overall effect. Through the innovations of the architect, however, Calvary Presbyterian becomes a bit atypical. Originally, components such as wooden columns topped by electric lights in place of traditional capitals reflect Schweinfurth's desire to incorporate modern conveniences within the context of accepted architectural themes. These features have now been replaced with more modern indirect lighting that highlights the spacial qualities of the sanctuary.

Calvary's rock-faced coarse finish set in an asymmetrical pattern, its large front and side gables perched above deep-set rounded stained-glass windows, the wide arch over the entranceway, and the squared-off bell tower crowned by battlements make the building a fine example of late Victorian Romanesque architecture.[29]

Just west of the Cleveland Playhouse on Euclid is Liberty Hill Baptist Church. Originally the Euclid Avenue Temple, this was an important center for the Jewish community in the first half of the twentieth century.

The Euclid Avenue Temple originated from the Israelitic Society. Founded in 1839, this was the first Jewish congregation in Cleveland. Disagreements over the religious traditions caused the congregation to split in 1842, but the various factions decided to reunite as the Israelitic Anshe Chesed Society in 1846. However, disagreements and clashes continued after this reunion and forty-seven members split from the group again to form the Tifereth Israel congregation in 1848. Those remaining in the Israelitic Society founded the Euclid Avenue Temple. The con-

11. Liberty Hill Baptist Church

(Originally Euclid Avenue Temple, 1912)
Architects: Lehman and Schmidt
Location: 8206 Euclid Avenue

gregation built their temple in 1912 and remained at that site until it relocated to the Fairmount Temple in Beachwood in 1956. The Euclid Avenue facility was then sold to the Liberty Hill Baptist Church congregation.[30]

Planned symmetrically and organized about a north-south axis, the structure is designed in the Neoclassical style by Lehman and Schmidt, who were also architects for the Cuyahoga County Courthouse. This building includes a semicircular auditorium seating 1,400. The overall exterior massing of the church is quite similar to that of St. Benedict Church on Dr. Martin Luther King, Jr. (MLK), Boulevard, though the materials are different and Liberty Hill Baptist has no towers.

Adjacent to the Cleveland Playhouse on the east is Emmanuel Episcopal Church. It was designed by Cram and Goodhue, promoters of the Gothic revival movement in the United States. However, the building was not completed according to the original design.

The founding members of the Emmanuel Episcopal congregation were originally associated with St. Paul Episcopal Church. In 1874, a group of St. Paul parishioners built their own chapel on Euclid Avenue near East 86th Street, and the facility remained under the auspices of the St. Paul congregation until recognized by the Episcopal Diocese of Ohio as Emmanuel Episcopal Church in 1876. The original Gothic-style frame structure was enlarged and moved slightly west to the present site in 1880. Despite religious disputes within the congregation, which eventually resulted in the formation of the Church of the Epiphany, the Emmanuel Episcopal congregation continued to grow. A new parish school was established

in 1890, and a chapel was built in 1892.[31]

The further expansion of the congregation led church officials to authorize the construction of a new church at the Euclid Avenue site in 1900. Designed by Ralph Adams Cram, this Gothic-style structure was built in stages. The original six bays of the nave and a temporary chapel were completed in 1902, and the remaining two bays and the interior of the church were finished in 1904. The bell tower remains to be completed. A wide front with shallow gables enclosing the nave, modified buttresses with finials, and perpendicular-style windows affirm the Gothic design.

Though small in number, members of the Emmanuel Episcopal congregation continue to play an active role in the neighborhood. Through the church, parishioners and area residents are provided with legal services and tutorial programs. The church is also home to a neighborhood food distribution center.[32]

13. EUCLID AVENUE CONGREGATIONAL CHURCH OF THE UNITED CHURCH OF CHRIST (1887)
Architect: Unknown
Location: 9606 Euclid Avenue

Begun as an outgrowth of a Sunday school started by Sally Cozad Mather in 1828, Euclid Avenue Congregational Church of the United Church of Christ has learned how to weather its transitional times. After meeting in various places for fifteen years, First Presbyterian Church of East Cleveland was organized in 1843, and the first permanent structure was built on what is now East 105th Street and Euclid Avenue.[33]

During the Civil War, the church separated from the presbytery over the slavery question and became known as an independent Presbyterian church. The small, brick church was soon outgrown, and in 1868 a new church on the corner of East 96th and Euclid, the present location, was dedicated. In 1872 a new constitution named the church Euclid Avenue Congregational Church of East Cleveland. Because the original design of the second building was never fully carried out, and because of the expanding congregation, a new structure had to be built within twenty years. The present structure, built of Ohio sandstone, was constructed between 1886 and 1887 on the site of the previous building. It was dedicated in September 1887.[34]

Inner-city struggle and change in the 1950s led Euclid Avenue Congregational U.C.C. to become part of a pilot program in an experiment to discover how an inner city church can become a strong, vital church and serve the needs of the community. By the 1980s, although members had moved to the suburbs and many of their children were affiliated with suburban churches, the church twice voted down the proposal to merge with a suburban church or relocate in the suburbs, believing its mission was to serve the neighborhood in which it had its beginnings. The church has developed an ambitious community outreach program that includes the creation of the Hough House Service Center and a day-care center.[35] More recently, the church has established a program for chemically dependent mothers.

Euclid Avenue Congregational U.C.C.'s well-proportioned, Romanesque-style building with its rounded arches, corbeling, and pyramid-capped towers creates an architectural landmark. Its history and continuing commitment to the community make it a significant neighborhood landmark.

14. EAST MT. ZION BAPTIST

(Originally Euclid
Avenue Christian
Church, 1908)
Architect: George
Kramer
Location: 9990 Euclid
Avenue

Built as Euclid Avenue Christian Church, today's East Mt. Zion Baptist, with its lantern over the sanctuary and green-colored stone, is an architectural landmark for Euclid Avenue's first African-American congregation.

Begun as an offshoot of the Disciples of Christ congregation from Franklin Circle Christian Church, the Euclid Avenue Christian Church congregation originated in 1843 when parishioners met for religious services in a maple grove located in the vicinity of Euclid Avenue and East 105th Street. This new congregation met in various members' homes until a church was erected in 1848 on Euclid Avenue east of East 105th Street. The congregation relocated to a new facility at 9990 Euclid Avenue in 1908 and remained there until moving to Cleveland Heights in 1955. The Euclid Avenue church was then sold to the East Mt. Zion Baptist congregation, which gained the distinction of being the first African-

American congregation to hold religious services on Euclid Avenue.[36]

The structure's green-colored rough stone and the decorated lantern over the sanctuary contrast nicely with the smooth-surfaced, undecorated Cleveland Clinic building across the street to the east. Architecturally, Syrian archways over various doors and windows, a coarsed-ashlar finish, and horizontal banding create a tasteful Romanesque-style exterior.[37] On the interior, finely crafted oak woodwork and glass windows created by J. R. Lamb Studios help to create an aesthetically pleasing place of worship. The church is also a good example of the Akron Plan popular during the era in which the church was constructed. This plan permitted the Sunday school rooms to be opened to the auditorium so that additional people could listen to a speaker or musical event.

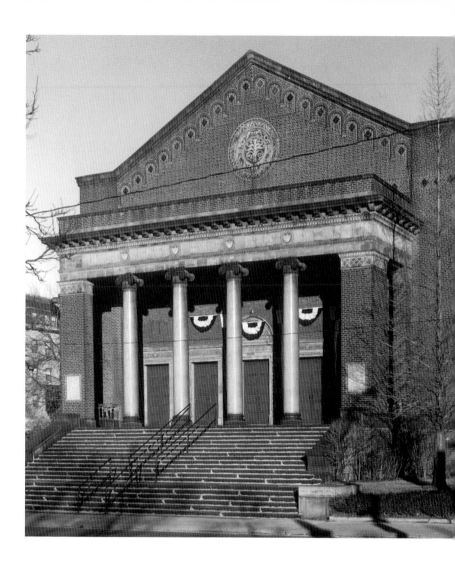

One block north of 105th and Euclid, Cleveland's second largest commercial district between World War I and World War II, is the Pentecostal Church of Christ, located on the northwest corner of 105th and Chester. Formerly it was the Fourth Church of Christ Scientist.

Founded in 1914, the congregation of the Fourth Church of Christ Scientist held its first services at the Woodward Masonic Temple hall.[38] By the end of World War I the congregation had gained enough financial support to build the present edifice on Chester Avenue. After nearly sixty years of use by the Fourth

15. PENTECOSTAL CHURCH OF CHRIST
(Originally Fourth Church of Christ Scientist, 1918)
Architects: Briggs and Nelson
Location: 10515 Chester Avenue

Church of Christ Scientist, the structure was sold to the congregation of the Pentecostal Church of Christ in 1980.

Designed by Briggs and Nelson, the church's main sanctuary can accommodate 1,600 people and the Sunday school can seat an additional 1,000. Stylistically, this church is neoclassical, possessing traces of Byzantine and Romanesque design. Flanked by two sets of doors on either side, the central doorway with a semicircular arch above stands out. Diamond details and varied brick patterns and corbeling below the gable ends give a human scale to this very large edifice.

16. Temple Tifereth Israel (The Temple)

Architect: Charles R. Greco

Location: University Circle and Silver Park

Overlooking Rockefeller Park to the east, The Temple acts as a gateway to the formerly Jewish neighborhoods that encircle the park and cultural gardens. Between World Wars I and II this area was the center of Cleveland's Jewish community, but after World War II the community moved to the eastern suburbs.

Congregation Tifereth Israel had been a well-established part of the greater Central–East 55th Street neighborhood when it decided to sell its Central Avenue Synagogue in the early 1920s and relocate to a new site on Ansel Road just west of East 105th Street. This relocation was prompted by the gradual movement of the congregation from the East 55th Street neighborhood to Wade Park and Cleveland Heights. Under the leadership of Rabbi Abba Hillel Silver, this reformed congregation erected a new synagogue in the University Circle area in 1923.

Designed by Boston architect Charles Greco, this religious facility served as the main temple until a new branch was dedicated in Pepper Pike in 1969. Nevertheless, the University Circle temple continues to be actively used by the congregation.[39]

All the architectural elements of The Temple—which include office, library, school, museum, and chapel—have been carefully placed within the unusually narrow, triangular site. The surface play between the seven prominent ribs that support the main dome and the dome skin and the color play between the dark woods of the balcony and ark and the lighter block walls create a visually exciting interior. On the exterior, visual stimulation is continued through the juxtaposition of Byzantine design and Romanesque detailing.

17. EPWORTH EUCLID METHODIST CHURCH (1926)
Architect: Bertram Goodhue; Walker and Weeks
Location: 1919 East 107th Street

The copper spire of Epworth Euclid Methodist Church provides a visual reference point to people using the Cleveland Fine Arts Garden and the institutions of the University Circle area.

The Epworth Euclid Methodist Church congregation at University Circle represents the merger of several of the oldest Methodist congregations in the city of Cleveland. The congregation of Euclid Avenue Methodist Episcopal Church is the oldest of the three merged congregations. Founded in Doan's Village on present-day East 105th Street near Euclid Avenue in 1831, Euclid Avenue Methodist Episcopal Church was originally called the Doan Street Methodist Episcopal Church.[40] The second oldest of the merged congregations is from the former Epworth Memorial Methodist Episcopal Church founded in 1850 as the Erie Street Methodist Episcopal Church. Initially located on present-day East Ninth Street south of Eagle Avenue, this congregation moved to larger quarters at the corner of Prospect Avenue and East 18th Street in 1875 and was then known as Christ Methodist Episcopal Church. In 1882, Christ Methodist Episcopal merged with Cottage Chapel and Missionary to create the Central Methodist Episcopal Church. After the congregation constructed a new building in 1893, the name was changed to Epworth Memorial.

In the early 1920s, a third merger took place. Epworth Memorial joined with Euclid Avenue Methodist Episcopal to create the Epworth Euclid Methodist Church. This group then constructed a new facility located at University Circle. The congregation commissioned Bertram Goodhue to design their new facility. After his death in 1924, the Cleveland architectural firm of Walker and Weeks worked with Goodhue's office to complete the project.[41]

Seemingly inspired by the Mont-Saint-Michel abbey in France, Goodhue designed Epworth Euclid with a massive space under the central spire as the controlling architectural element in the church. Additional spaces in the form of nave and transepts around this fleche form a cruciform plan. The Art Deco patterned copper on the lower part of the spire contrasts with more traditional French Gothic–style elements, such as pointed arches, buttresses, and a rose window. This deco theme is continued in the sculptures by Leo Friedlander, who also provided artwork for Rockefeller Center in New York City. The high vaulted interior ceilings, a richly carved chancel rail, and stained-glass windows created by the studios of Bonawit and Wilbert and R. Toland Wright give the church a simple elegance. Epworth Euclid is essentially a modern building that alludes to the Gothic tradition.

18. AMASA STONE CHAPEL (1911)
Architect: Henry Vaughan
Location: Euclid Avenue opposite Wade Park

Located on the campus of Case Western Reserve University across Euclid Avenue from the Cleveland Orchestra's home in Severance Hall, the Amasa Stone Chapel, with its 140-foot tower, serves as a point of orientation in University Circle. The chapel also helps to delineate the urban wall surrounding the Wade Park Lagoon in front of the Cleveland Museum of Art.

Clara Stone Hay and Flora Stone Mather commissioned this chapel in 1911 in memory of their father, Amasa Stone, a Cleveland businessman and entrepreneur who was an important leader in both the railroad and steel industries.[42] Stone was also interested in education, and in 1881 he confirmed his commitment financially by establishing Adelbert College at Western Reserve University in memory of his son who had died in a swimming accident. Thus, Clara Stone Hay and Flora Stone Mather were following a family commemorative precedent by creating a chapel for the university.

Designed by Henry Vaughan of Boston, once designer for the National Cathedral in Washington, D.C., the Indiana limestone chapel is emblematic of English Gothic design popular at the turn of the century. Typical of this style are the chapel's flying buttresses, pointed windows, and crockets. The tower, constructed without a spire, is very similar to that seen in Magdalen College, Oxford, England. Providing a bit of local distinction, a bust of Amasa Stone was moved from its location at the Bank Street railroad station in downtown Cleveland and placed over the rear entry of the chapel.

Of particular interest is the south window, a memorial to Flora Stone Mather. The window, rich in ornamentation and painted details, is the only local authenticated work by Charles Eamer Kempe, an English stained glass artist committed to carrying out medieval traditions in the twentieth century. Kempe's efforts reflect the aesthetic ideals of the English Arts and Crafts movement based on the medieval ideal of labor as an enjoyable handicraft. Kempe's designs, in contrast to the day's prevailing obsession with natural depth, emphasize abstraction and possess a two-dimensional quality.

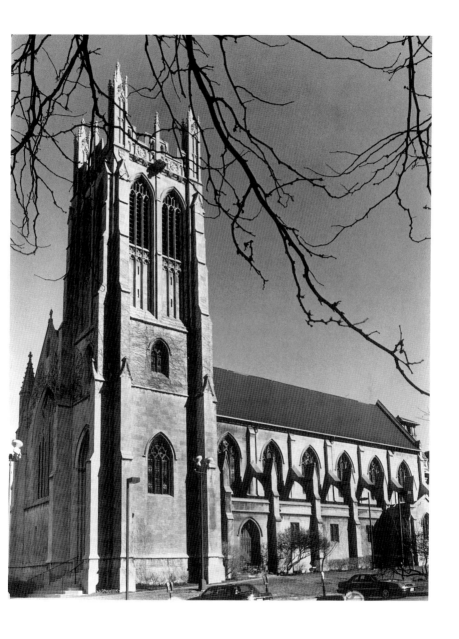

The massive Gothic revival Church of the Covenant is situated near the eastern edge of the Case Western Reserve campus on the north side of Euclid Avenue. The Church of the Covenant represents the merging of three Presbyterian congregations within a fourteen-year period, beginning in 1906 when the Euclid Avenue Church, founded in 1853, joined with the Beckworth Memorial Presbyterian Church, organized in 1885. This newly formed Euclid Avenue Presbyterian Church purchased a parcel of land adjacent to the Woman's College at Western Reserve University and moved into their new building in 1909.[43] In 1920, the Second Presbyterian Church, founded in 1837, joined the Euclid Avenue Presbyterian congregation to create the Church of the Covenant. The final merging of the congregations took place in 1928 when Dr. Philip Smead Bird became the first minister of the joint congregation; before that time each congregation maintained its own minister.

Architects Cram and Ferguson designed the Church of the Covenant in the

19. Church of the Covenant
(1909, 1972)
Architects: Cram and Ferguson,
Conrad and Fleischman
Location: 11205 Euclid Avenue

style of English Gothic. The sanctuary facade is massive and simple; it consists of a single deeply recessed doorway with a large rose window above framed by two large octagonal turrets. For a Gothic structure, typically light and airy, the amount of stone seems excessive. However, the buttresses in combination with accentuated waterlines and window tracery tend to lighten the structure. The 140-foot tower divides the private space of the parish house and the public space of the sanctuary.

Spiritually, the congregation attempts to "reach out to all persons." The congregation has therefore directed its energy and funds to the needs of local university students, Cleveland citizens, and overseas missionary efforts.[44] Conrad and Fleischman's 1972 community education building addition helps serve these purposes and is a contemporary, contrasting complement to the original, traditional design.

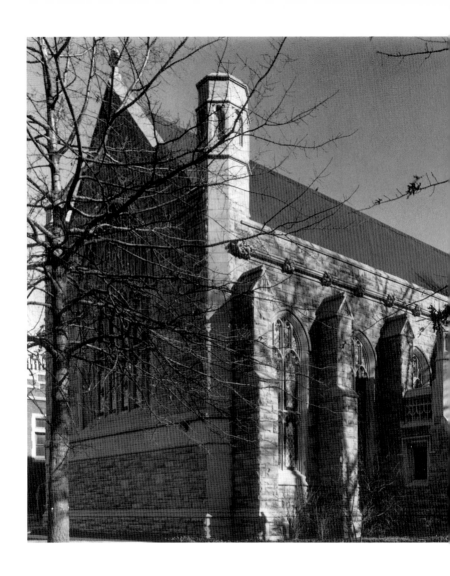

20. FLORENCE HARKNESS CHAPEL
(1902)
Architect: Charles Schweinfurth
Location: Bellflower Road

Located immediately behind the Church of the Covenant in the midst of late nineteenth-century campus buildings is the Florence Harkness Chapel. A memorial to Florence Harkness Severance, the daughter of Stephen Harkness and the wife of Louis H. Severance, this chapel combines architectural elements associated with both Romanesque and Gothic designs. Pointed windows, often associated with the Gothic style, are placed within the Romanesque-influenced coarsed-ashlar wall surfaces. Small, deep-set windows in the study rooms and heavy exterior buttresses emulate the fortresslike effect often associated with Romanesque design. Encompassing both styles, the hammer beam roof with its highly polished trusses helps to distinguish the interior space of the chapel. Eric Johannesen, in his book *Cleveland Architecture, 1876–1976,* suggests that the chapel, however, relies more directly on the sixteenth-century Tudor style that became the primary source of the popular idiom of the collegiate Gothic.[45]

21. Mt. Zion Congregational Church (1955)

Architects: Carr and
Cunningham
Location: 10723 Magnolia
Drive

Mt. Zion Congregational Church was founded by the Reverend J. H. Muse in 1864 as an outgrowth of an earlier prayer group begun by Edward Woodliff. This newly established African-American congregation, initially affiliated with Plymouth Congregational Church, had its first meetinghouse on East Ninth Street opposite Webster Avenue just south of Carnegie. Unfortunately, unforeseen mortgage expenses forced Mt. Zion Congregational to vacate this meetinghouse and relocate to another new, less expensive structure on East 31st Street directly south of Cedar Avenue. The group remained at the location until a fire destroyed the facility in 1923. It was at the East 31st Street address that the famous Mt. Zion Congregational Church Lyceum had its beginnings. The purpose of the lyceum was to discuss and debate issues important to African-American society.[46] The congregation also established the first African-American Girl Scout troop in Cleveland and a day nursery for children of working women.

The congregation decided after the fire of the early 1920s to purchase the

former Temple Tifereth Israel building at the corner of Central Avenue and East 55th Street. Financial difficulties during the Great Depression compelled the group to give up the former temple in 1938 and relocate to another site at 9014 Cedar Avenue. The Mt. Zion congregation later moved to the Cedar Avenue branch of the YMCA at 7615 Cedar Avenue, where they remained until 1954. The congregation then purchased an old mansion on Magnolia Drive and used it for their church. Within a year, plans were unveiled for a new sanctuary costing approximately $213,000. Under the guidance of the Reverend Richard T. Andrews, the mansion was renovated and a new sanctuary was constructed to serve as a combined educational and social facility.[47] This church is a good example of modern design adapted to local conditions. Uniform brick surfaces are coordinated with plain windows and doors to create a well-balanced, well-proportioned building.

22. Holy Rosary Roman Catholic Church (1905)

Architects: William P. Ginther, A. E. Sprackling
Location: 12021 Mayfield Road

Holy Rosary Roman Catholic Church is located on Mayfield Road in the heart of Cleveland's Little Italy. Established in 1892 by Father Joseph Strumia, Holy Rosary held its first services in D'Errico Hall in eastern Cleveland. A temporary chapel was erected at the corner of Mayfield and East End roads later in 1892 and served the congregation until the completion of the present church in 1909.[48] The "temporary" chapel continues to serve the predominately Italian congregation as a renovated recreation hall.

Rounded arches, quoins in the bell tower, and pilasters suggest a Romanesque influence, but the overall form and symmetry and the open belfry with rounded cupola suggest an Italian neoclassical flavor. A statue of Our Lady of the Holy Rosary in the central bay is flanked by statues of Matthew, Mark, Luke, and John. On the interior, the main altar is adorned with a bas relief of the Last Supper, and a baptismal font is decorated with a scene of the baptism of Jesus by John the Baptist. Except for the single tower, the overall composition and detail of Holy Rosary is similar to St. Adalbert on East 83d Street designed by William Ginther five years later.

23. First Church of Christ Scientist (1930)

Architects: Walker and Weeks
Location: 2200 Overlook Road

Perched atop the hill overlooking the city and adjacent to the old mansions and new apartments of Cleveland Heights is First Church of Christ Scientist, one of the architectural firm of Walker and Weeks's finest neoclassical structures. From here, looking west, one can see in a single glance all of the structures previously described.

The First Church of Christ Scientist was incorporated by the Reverend George A. Robertson in 1888 and received its charter from the state of Ohio in 1891. Services were held at various locations, including the Nottingham Building and the Pythian Temple, until the congregation moved into its own church building at the corner of Cedar Avenue and present-day East 46th Street in 1901, now the home of Lane Metropolitan Christian Methodist Episcopal (C.M.E.) Church. In 1914, the congregation moved into the Duchess Theater, where they remained until 1915 when the group purchased the former Euclid Avenue Methodist Church at Euclid Avenue and East 93rd Street for their new home. In 1928, the congregation purchased the residence of Mrs. Howell Hinds and the surrounding four acres of

land on the west side of Overlook Drive to serve as the site of a new religious facility.[49] The group moved to this new house of worship in 1931.

The building's extended front portico supported by four modified Corinthian capitals, a slightly raised podium on the front facade, and an enlarged triangular cornice above the main portico convey the designers' neoclassic intent. The auditorium is octagonal in form, a form often used in Christian Scientist churches and one also used in Severance Hall, a building designed by the same architects. This form was first introduced to the United States by Robert Mills, who sought to house large congregations in a comfortable auditorium with good sight lines. The Monumental Church in Richmond, Virginia, is the sole surviving octagonal church designed by Mills. In Europe and Asia the octagonal form was used quite early—for example, in San Vitale in Ravenna, Italy, begun in A.D. 540. First Church's tall, separate tower is illuminated at night and can be seen from many distant parts of the city. The elevated site on the edge of the Appalachian escarpment provides an ideal setting for this landmark building.

24. GARFIELD MEMORIAL MONUMENT (1890)
Architect: George Keller
Location: Lake View Cemetery

The James A. Garfield Memorial is located in Lake View Cemetery high on a hill overlooking Lake Erie and the city of Cleveland. The Garfield National Monument Association was established under the guidance of Henry Payne, Joseph Perkins, and Jeptha Wade. In 1883 the group sponsored a design competition that was won by George Keller of Hartford, Connecticut. Construction of the monument began in 1885, and it was dedicated on Memorial Day 1890, with President Benjamin Harrison, former President Rutherford Hayes, and Vice President Levi Morton in attendance.[50]

This monument represents a combination of Byzantine, Gothic, and Romanesque designs. Constructed of Ohio sandstone, this structure functions as both a tomb and a memorial. The central tower is 180 feet high with 50-foot diameter and rises from an extended square base and terrace area. Five life-size reliefs of James A. Garfield during different periods of his life are placed along the exterior of the base itself. The Memorial Room contains a lifelike marble statue of President Garfield standing in front of a marble chair. This particular room is noted for its polished red granite columns which support the large dome above. The crypt is located directly below the Memorial Room.

The vast openness of the Memorial Room is a direct reflection of Byzantine design, while the buttresses found in the perimeter aisle along with the point openings within the entrance portal and surrounding porch windows are reminiscent of later Gothic detail. The round main tower with its conical-shaped dome and secondary octagonal towers is characteristic of Romanesque style. Symbolism played an important role in the building's design, and it is considered to be the first true mausoleum in America. According to Eric Johannesen, the design is thoroughly characteristic of the date of its conception, 1883.[51]

At the bottom of the hill below the Garfield Memorial and overlooking a picturesque lake is the little neoclassical Wade Memorial Chapel. This chapel was erected by the Wade family as a memorial to the well-known Cleveland businessman and entrepreneur Jeptha H. Wade. The structure is unique in that it is located at the edge of a hill; the crypt is placed on a special sandstone platform slightly below the top of the hill so that the platform is hidden from the front driveway.[52]

The Wade Memorial Chapel was designed by Hubbell and Benes, who were also architects for the Cleveland Museum of Art. The neoclassic architectural elements include the extended front portico supported by fluted columns topped by

25. WADE MEMORIAL CHAPEL (1900)
Architects: Hubbell and Benes
Location: Lake View Cemetery

Ionic capitals, a low-slung pediment roof, and a wide unadorned frieze below the dentilated roof cornice. The interior of the memorial is especially significant. The large Tiffany stained-glass window opposite the entrance portrays the fulfillment of the divine promise. Prior to its installation here, the work was shown at the 1900 World Exposition in Paris. Tiffany's stained-glass works differ from medieval glass in that Tiffany attempted to convey a three-dimensional image through the use of layers and variations in shading in the opalescent glass. The glass mosaics by Frederick Wilson, Tiffany's principal designer, are placed within the marble walls of the interior and focus on biblical life.[53]

CHAPTER TWO

North Central Cleveland

The North Central community is made up of three neighborhoods: Goodrich-Kirtland, Hough, and St. Clair–Superior.

The Goodrich-Kirtland neighborhood is bound on the north by Lake Erie, on the east by East 55th Street, on the south by Chester Avenue, and on the west by the Innerbelt. Major east-west roads are St. Clair, Superior, Payne, and Chester avenues. This neighborhood was formerly home to Irish and German immigrants and was composed of small shops and houses. With the construction of the Pennsylvania Railroad line, the area was transformed into separate districts—industrial north of St. Clair and industrial-commercial south of St. Clair. Many of the old major neighborhood institutions are still scattered along Superior, hinting at the area's former character. Cleveland's small Asian community is nestled between the railroad and the Innerbelt along Payne Avenue.

TOUR

Begin the tour at the Innerbelt-Superior interchange and travel east on Superior Avenue. At East 36th and Superior, note the modern ST. NICHOLAS BYZANTINE CROATIAN CATHOLIC CHURCH (26) on the northwest corner of the intersection.

Continue on Superior Avenue until East 40th Street and note NORTH PRESBYTERIAN CHURCH (27) on the northeast corner. The building resembles a school more than a church. Then turn north (left) onto East 40th. Near the intersection of East 40th and St. Clair Avenue is ST. PAUL CROATIAN ROMAN CATHOLIC CHURCH (28) to the east. At the intersection of St. Clair and East 40th turn east (right).

Travel on St. Clair for one block and then turn south (right) onto East 41st Street. Travel on East 41st for one block. At Superior, turn east (left) and note on the northeast corner IMMACULATE CONCEPTION ROMAN CATHOLIC CHURCH (29), a large Gothic edifice with Victorian gables above the portals. Travel on Superior for five blocks. As you pass East 51st Street, notice St. Andrew Roman Catholic Church. With its Spanish flavor and the Solomonic columns on the front facade, St. Andrew's does not quite fit in with its surroundings.

At East 53d Street turn north (left). Travel on East 53d for only one block and then turn east (right) at Spencer. Take Spencer for one block. Turn south (right) onto East 55th Street. At the southwest corner note St. Paul Lutheran Church. Travel south on East 55th. As soon as you pass Superior, the east side of East 55th is in the Hough neighborhood while the west side is still in Goodrich-Kirtland. Hough is bound on the north by Superior Avenue, on the east by Rockefeller Park, on the south by Chester Avenue, and on the west by East 55th Street. Hough and Wade Park avenues are major east-west roads; East 79th is the major north-south street.

Named after early district landowners Oliver and Eliza Hough, the Hough neighborhood became a fashionable residential district in the mid-1870s and was characterized by large single-family homes. Between 1920 and 1960 it was a pre-

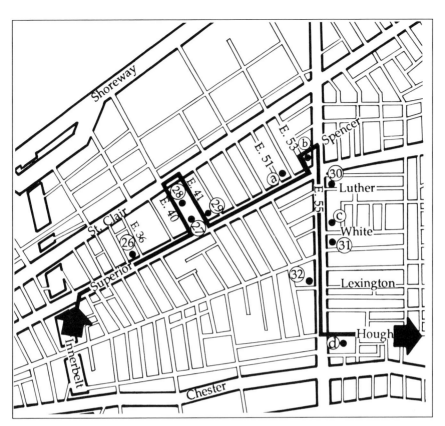

GOODRICH-KIRTLAND

26. St. Nicholas Byzantine Croatian Catholic Church
27. North Presbyterian Church
28. St. Paul Croatian Roman Catholic Church
29. Immaculate Conception Roman Catholic Church
30. Willson United Methodist Church
31. St. James Anglican Episcopal Church
32. Fellowship Baptist Church
 a. St. Andrew Roman Catholic Church
 b. St. Paul Lutheran Church
 c. Corinthian Baptist Church
 d. Emmanu-El A.M.E. Zion Church

dominantly white, working-class neighborhood. Between 1950 and 1960 Hough changed drastically; the neighborhood went from having a 5 percent African-American population in 1950 to having a 74 percent African-American population in 1960. By 1965 Hough was a neighborhood in "crisis," culminating with the July 1966 riots. Reflecting the city's—and nation's—pattern of racial tension and frustration, the Hough riots occurred over a one-week period and resulted in four deaths, thirty injuries, 300 arrests, and 240 fires.[1] The neighborhood has undergone significant rehabilitation since then. New, encouraging signs include the large multifamily Lexington Village, Hough Norwood Family Health Care Center, Martin Luther King, Jr., Plaza, Giddings Elementary School, and Martin Luther King, Jr., High School, as well as the construction and rehabilitation of several large single-family houses.

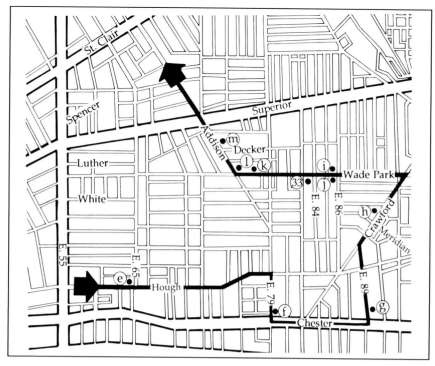

HOUGH

33. Fidelity Baptist Church
e. Hough Avenue United Church of Christ
f. Gesthsemane Baptist Church
g. University Church of Christ
h. Crawford Road Christian Church

i. Nazarene Baptist Church
j. St. Matthew United Methodist Church
k. Greater Avery A.M.E. Church
l. Bethlehem Seventh Day Adventist
m. New Jerusalem Baptist Church

After traveling south on East 55th for a block past Superior, note on the northeast corner of the East 55th Street–Luther Avenue intersection **WILLSON UNITED METHODIST CHURCH (30)**, a Romanesque revival building with newer glass-block windows.

Continue to move south on East 55th Street for another block. When crossing White, note **Corinthian Baptist Church** in the northeast corner. Built in 1894 as Zwhite German Baptist, the building has belonged to the Corinthian congregation since 1979. One block south of Corinthian Baptist, note **ST. JAMES ANGLICAN EPISCOPAL CHURCH (31)**, a small stone-and-frame building that would look more at home in a small English village than on East 55th Street.

After two more blocks, look to the right and notice **FELLOWSHIP BAPTIST CHURCH (32)** at Lexington and East 55th. Located in the Goodrich-Kirtland neighborhood, the church originally housed a German Lutheran congregation.

A few blocks farther south at Hough Avenue, turn east (left). Note **Emmanu-El African Methodist Episcopal (A.M.E.) Zion Church** to the south. Travel

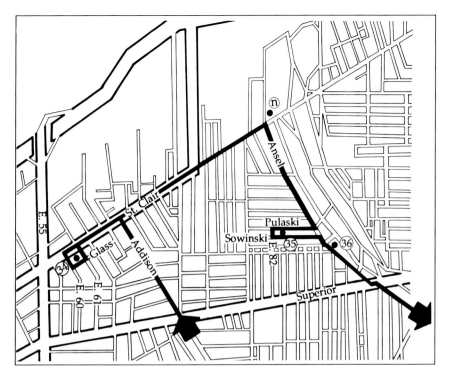

St. Clair–Superior ⌂

34. St. Vitus Roman Catholic Church
35. St. Casimir Roman Catholic Church

36. St. Mary Seminary
 n. St. Philip Neri Roman Catholic Church

east on Hough until East 65th Street. Here, at the northwest corner of the intersection, note **Hough Avenue United Church of Christ**. This blackened sandstone building with its unique lantern was done in the Richardson Romanesque style popular at the turn of the century. Continue to move east until East 79th Street. Turn south (right) at East 79th.

Travel on East 79th until Chester Avenue. Opposite Home Avenue note **Gesthsemane Baptist Church** to the east. Turn east (left) onto Chester Avenue. Travel on Chester until East 89th Street.

Turn north (left) onto East 89th. When turning, note the modern **University Church of Christ** to the east. Travel on East 89th Street and cross Hough Avenue. When East 89th crosses Hough it becomes Crawford Road. Continue on Crawford Road. Shortly after passing Meridian Road on the left, note **Crawford Road Christian Church** on the right. Built in 1907, it was the outgrowth of the Cedar Avenue Christian Church founded in 1883. Continue to move northeast on Crawford Road until Wade Park Avenue.

Turn west (left) onto Wade Park. After passing East 86th Street, note **Nazarene Baptist Church** (built as Church of the Holy Spire in 1893) to the north and **St. Matthew United Methodist Church** (constructed in 1907) to the south. Following St. Matthew's, at the southeast corner of East 84th Street and Wade Park, is **FIDELITY BAPTIST CHURCH (33)**, a vernacular-style frame church constructed in 1911. Continue west on Wade Park. After crossing East 79th Street, note **Greater Avery A.M.E. Church** followed by **Bethlehem Seventh Day Adventist** at the corner of Wade Park and Addison to the north.

Turn north (right) onto Addison. After two blocks note **New Jerusalem Baptist Church** at the northeast corner of Addison and Decker. After Addison crosses Superior, enter the St. Clair–Superior neighborhood. The St. Clair–Superior neighborhood is defined on the north by Lake Erie, on the east by Rockefeller Park, on the south by Superior Avenue, and on the west by East 55th Street. East 71st Street, Addison, and Ansel Road are major north-south roads. Continue on Addison until it ends at St. Clair. At St. Clair turn west (left) and continue on to East 60th. Turn south (left) on East 60th and travel for one block. At East 60th's intersection with Glass Avenue, turn east (left) and travel on Glass for one block.

Turn north (left) on East 61st Street. When turning, note **ST. VITUS ROMAN CATHOLIC CHURCH (34)**. Travel north on East 61st for one block and then turn east (right) back onto St. Clair. Travel east on St. Clair until its intersection with Ansel Road. At Ansel, turn south (right). When turning, note the modern edifice and modified rose window of **St. Philip Neri Roman Catholic Church** on the northeast corner. Continue to travel on Ansel for six blocks and then turn west (right) onto Pulaski.

Travel on Pulaski for one block and then turn south onto East 82d Street. On the east side of East 82d note **ST. CASIMIR ROMAN CATHOLIC CHURCH (35)** with its tall twin brick towers. After passing the church, turn left (east) on Sowinski and travel for one block. Then turn south (right) onto Ansel Road. After one block, look to the east and note **ST. MARY SEMINARY (36)**, a collection of classical forms put together in an eclectic manner.

Continue to follow Ansel Road to Superior. Here this tour ends. One block to the east (left) Dr. Martin Luther King, Jr., (MLK) Boulevard provides easy access to the Shoreway via Rockefeller Park.

26. ST. NICHOLAS BYZANTINE CROATIAN CATHOLIC CHURCH (1972)
Architect: Berj A. Shakarian
Location: 3431 Superior Avenue

Nestled in among the older buildings and a mix of single-family, multifamily, commercial, industrial, and public uses of property along Superior Avenue is St. Nicholas Byzantine Croatian Catholic Church. St. Nicholas's was established by Father Mile Golubic in 1901 to serve the neighborhood's Croatian community. The original parish consisted of fifty families who had moved from the Zunberek province of Croatia. Their first church was located in a former Protestant church at the corner of St. Clair Avenue and East 41st Street; the parish moved to Superior Avenue in 1913. When Cleveland architect Berj Shakarian designed the present church in 1972, it became the first ethnic church to be built in the city of Cleveland in over a decade.[2]

Although stained-glass windows near the entrance of the church offer a semblance of "tradition," function rather than historic ornamentation characterizes this religious facility. The front facade is made up of a series of smooth, unbroken brick planes that are separated by narrow continuous slit windows in the modern idiom. These planes step both down and back, visually directing the eye to the main entry. There, plain, unadorned modern elements provide a contrast to the more elaborate bell tower that frames the entry on the left.

27. NORTH PRESBYTE-RIAN CHURCH (1887)
Architect: Unknown
Location: 4001 Superior
Avenue

Anchoring the northeast corner of East 40th Street and Superior Avenue is North Presbyterian Church. Begun in 1859 as a Sunday school branch for the Old Stone Church, North Presbyterian was the direct result of the migration of members of the Old Stone congregation out of the immediate downtown neighborhood. Initially called the Wassonville Mission, this Sunday school was located on St. Clair Avenue near present-day East 41st Street until it moved to a former mission chapel on East 36th Street directly north of Superior Avenue in 1867; this chapel served as the main sanctuary until the late 1880s.[3]

In 1870, the Sunday school was recognized as a complete Presbyterian church, and the original congregation, made up of fifty former members of the Old Stone Church, named their new church after the Old North Church in Boston. In 1887 the congregation moved into the present church located on Superior Avenue at

East 40th Street.[4] This structure, which still serves the North Presbyterian congregation, is a blend of Gothic and Romanesque styling. Gothic elements like pointed arches, a central rose window, finials, and spires contrast with the building's more Romanesque characteristics, such as the rounded arch entranceway with jamb shafts and the squared-off bell tower with pyramidal roof.

North Presbyterian was a leader in the greater Cleveland Sunday school movement; Boulevard, Glenville, and Westminster churches all originated from North. The church has been committed to domestic missions throughout its history. During the depression of the 1930s, the congregation offered aid to those in need; more recently, the group has offered child-care services, emergency food programs, and recreational activities for residents of the Goodrich-Kirtland neighborhood.

28. ST. PAUL CROATIAN ROMAN CATHOLIC CHURCH (1903)
Architect: Unknown
Location: 1369 East 40th Street

In the midst of an interesting industrial, commercial, and residential urban neighborhood stands the modest, well-maintained, and well-proportioned St. Paul Croatian Roman Catholic Church. Established by Father Milan Sutlic in 1901 to serve the Croatian immigrants within the greater East 40th–St. Clair area, the St. Paul Roman Catholic congregation built its first and only church in 1903 and held its first service on Easter Sunday 1904. A brick parish school was added to the complex just prior to World War I.[5]

Architecturally, the church is basically a Gothic meetinghouse. The pointed arches over the entry doors with shallow jamb shafts, the pointed stained-glass windows, and the louvered belfry capped by a conical copper spire surrounded by finials are indicative of Gothic styling. However, the corbel brick effect beneath the gabled edge of the roof is a Romanesque characteristic and the squared-off bell tower is classical in detail.

The St. Paul congregation was instrumental in helping Croatian immigrants find homes and employment in Cleveland following World War II.[6] Today it continues to serve as an important social service center catering to the needs of Croatians throughout northeastern Ohio. The church still assists in relocating new immigrants and in helping the community's older residents find nursing home facilities.

29. IMMACULATE CONCEPTION ROMAN CATHOLIC CHURCH (1873)
Architect: Thomas Thorpe
Location: 4129 Superior Avenue

Immaculate Conception, one of the oldest Catholic parishes in Cleveland, had an unusual beginning. During the building of the original St. John Cathedral, a temporary structure, the Chapel of Nativity, was erected adjacent to the construction site so that the congregation could keep tabs on the cathedral's progress, as well as have a house of worship in the meantime.

In 1855, after the completion of St. John Cathedral, Bishop Rappe had the temporary church building moved to the corner of Superior Avenue and East 41st Street. The relocated church soon became known as Immaculate Conception. This original frame church was replaced by the present structure, which was begun in 1873. However, high construction costs led church officials to halt construction of the facility from 1875 until 1880. The decade of the 1880s witnessed the completion of the interior stone arches, piers, and columns. The towers were added in the 1890s.[7]

Such architectural elements as pointed arches above the window and door openings, a large front gable with niche and statue, and recessed portals with gables and jamb shafts indicate a Gothic-style design, as do the modified crenelation with finials on the taller tower and the triangular gables and crockets on the shorter tower. All elements work together in this large structure to form one of Cleveland's finest examples of a Victorian Gothic–style church.

30. WILLSON UNITED METHODIST CHURCH (1893)

Architect: Unknown

Location: 1561 East 55th Street

Located on the East 55th Street (formerly Willson Avenue) commercial-institutional strip, Willson United Methodist rests on the northeast corner of the Luther Avenue–East 55th intersection. Founded in 1857, the Willson United Methodist Church congregation erected the present building in 1893.[8] This church's architecture was influenced by the Richardsonian Romanesque design popular in the United States during the late nineteenth and early twentieth centuries. The building's rough-faced stone exterior, wide front and side gables, short bell tower with pyramidal roof, and round arches above the front and side entrances are all indicative of the style developed by American architect H. H. Richardson in the late nineteenth century. This church exhibits a stepped arcade effect in the main front windows (originally without glass block) and a modified Palladian side window. These design devices serve to offset the overall severity of the harsh planes of the exterior walls.

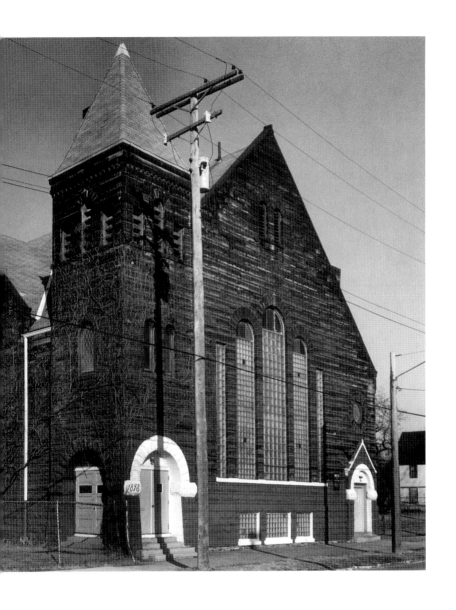

**31. St. James Anglican
Episcopal Church
(1890)**
Architect: H. B. Smith
Location: 1681 East 55th
Street

With several other churches—Willson United Methodist Church, Corinthian
Baptist Church, and Emmanu-El A.M.E. Zion—St. James Anglican Episcopal
helps form the urban wall that defines the western edge of the Hough neighborhood. St. James's, however, has a more human scale than do the adjacent
structures.

St. James Anglican Episcopal Church was established as a satellite of Trinity
Episcopal Church in 1857 by the Reverend Gideon B. Perry. During the Civil War
years, growth of the congregation necessitated the erection of a new brick structure. Built in 1865 at the corner of Superior Avenue and present-day East 26th
Street, this church served the congregation until the present stone church facility
was dedicated by Bishop Leonard in 1890. The interior of the church was modernized in 1938.[9]

The straightforward use of rough-cut stone and the building's squat mass suggest a Richardsonian Romanesque style, while the extended parapets perched atop
the main gables and front entrance portico are more indicative of the Gothic revival efforts of the time. The amalgamation of the Richardsonian Romanesque
and Gothic revival styles is typical of architectural trends at the end of the nineteenth century.

32. Fellowship Baptist Church

(Originally Grace Lutheran Church, 1908)
Architect: Unknown
Location: 1754 East 55th Street

Situated on the northwest corner of East 55th and Lexington, Fellowship Baptist Church, built as Grace Lutheran Church and former home of the First Assembly of God, defines the eastern edge of the Goodrich-Kirtland neighborhood along with St. Paul Evangelical Lutheran.

Founded by the Reverend H. P. Eckhardt in 1898 to serve Cleveland's German Lutheran community and its English-speaking religious school, Grace Lutheran Church initially consisted of both East Side and West Side members. However, within a few months of its formation, West Side parishioners decided to break away and establish their own church. Those remaining became the first Grace Lutheran congregation and built a small frame church at the corner of Lexington Avenue and East 55th Street later the same year.[10] The expansion of the Grace Lutheran congregation at the turn of the century necessitated the construction of

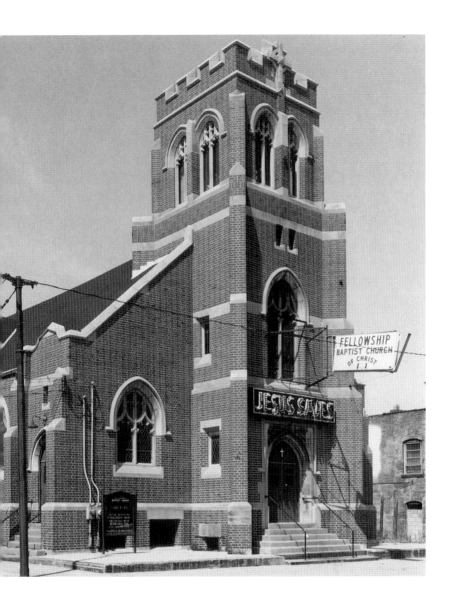

a new brick facility at 1754 East 55th Street in 1908. The original frame sanctuary was dismantled and donated to Grace Lutheran Church in Elyria.

The movement of the congregation toward the eastern suburbs after World War I prompted the congregation to move to its present location on Cedar Road in Cleveland Heights in 1926. The First Assembly of God then occupied the church building on East 55th Street. This congregation sandblasted and waterproofed the entire building in 1953. In 1964, Fellowship Baptist Church, founded in the early 1900s at the Phillis Wheatley Association auditorium on Cedar Avenue, bought the building.[11]

A squared-off bell tower topped by a crenelated cornice, tracery in various windows, pointed arches, and wall buttresses mark this building as a part of the American Gothic revival that took place around the turn of the century.

33. FIDELITY BAPTIST CHURCH (1911)
Architect: Sidney R. Badgley
Location: 8402 Wade Park Avenue

Located at the southeast corner of East 84th Street and Wade Park Avenue, Fidelity Baptist Church is set among many small churches in this predominantly residential neighborhood. Fidelity Baptist Church, originally called Fidelity Free Will Baptist Church, was organized in 1892 by the Reverend T. C. Lawrence at the corner of Wade Park Avenue and present-day East 84th Street.[12]

Built in 1911 under the direction of Cleveland architect Sidney R. Badgley, who also designed several other Cleveland churches, the church's steep-pitched gable dormers help break the severity of the roof's slope. Its front gable and one-story projecting bays topped by traditional pyramidal roofs and welcoming front porch uniquely identify this landmark structure.

Fidelity Baptist continues to maintain its tradition of service to the community. The church provides a wide variety of youth programs, leadership sessions, and weekly Bible classes for its members. The extended arm of the church's ministry provides emergency provisions for more than 10,000 families annually and provides counseling for drug abuse and mental illness.

Located one block south of the neighborhood's commercial strip on St. Clair Avenue, St. Vitus Roman Catholic Church has had a strong influence on the maintainance of this Slovenian community's character. Small, well-cared-for homes and gardens line the streets adjacent to the church.

Organized in 1893 by Father Vitus Hriber as the first Slovenian parish in the city of Cleveland, St. Vitus Roman Catholic Church held its first services in the chapel of the St. Peter School at the corner of Superior Avenue and East 18th Street. In 1894, under the direction of Father Hriber, the congregation erected its first frame church on Norwood Avenue. In 1906 the parish was divided; some of the parishioners were transferred to the newly established Our Lady of Sorrows Church while the rest remained at St. Vitus's. This arrangement proved short-lived, and in 1907 the St. Vitus parish was reunited.[13]

St. Vitus's commitment to education began when a school and convent were erected next to the church in 1902. A new school was built in 1913 and the

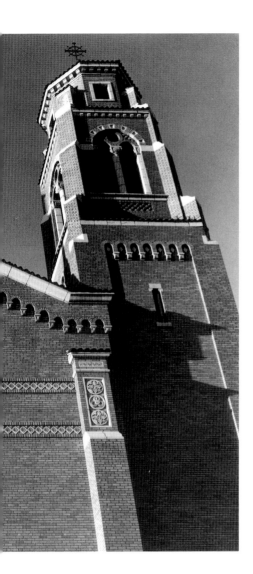

34. St. Vitus Roman Catholic Church (1932)
Architect: William Jansen
Location: 6019 Glass Avenue

convent was enlarged to provide more space for additional teachers in 1919; however, the commitment and subsequent high cost involved in educating the children of the parish prevented the St. Vitus congregation from building a more modern sanctuary until the early 1930s. Under the guidance of Father Bartholomew Ponkivar, the congregation authorized the construction of a new church in 1932.[14]

Based on Romanesque-Lombard design, the church was built in the traditional cruciform pattern and is able to seat 1,500 worshipers. Fourteen decorative columns serve to separate the 141-foot nave from the side aisles, and galleries in each of the 100-foot transepts were designed to seat the parish children.[15] Specific details associated with this Lombard design include the twin 100-foot ornamental towers topped by octagonal cupolas, the terra-cotta molded pediment visually supported by unadorned pilasters with ornate capitals, and the bas reliefs and ornamentation found above the main entrances.

35. St. Casimir Roman Catholic Church (1918)

Architect: William Jansen

Location: 8223 Sowinski Avenue

Located opposite an open space in a predominantly residential area, St. Casimir Roman Catholic Church dominates the east side of 82d Street between Sowinski and Pulaski avenues. St. Casimir's was established in 1891 by Father Benedict Rosinski for the Polish-speaking parishioners living in the northeast section of Cleveland. A brick combination church-and-school was built in 1892 and served the parish until the present church was constructed in 1918 under the direction of Father Carl Ruszkowski and Father John Solinski.

This stone-trimmed brick edifice, measuring 155 feet by 64 feet, can seat 1,200. It has a three-aisled cruciform configuration that was enlarged and renovated in 1937. The nave with a corbeled gable end, two symmetrically placed towers with open belfries, and a rounded entrance arcade are some of the elements that exemplify the building's Romanesque design.

St. Mary Seminary is located on the western rim of Rockefeller Park, part of a long chain of parks extending from Gordon Park on the lakefront to Shaker Lakes Park in Shaker Heights.[16] Placed next to the park's pathways, playgrounds, and rebuilt lagoon, St. Mary's overlooks one of the most picturesque areas in the city.

St. Mary Seminary traces its origins to Father Louis De Goesbriand, who served as its first superior in 1848. Located on what is now East Sixth Street, St. Mary's enrolled ten students during its first year. By 1872, church officials were considering the erection of a new seminary, but the financial panic of 1873 forced the church to redirect its energies. However, the steady increase in enrollment encouraged officials to build a new three-story brick addition to the East Sixth Street facility in the 1880s. This addition offered only a temporary solution to the pressing need for more school space, so in 1922 church officials decided to build a new, modern seminary complex on Ansel Road. St. Mary's became a fully accredited member of the Association of Theological Schools in 1971 and since 1985 has offered a five-year program in theology.[17]

36. St. Mary Seminary (1924)
Architect: Franz Warner
Location: 1227 Ansel Road

This seminary can accommodate up to 155 students and their professors. The plan of the seminary is organized around an axis through the chapel which is separated from the classroom area by two monastic courts. The chapel is especially noteworthy because it contains decorative ceiling beams, stained-glass windows imported from Munich, and an impressive mosaic that covers the apse.

The projecting central pavilion possesses a curved gable in rococo style; the pediment outline, similar in form to that found in the Zwiefalten, Bavaria, church by Johan Fiscurt, is flanked by octagonal twin towers. Other details include the richly adorned stone entranceway, in the style of the Italian Renaissance, and decorative urns on the twin belfries. The central dome is supported by pendentives and is reminiscent of earlier Byzantine churches. Thus, St. Mary Seminary may be linked to the romantic classical style that emerged from the renewed study of antiquities in the eighteenth century. During this period, architects borrowed elements from many styles and assembled them in new and imaginative compositions.

Located along the edge of Lake Erie, the Northeast community is comprised of Glenville–Forest Hill, North and South Collinwood, and Euclid Green.

The Glenville–Forest Hill neighborhood is defined on the north by Lake Erie, on the east by East 131st Street and the city of East Cleveland, on the south by Wade Park Avenue, and on the west by Rockefeller Park. East 105th Street, Parkwood Avenue, and Eddy Road are major north-south roads; St. Clair Avenue and Superior Avenue are major east-west streets.

Glenville, a predominantly Irish settlement, was incorporated as a village in 1870; it was annexed to the city of Cleveland in 1904. Earning its name from its woody landscape and many streams, Glenville, located next to the lake, was a popular location for Cleveland's elite at the end of the nineteenth century. However, as the city's industrial base expanded east along the railways during mid-century, many of the prosperous Jewish families moved to the eastern suburbs, and Glenville's character began to change. By 1950, 90 percent of Glenville's population was African-American.[1] During the 1960s and 1970s this neighborhood, like Hough, suffered racial tensions. But with a new East Side Market at East 105th Street and St. Clair, a rehabilitated Forest Hills Park, and a significant amount of new housing, a new community spirit has emerged in the eighties and nineties.

Forest Hill was originally the summer home of the John D. Rockefeller family. After the death of Laura Spelman Rockefeller in 1915, the Forest Hill estate was visited infrequently; under the custody of John D. Rockefeller, Jr., the estate was broken up in the 1920s. New York architect Andrew J. Thomas designed the eighty-one French Norman–style houses that were built in 1925 as part of a projected 600-home development known as Forest Hills Park. Today, as the neighborhood has grown around this residential community, Forest Hills Park marks the center of the old Rockefeller estate.[2]

TOUR

Begin this tour at the intersection of MLK Boulevard and Superior Avenue traveling east on Superior. Turn south (right) onto East Boulevard. When turning, note the impressive edifice of **ST. MARK PRESBYTERIAN CHURCH (37)** to the east. Located across from the Cultural Gardens in Rockefeller Park, this church was built in 1911. Continue on East Boulevard for one block. Turn east (left) onto Ashbury Road. Continue on Ashbury until East 110th Street.

At East 110th turn north (left). After two blocks look west and note **Bethel A.M.E. Zion Church,** founded in 1940 and rebuilt in 1958. At the next block look east. Located just opposite Hull Avenue is **New Wood Missionary Baptist Church.** Built in 1925, the building's brick walls are now covered with ivy. A tree growing out of the church's copper-capped bell tower makes this an interesting landmark. Continue on East 110th for one more block and then turn west (left) onto Superior Avenue.

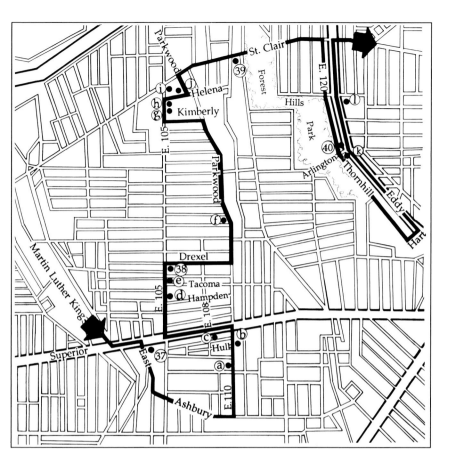

GLENVILLE–FOREST HILL ⬆N

37. St. Mark Presbyterian Church
38. Cory United Methodist Church
39. St. Aloysius Roman Catholic Church
40. Greater Friendship Baptist Church
a. Bethel A.M.E. Zion Church
b. New Wood Missionary Baptist Church
c. Calvary Church of God and Christ
d. Bethany Baptist Church
e. Greater Abyssinia Baptist Church

f. Parkwood Christian Methodist
   Episcopal Church
g. Glenville Seventh Day
   Adventist Church
h. Glenville Presbyterian Church
i. Central Christian Church
j. Morning Star Baptist Church
k. Christ Temple
l. Second Mount Olive Baptist

Travel on Superior for one block and note **Calvary Church of God and Christ** at the southeast corner of East 108th Street and Superior Avenue. Stay on Superior for one more block and then turn north (right) onto East 105th Street.

Proceed north on East 105th for four blocks and then look east to **Bethany Baptist Church** at the corner of East 105th and Hampden. At the next block look east again to note **Greater Abyssinia Baptist Church** and its new addition at the corner of East 105th and Tacoma. Stay on 105th until Drexel. Turn east (right) at Drexel and note on the southeast corner of the intersection the large **CORY UNITED METHODIST CHURCH (38),** originally constructed as a Jewish temple.

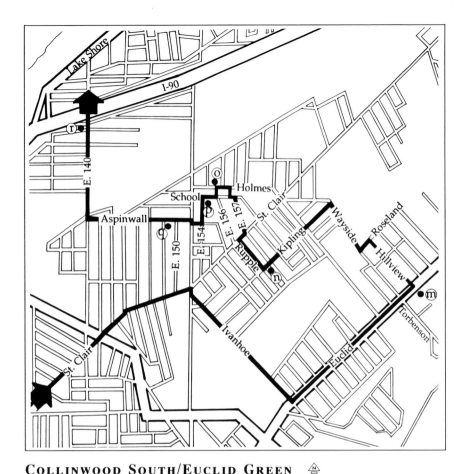

COLLINWOOD SOUTH/EUCLID GREEN

m. Good Shepherd Baptist Church
n. Holy Redeemer Roman Catholic Church
o. St. Mary of the Assumption Roman Catholic Church
p. Collinwood Christian Church
q. Greater New Calvary Baptist Church
r. Golden Rule Church of God

Travel on Drexel for two blocks and then turn north (left) onto Parkwood Avenue. After four blocks look to the west to see **Parkwood Christian Methodist Episcopal Church,** noting the Star of David motif. Continue on Parkwood for nine more blocks and then turn west (left) onto Kimberly.

Travel on Kimberly for one block. At East 105th turn north (right) and stay on it for two blocks. After one block, look east and note the **Seventh Day Adventist Church** at the corner of East 105th and Elgin.

Turn east (right) at Helena. When turning, note **Glenville Presbyterian** at the southeast corner of the intersection and **Central Christian Church** to the northeast. Travel on Helena for one block and then turn north (left) onto Parkwood. Bear left on Parkwood and look to the west to see **Morning Star Baptist Church.** Founded in 1917, it is located near the new East Side Market. Turn east (right) onto St. Clair Avenue.

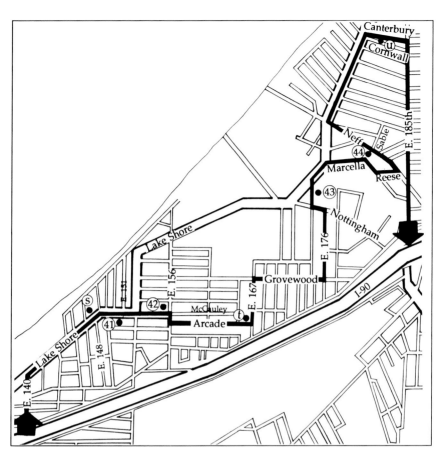

COLLINWOOD NORTH

41. St. Jerome Roman Catholic Church
42. Immanuel Presbyterian Church
43. St. John Lutheran Church
44. Our Lady of Perpetual Help Roman
    Catholic Church

s. Christian Fellowship Center
t. Wesleyan Methodist Church
u. Beachland Presbyterian Church

Travel on St. Clair until its intersection with East 109th Street. Here, look to the southeast corner of the intersection and note ST. ALOYSIUS ROMAN CATH-OLIC CHURCH (39) built in the early Christian style. Continue on St. Clair for five more blocks and then turn south (right) onto East 120th, which becomes Thornhill. At Thornhill and Arlington, look east to see the imposing GREATER FRIENDSHIP BAPTIST CHURCH (40), built as the First Evangelical and Reformed Church in 1926, located opposite Forest Hills Park.

Continue on Thornhill for two more blocks then turn east (left) onto Hart. After one block turn left and follow the curve (north) onto Eddy Road. After passing four blocks on the right, look to the west and note **Christ Temple.** Travel on Eddy for three more blocks and look east to see **Second Mount Olive Baptist Church,** originally built as Sieb Sachs Evangelical Lutheran Church.

Continue on Eddy until St. Clair. Turn east (right) onto St. Clair to enter

Collinwood South. The Collinwood South neighborhood is bound on the north, south, and west by railroad tracks and on the east by Cleveland city limits. St. Clair Avenue is the major east-west street; Coit Road, East 152d Street, and Ivanhoe are the major north-south roads. Annexed to the city of Cleveland in 1910, Collinwood was home to large Italian, Irish, and Slovenian populations. Its proximity to the railroad switching yards made Collinwood an important industrial center during World War II. During the same period, Five Points business property—the intersection of East 152d, St. Clair, and Ivanhoe—was some of the most valuable commercial land in Cleveland. Following the war, the area became home to many African-Americans, and by the end of the 1980s the neighborhood was a rather uneasy blend of different ethnic and racial groups, though it remains physically one of the city's best neighborhoods.[3]

Continue on St. Clair until Five Points. Turn northeast (right) onto Ivanhoe. Take Ivanhoe for five blocks. Enter the Euclid Green neighborhood and then turn east (left) onto Euclid Avenue. Euclid Green, a triangular-shaped neighborhood, is bound on the northwest by railroad tracks and on the northeast and south by Cleveland city limits. Euclid Avenue is the major east-west road; Green Road and Belvoir Boulevard are the major north-south roads.

Continue on Euclid until Hillview Drive. Here, opposite Hillview, is **Good Shepherd Baptist Church.** Although it is fronting Euclid Avenue, this church is only accessible by Torbenson Drive to the west. Built in 1958, the church rests on the side of a hill, and its open sanctuary of glass looks out onto the landscaped setting.

Turn north (left) onto Hillview. Take Hillview until it ends at Roseland. Turn west (left) onto Roseland. Follow Roseland for one block and then turn north (right) onto Wayside. Take Wayside for three blocks and then turn west (left) onto Kipling, entering the Collinwood North neighborhood. Collinwood North is bound on the north by Lake Erie, on the east by Cleveland city limits, on the south by railroad tracks, and on the west by East 131st Street. Lake Shore Boulevard is the major east-west road; East 152d Street, Neff Road, and East 185th Street are the major north-south roads.

Follow Kipling until Rupple. Before turning right on Rupple, note **Holy Redeemer Roman Catholic Church,** built in 1959. Located near a now-empty elementary school, the complex includes a church, school, rectory, and faculty house. Stay on Rupple for one block and then turn east (right) onto St. Clair. After one block on St. Clair, turn north (left) onto East 157th Street. Take East 157th for a block and then turn west (left) at Holmes.

Travel on Holmes for one block and then note **St. Mary of the Assumption Roman Catholic Church** at the northwest corner of the Holmes–East 156th Street intersection. The congregation's original structure, built in 1908, is located directly east of it. This 1957 church's copper-clad bell tower is a local landmark.

Turn south (left) onto East 156th. Travel on it for one block and then turn west (right) onto School Street. Take School Street for one block and then turn south (left) onto East 154th Street. When turning, note **Collinwood Christian Church** at the southeast corner of the intersection. Organized in 1878, this was the second church in the original village of Collinwood.

Take East 154th Street for one block and then turn west (right) onto Aspinwall. After two blocks, look to the south and note **Greater New Calvary Baptist Church** at the southwest corner of the Aspinwall–East 150th intersection. Built of buff-colored sandstone in the Richardsonian Romanesque style in 1893, this church first housed the First Congregational Church of Collinwood. Organized in 1876, it was the village's first church.[4] The building became Greater New Calvary Baptist Church on January 3, 1971.

Continue on Aspinwall until East 140th Street. At East 140th, turn north (right). Travel north for six blocks. Here on Diana, just west of East 140th, is **Golden Rule Church of God.** Located opposite Longfellow Elementary School, it is scaled to fit into the context of the surrounding residential neighborhood. Continue to move north until Lake Shore Boulevard. Turn east (right) at Lake Shore. Travel on Lake Shore until East 148th Street. Here, look to the north and note **Christian Fellowship Center.** Continue on Lake Shore until East 151st. Here, opposite East 151st is St. Jerome Roman Catholic Church (41), a modern adaptation of the English Gothic revival style.

Continue on Lake Shore until it runs into Macauley. Travel on Macauley for one block and then turn south (right) onto East 156th Street. When turning, note Immanuel Presbyterian Church (42) on the left. Built in 1924, this church is connected at the transept to the earlier church constructed in 1906.

After one very short block on East 156th, turn east (left) onto Arcade. Travel on Arcade until it ends at East 167th Street. At the northwest corner of this intersection is **Wesleyan Methodist Church,** a small neighborhood church.

Turn north (left) onto East 167th and travel on it for two blocks. At Grovewood turn east (right) and travel on it for six blocks. Turn north (left) at East 176th Street. Travel on it until it is intersects with Nottingham. Dominating the view to the north is St. John Lutheran Church (43). Founded in 1890, the present church building was dedicated in 1954. The building wraps around itself to create an inner courtyard garden. Opposite the church is St. John Nottingham Lutheran School. Both of these buildings are landmarks in this pleasantly scaled neighborhood with its brick streets.

Turn west (left) onto Nottingham. After one block turn north (right) onto Lake Shore Boulevard. Continue on Lake Shore as it curves into Marcella. Then bear right on Marcella until Reese. Take Reese to the left one block. Then turn left again onto Neff. At Neff turn northwest (left) and travel on it to Sable. Here look left and notice Our Lady of Perpetual Help Roman Catholic Church (44), a religious home to people of Lithuanian descent.

Continue on Neff until Lake Shore Boulevard. Turn northeast (right) onto Lake Shore and continue on it for seven blocks. Here on a point of land created by Canterbury and Cornwall's intersection with Lake Shore is **Beachland Presbyterian Church.** This small, well-scaled building shows a James Gibb influence through its steeple and the fanlight over the main entrance. It could easily fit into the fabric of some small New England town.

The tour ends here, only a few blocks west of the Cleveland-Euclid city line. Travel east on Canterbury or Cornwall to East 185th Street, then turn right (south) on East 185th Street to secure access to Interstate-90, about ten blocks south.

37. St. Mark Presbyterian Church

(Originally Boulevard Presbyterian
Church, 1911)
Architect: Unknown
Location: 1319 East Boulevard

Boulevard Presbyterian Church, founded in 1897, erected its East Boulevard religious facility in 1911.[5] This church served the Boulevard Presbyterian congregation until the late 1940s, when church officials decided to disband the congregation and sell the building. A dwindling membership based in large part on the move to the suburbs necessitated such action. The Boulevard Presbyterian congregation received $35,000 in cash plus additional real estate holdings from the new occupants, the congregation of St. Mark Presbyterian Church.

St. Mark Presbyterian Church, an African-American congregation, was founded in 1918 at 5507 Thackeray Avenue between Ayer and Central just east of 55th Street. The group remained at the Thackeray Avenue location from 1918 until 1945, when the congregation initiated a building fund for a new church facility. Ms. Jane E. Hunter, founder of the Phillis Wheatley Association, was active in

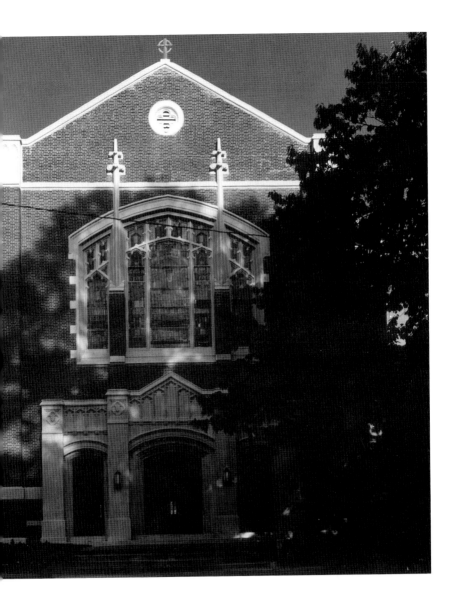

this fundraising effort.[6] The high cost of new construction prompted the St. Mark congregation to buy the former Bethlehem Evangelical Lutheran Church building at 10301 Garfield Avenue in the northern part of Glenville in 1950. A fire in 1951 destroyed the sanctuary; church officials purchased the former Boulevard Presbyterian Church structure later that same year.

The church is neoclassical with Romanesque and English Gothic elements. The English Gothic details include the decorative stone screen above the entrance on the front facade and the large gable crowned by a stone parapet featuring a stone cross. The enlarged pilasters flanking the entrance are topped by finials in a fleur-de-lis pattern. Romanesque style elements in this building include the rounded arches above the recessed tripartite portals and the light stone waterlines, lintels, and sills that provide a pleasing contrast to the dark-brown brick exterior.

38. CORY UNITED METHODIST CHURCH

(Originally Anshe Emeth Synagogue, 1921)
Architect: Albert S. Janowitz
Location: 1117 East 105th Street

Located on East 105th Street at Drexel Road, Cory United Methodist is one of the most imposing landmarks on the southern end of this neighborhood's commercial spine.

Cory United Methodist is one of the earliest established African-American congregations in the city of Cleveland. Founded in 1875 by the Reverend Henry Steen, this church was originally known as Cory Chapel and was named in honor of the Reverend J. B. Cory, a local Methodist missionary. The congregation held services in a number of private homes and public halls until the group purchased a building at the corner of what is now Central Avenue and East 37th Street in 1890. In 1911, the congregation moved to a larger structure at the corner of Scovill Avenue and East 35th Street. A fire at this location in 1921 led to the renovation of the entire building. Because of the growth of the congregation—from just several hundred members during the Great Depression to over 3,000 by the early 1950s—this refurbished structure proved to be too small, so church

leaders initiated a long-term fundraising campaign.[7] By 1946, the church had accumulated enough funds to purchase the Anshe Emeth Synagogue at 1117 East 105th Street.

Constructed for the Jewish congregation in 1921, the southern portion of this imposing classical structure served as the Cleveland Jewish Center, which housed educational, social, recreational, and cultural activities in addition to the worship services. The northern auditorium, capped by a circular dome, can seat 2,400. The block-long brick building has a frieze just below the roofline inscribed with the names of Jewish prophets and scholars.[8] A massive front portico supported by four freestanding columns is a notable architectural feature of this large structure.

Cory United has occupied the structure since 1946 and has maintained its active role in the local community. The church not only provides religious services and programs, but it also continues to offer a wide variety of recreational and social activities for its parishioners and others.

39. ST. ALOYSIUS ROMAN CATHOLIC CHURCH (1922)

Architect: William Jansen
Location: 10932 St. Clair Avenue

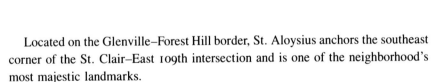

Located on the Glenville–Forest Hill border, St. Aloysius anchors the southeast corner of the St. Clair–East 109th intersection and is one of the neighborhood's most majestic landmarks.

Founded in 1898 by Father Joseph F. Smith to serve the Irish Catholic community in Glenville, the original parish met in a small frame church on what is now East 105th Street. Under the guidance of Father Smith and Father Thomas F. Mahon of St. Thomas's parish, the congregation purchased a parcel of land near the corner of St. Clair and Lakeview for the purpose of building a new church. A three-story brick church-and-school was built in 1902 and served the congregation until this larger structure was built in 1922; the present 1,250-seat church was consecrated in 1925.[9]

Based on the form of an early Christian church, William Jansen's design is the neoclassical style of the Italian Renaissance. Rounded arches above the side and main windows, paired pilasters with modified Corinthian capitals flanking the main entrance, and an enlarged triangular pediment above the second-floor facade help create a neoclassical image. The church is entered through hammered-bronze doors, and its impressive interior, supported by fourteen columns, is graced by the stations of the cross, also done in hammered bronze.

40. GREATER FRIENDSHIP BAPTIST CHURCH
(Originally First Evangelical and Reformed Church, 1926)
Architects: Corbusier, Lenski and Foster
Location: 12305 Arlington Avenue

Facing Forest Hills Park across Thornhill Avenue, Greater Friendship Baptist Church was originally built as First Evangelical and Reformed Church. Established in 1835 by the Reverend F. J. Tanke, the church was first known as Schifflein Christi, or Little Boat of Christ, and was then located at the corner of present-day East Ninth Street and Hamilton Avenue.[10] Internal disputes within the congregation led one group to form Zion Evangelical Lutheran Church in 1843.

Under the leadership of the Reverend George Moench, the Schifflein Christi congregation erected a new sanctuary in 1876 at what is today East 17th Street and Superior Avenue. The death of the Reverend George Maul, pastor of the Ebenezer Evangelical Church, led to the merger of Ebenezer Evangelical and Schifflein Christi in 1923. The newly enlarged congregation embarked on a church building campaign in 1925. Under the guidance of the Reverend J. C. Hansen, First Evangelical commissioned Corbusier, Lenski and Foster, the architects of the B. F. Keith Building at Playhouse Square, to design their new church facility on Arlington Avenue. First Evangelical later merged with Glenville Evangelical Reformed Church in 1953 and then with Fellowship United Church of Christ, Wickliffe, in 1969.[11] Greater Friendship Baptist Church currently occupies the facility.

Built in a cruciform design, the sanctuary can accommodate 1,000 people if the classroom doors are fully opened onto the main auditorium; when the doors are closed, the sanctuary seats 650. The gymnasium is equipped to seat 400 and contains showers, individual lockers, and six bowling alleys. In the basement are dining rooms, a kitchen, and additional space for club rooms. Constructed of Briar Hill sandstone, the well-proportioned, solid, eclectic structure has an impressive Gothic entry and rose window. The building is set off by a single tall bell tower with louvered Romanesque-style openings. As the tallest, largest, and most architecturally refined structure in the area, Greater Friendship Baptist Church is an important neighborhood landmark.

Just before Lake Shore Boulevard curves north from East 152d Street, the imposing St. Jerome Roman Catholic Church dominates this residential and commercial street in North Collinwood. From the church one can see Lake Erie one block to the north.

The St. Jerome parish traces its origins to St. Joseph Roman Catholic Church in Collinwood. Founded in 1877 by Father Anthony Martin of Euclid, St. Joseph's served the needs of local immigrants until the World War I era, when parishioners in the northern section of the parish requested their own church. In 1919, Father Leo O. Hammer established the parish of St. Jerome and authorized the construction of a frame church building on the corner of Lake Shore Boule-

41. St. Jerome Roman Catholic Church (1950)
Architect: William Koehl
Location: 15200 Lake Shore Boulevard

vard and East 150th Street.[12] The growth of the congregation in the 1930s and 1940s created the need for larger facilities. In 1949, the parish's building-campaign goal was reached, and ground breaking for the new church took place in early 1950.

Constructed of multicolored Tennessee quartzite with Indiana limestone trim, this 850-seat church is a modern adaptation of the English Gothic style. The large, pointed narthex windows with tracery and the buttressed walls are examples of the building's Gothic features. The interior contains a marble altar, a wrought-iron vestibule screen, and stained-glass windows.

42. Immanuel Presbyterian Church (1925)

Architect: Herman Maurer
Location: 326 East 156th Street

Located on the corner of Macauley and East 156th Street, Immanuel Presbyterian stands out in this residential neighborhood. The church was founded by the Reverend Frank N. Riale as a mission and Sunday school in 1903. Sponsored by the Calvary Presbyterian Church, located at the corner of Euclid Avenue and East 79th, this mission began in a small rented room on Waterloo Road in the Collinwood neighborhood. The church received full recognition in 1908 and adopted its present name in 1909. However, no sooner had the congregation been established when tragedy struck: fifty-seven Immanuel Sunday school children died in the infamous Collinwood school fire of 1908.[13]

Growth of the congregation during the 1920s prompted church officials, led by the Reverend George A. Mackintosh, to erect a new main sanctuary at a cost of $125,000.[14] The original chapel was subsequently renovated for classroom space. In the 1930s, under the leadership of the Reverend Leroy C. Hensel, the congre-

gation initiated a series of new social programs designed to relieve the suffering of the poor. Reverend Hensel also helped increase the membership of Immanuel Presbyterian and eradicate the building debt.

A further remodeling effort to modernize the chapel was initiated in 1961. One focal point of this refurbishing project was the installation of an impressive stained-glass window designed by Rudolph Sandon and featuring an image of the head of Jesus.[15]

Gothic styling is evident in the pointed arches located above the sanctuary windows and above the rose window on the front facade, and quatre-foil tracery is found within many of the church windows. The modified stepped gable and smooth-cut stone lintels and sills are more commonly associated with the Romanesque.

43. ST. JOHN LUTHERAN CHURCH (1954)

Architects: Ward and Conrad
Location: East 176th Street and
Nottingham Road

St. John Lutheran Church is located at the triangular intersection of Nottingham Road, East 176th Street, and Lake Shore Boulevard. The church was established by the Reverend Martin Ilse in 1892 to serve the residents of Collinwood. The growth of the congregation after World War II prompted the Reverend Walter J. Luecke to authorize the building of a new main sanctuary in 1954. Designed in a modern style, and seating more than 500, the church cost more than $200,000. The structure is noted for its large stained-glass window featuring an image of Jesus. The window is lit from within, making it visible to passersby at night.[16]

This modern building with smooth planes of light-colored brick surfaces and simple unadorned openings creates a distinctive, streamlined appearance. Containing little historic ornamentation, except for the smooth-cut stone lintels and sills around the windows and the stone caps along the roofline, the overall design effect is horizontal. However, the portico near the main entrance and the free-standing slender bell tower at the south end provide vertical contrasts and draw attention to the entry located behind the sanctuary.

44. OUR LADY OF PERPETUAL HELP ROMAN CATHOLIC CHURCH (1950)

Architects: Michael G. Boccia and Stanley Kudokas
Location: 18022 Neff Road

Our Lady of Perpetual Help was founded as a Lithuanian parish in 1930 by Father M. Karaziskis. Significant growth of the congregation after World War II necessitated the construction of a new sanctuary in 1950.[17] Under the direction of Michael Boccia, with the assistance of Lithuanian designer Stanley Kudokas and the general contractor Juozas Augustinauicius, the church was completed in 1952. An auditorium, school, and convent were later additions.

This modern, simple structure has strong forms based on the Romanesque tradition. The few openings in the smooth wall planes are outlined in a light-colored stone to contrast with the color of the darker brick building mass. The rectory and religious school are attached to the rear of the sanctuary on the north and form a front courtyard.

The South Central region of Cleveland is composed of three neighborhoods: Central, Fairfax, and Kinsman.

Central is bound on the north by Carnegie Avenue, on the east by the old Pennsylvania Railroad tracks, on the south by Rapid Transit tracks, and on the west by Interstate-77. Central and Woodland avenues are major east-west roads; East 55th Street is the major north-south road. Among the oldest residential neighborhoods in the city, Central changed significantly with the advent of public housing, urban renewal, and the construction of the interstate highway system following World War II.

TOUR

Begin the tour traveling east on Central Avenue after exiting I-77 at East 22d Street. Turn south (right) at East 22d and travel for two blocks. Turn east (left) onto Woodland Avenue. After the Boy Scouts of America building is the now-empty Victorian Gothic structure of **ST. JOSEPH FRANCISCAN ROMAN CATHOLIC CHURCH (45).** Stay on Woodland for one block and then turn north (left) at East 30th Street.

Travel on East 30th for two blocks and turn east (right) onto Central. When turning note **ST. PHILIP CHRISTIAN CHURCH (46),** a very modern building, on the southeast corner.

Travel on Central for six blocks and then turn south (right) at East 38th Street. Travel on East 38th for one block and then turn east (left) at Community College Avenue. When turning note **TRIEDSTONE BAPTIST CHURCH (47)** on the southwest corner. This structure was originally built for an Orthodox Jewish congregation.

Stay on Community College for two blocks and then turn north (left) onto East 40th Street. After one block notice on the corner of Central and East 40th **ST. JOHN A.M.E. (48),** the oldest Protestant African-American congregation in the city. Continue on East 40th for one more block and then turn east (right) onto Cedar. Travel on Cedar for two blocks. At the northeast corner of the intersection with East 46th Street, note **LANE METROPOLITAN C.M.E. CHURCH (49),** which originally housed the First Church of Christ Scientist congregation. Continue on Cedar for one more block and then turn south (right) onto East 49th Street.

When turning note **ST. ANDREW EPISCOPAL CHURCH (50)** to the east. Travel south on East 49th Street until Central Avenue. Turn east (left) onto Central and travel on it for one block.

At East 55th Street turn south (right) and notice **FRIENDSHIP BAPTIST CHURCH (51)** to the southeast. This church formerly housed the congregation of Temple Tifereth Israel. Continue on East 55th Street for two blocks. At the southeast corner of Scovill and East 55th is **SHILOH BAPTIST CHURCH (52),** originally the home of another Hebrew congregation, B'nai Jeshuran. Take East 55th Street

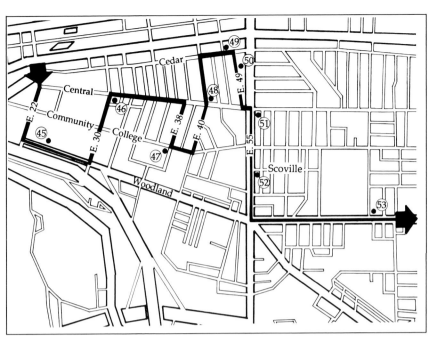

CENTRAL

45. St. Joseph Franciscan Roman Catholic Church
46. St. Philip Christian Church
47. Triedstone Baptist Church
48. St. John A.M.E. Church
49. Lane Metropolitan C.M.E. Church

50. St. Andrew Episcopal Church
51. Friendship Baptist Church
52. Shiloh Baptist Church
53. Holy Trinity and St. Edward Roman Catholic Church

for three more blocks and then turn east (left) onto Woodland Avenue. Travel on Woodland past Woodland Cemetery and note twin-towered **HOLY TRINITY AND ST. EDWARD ROMAN CATHOLIC CHURCH (53)** on the left. Continue on Woodland and enter the Fairfax neighborhood.

Fairfax is a triangular-shaped transitional neighborhood characterized by larger-scale buildings to the north and smaller-scale ones to the south. It is bound on the north by Carnegie Avenue, on the southeast by Rapid Transit tracks, and on the southwest by the old Pennsylvania Railroad tracks. Quincy and Cedar avenues are major east-west roads; East 79th, East 83d, and East 89th streets are major north-south roads.

Continue on Woodland until East 83d Street. Turn north (left) and note **Open Door Missionary Baptist Church** on the northwest corner of the intersection. Travel north on East 83d past Quincy. Opposite the recreation center to the east is **ST. ADALBERT ROMAN CATHOLIC CHURCH (54)**, a classical-style structure resembling the cathedral in Salzburg, Austria. Continue on East 83d for one more block and then turn west (left) onto Golden.

Travel west on Golden for nine blocks and then turn north (right) onto East 71st Street. Travel on East 71st for one block and then turn east (right) onto Cedar.

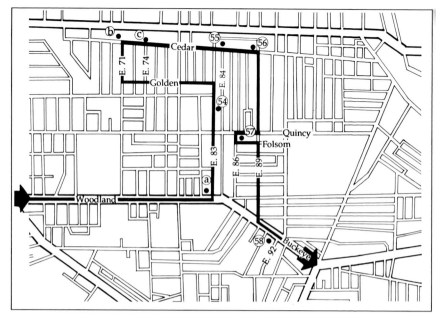

FAIRFAX/KINSMAN

54. St. Adalbert Roman Catholic Church
55. St. James A.M.E. Church
56. Antioch Baptist Church
57. Olivet Institutional Baptist Church
58. St. Elizabeth Roman Catholic Church

a. Open Door Missionary Baptist Church
b. Mount Gillion Baptist Church
c. Messiah Baptist Church

When turning note **Mount Gillion Baptist Church** on the northwest corner of the intersection.

Travel on Cedar for two blocks. Here, opposite East 74th Street, is **Messiah Baptist Church.** Continue on Cedar. Opposite 84th Street is **St. James A.M.E. Church (55),** originally constructed as Trinity Congregational Church. Travel on Cedar for four more blocks and then turn south (right) at East 89th. When turning note **Antioch Baptist Church (56)** at the northwestern corner of the intersection.

Travel south on East 89th for one block and then turn west (right) onto Quincy. Travel on Quincy for one block and note the modern **Olivet Institutional Baptist Church (57)** opposite East 87th and East 88th streets.

Continue on Quincy until East 86th Street and then turn south (left). Travel on East 86th for one block and then turn east (left) on Folsom. Travel on Folsom for one block and then turn south (right) onto East 89th Street. Continue on East 89th and enter the Kinsman neighborhood. This triangular neighborhood is bound in by tracks on all three sides—Rapid Transit to the north and railroad to the southeast.

Continue to move south on East 89th until it intersects with Buckeye Road. Turn east (left) onto Buckeye and travel on it for two blocks. At the southwest corner of the Buckeye–East 92d intersection is **St. Elizabeth Roman Catholic Church (58),** a classical structure in the Italian baroque style originally built for Hungarian immigrants who once dominated this neighborhood. This ends the tour of South Central Cleveland.

To leave the neighborhood, continue up Buckeye Road for several blocks until it intersects with Woodhill Road and Shaker Boulevard. There artereal streets are linked to the major highway network. To commence the tour of Buckeye-Woodland (chapter 6), take Woodland north (left from Buckeye) until it intersects with Fairhill Road. Turn right onto Fairhill and follow the Tour directions.

45. ST. JOSEPH FRANCISCAN ROMAN CATHOLIC CHURCH (1871)

Architects: Cudell and Richardson
Location: 2543 East 23d Street

St. Joseph Franciscan Roman Catholic Church, a landmark visible from the interstate system, acts as a visual gateway to the downtown. Established in 1855 by Father John H. Luhr for the local German community, the first church and school were built in 1857 at the corner of Orange Avenue and present-day East 25th Street.[1] These original buildings were operated by Father Luhr and the St. Peter parish until Father Anthony Krasney became St. Joseph's first spiritual leader in 1862.

In 1863, a new frame church was built at the corner of Woodland Avenue and East 23d Street. The Franciscan friars assumed control of the parish in 1867 and authorized the construction of a new monastery on Chapel Avenue at East 23d. This was followed by the erection of a new main church facility on Woodland Avenue at East 23d in 1871. In 1893, a Romanesque-style friary was added to the rear of the church.[2] The church remained at this location until it was closed in 1986.

St. Joseph's is of the German Gothic style, yet it also has a Victorian flavor. The exterior form of the narthex area with the central tower and hip roof tends to the Romanesque. Behind the narthex is a tall, simple nave terminated by a three-sided apse. Both the nave and apse have large, strongly colored glass clerestory windows, now boarded up, that filled the interior with glorious light. There are no transepts; the interior, in the French Gothic style, is quite simple except for the intricately carved wood altar and side shrines.[3]

Through efforts in the 1980s by the Friends of St. Joseph and other interested groups, the church has temporarily been saved from demolition. These groups plan to renovate the structure to better serve the needs of the local neighborhood and retain one of Cleveland's most visible sacred structures.

Located on East 30th Street, St. Philip Christian Church provides a transition from the larger scale of Cuyahoga Community College to the west to the smaller scale of the residential area to the east. St. Philip's is an example of a contemporary design intended to withstand the tensions of urban living.

St. Philip Christian Church originated in a store on Woodland Avenue in 1954.[4] Growth of the congregation necessitated the construction of a new facility, and in 1968 the present church was built under the guidance of architect Frederick S. Toguchi.

Made of a series of attached precast concrete panels placed over a preset foun-

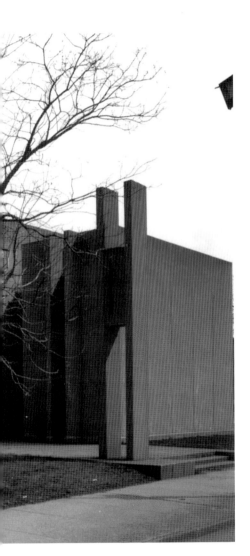

46. St. Philip Christian Church (1968)

Architect: Frederick S. Toguchi

Location: 2303 East 30th Street

dation, the building is composed of horizontal wall surfaces that have been incorporated with deep-set vertical doors and windows to create a balanced building composition. The church contains virtually no historic ornamentation, for, with the exception of the rather unique detached bell tower erected on the street level, function rather than tradition serves to distinguish this edifice. On the interior, the balcony is crucial to the design. It divides the space into two large areas and acts as a central focal point for each of them. The specially designed altar complements the narrow width of the church.[5]

47. TRIEDSTONE BAPTIST CHURCH
(Originally Oheb Zedek Hungarian Orthodox Synagogue, 1905)
Architect: Albert S. Janowitz
Location: 3782 Community College Avenue

This yellow-brick building was originally constructed as Oheb Zedek Hungarian Orthodox Synagogue in this once-Jewish neighborhood. Now an African-American church, Triedstone Baptist faces a field of vacant, deteriorating houses near the city's center. But the church is alive; Triedstone Baptist is a symbol of hope for the neighborhood.

Oheb Zedek is the largest Orthodox Jewish congregation in the greater Cleveland area. Founded in 1904 when forty Hungarian immigrants split with the B'nai Jeshuran congregation, Oheb Zedek chose Henry A. Liebowitz to serve as the synagogue's first rabbi.[6] One of the first steps taken by the congregation in 1905 was the erection of a new synagogue on what was then Scovill Avenue and East 38th Street.

The eventual movement of the congregation away from the Scovill Avenue neighborhood to Glenville at the time of World War I led this group to build a second synagogue on what is now Parkwood Avenue in 1922. Oheb Zedek remained at this location until the congregation moved to its present site on Taylor Road in Cleveland Heights in 1955.[7]

Triedstone Baptist Church bought the synagogue on Community College Avenue in 1921 and has remained at that site.[8] Initial modifications were made in the early 1920s so that the building would better conform to the religious needs of its new occupants. In 1958, the church added a glassed-in courtyard and a fellowship hall. Even though modifications have been made, several elements serve to distinguish this building's original function as a synagogue. The double choir windows on the front facade symbolize the tablets of Moses, and the Star of David in the gabled brickwork reflects the structure's intended religious purpose. Similarly, the interior balcony was designed to separate the men from the women in the Orthodox congregation.

48. St. John African Methodist Episcopal Church (1908)
Architects: Badgley and Nicklas
Location: 2261 East 40th Street

St. John A.M.E. Church has an imposing structure and an active congregation, making it a neighborhood landmark structurally, socially, and culturally. It also has the distinction of being the oldest African-American Protestant congregation in the city of Cleveland. Established by Father Quinn in 1830 on West Ninth Street, the group moved several times before settling on its present site on East 40th Street in 1908.[9]

An eclectic neoclassical structure, the building's main perpendicular-style windows, parapets, and front porticos give it an English Gothic appearance, while hoodmolds and reverse corbiesteps and extended waterlines are more reminiscent of Romanesque detail. The overall horizontal effect of the main block of the church is broken up by the two towers of differing heights, a common feature in Romanesque revival churches in America at the turn of the century. The front porches over the doors of the main facade have an almost Tudor character.

The St. John A.M.E. congregation has had a long tradition of supporting civil rights activities in Cleveland. It was also one of the first African-American churches to oppose segregation within its own religious sect. Its location in the Central neighborhood has made St. John A.M.E. a natural focus for recreational and social activities of African-Americans since the 1920s.[10]

Lane Metropolitan C.M.E. Church is a distinctive classical-style building prominent on the northeast corner of East 46th Street and Cedar Avenue. Built as the First Church of Christ Scientist, it is loosely modeled after the Pantheon in Rome.

The Christian Science religious movement originated in Boston under the leadership of Mary Baker Eddy in 1866 and was introduced to Cleveland by General Erastus N. Bates in 1877.[11] The Christ Scientist congregation held religious services in a number of different houses and halls until the First Church of Christ Scientist was completed in 1901.

Located at the intersection of what is now Cedar Avenue and East 46th Street, the congregation remained at this location until moving to the former Euclid Av-

**49. Lane Metropolitan
Christian Methodist
Episcopal Church**
(Originally First Church of
Christ Scientist, 1900)
Architect: George Hammond
Location: 2131 East 46th Street

enue Methodist Church facility at East 93d Street in 1918. Then, in 1931, it moved to its present location on Overlook Road. The Lane Metropolitan C.M.E. congregation bought the East 46th Street church in 1919 and remains there today.[12]

Designed by George Hammond, who was also the architect for the Ameritrust Building at East Ninth and Euclid, the building's overall symmetrical design with its monumental proportions, extended front portico supported by composite fluted columns, and unadorned entablature is neoclassic in style. Most Christian Science churches in Cleveland and elsewhere have a similar character, because classicism was considered to be a rational style and Christian Science a rational religion.

50. St. Andrew Episcopal Church (1916)
Architect: Charles Schneider

Location: 2171 East 49th Street

Tucked away on a side street in a diverse neighborhood is St. Andrew Episcopal Church, the first recognized African-American Episcopal congregation in the city of Cleveland. Founded with fifty members in 1890 as an outgrowth of Trinity and Grace Episcopal churches, St. Andrew's received formal parish status in 1892. The group first held services at St. Peter's on Chapel Street and then met at a former Swedish church on Central Avenue at East 24th Street. The congregation remained at the Central Avenue site until the expansion of St. Vincent Charity Hospital in 1915 necessitated relocation.[13]

The present church was erected in 1916 and reflects a Gothic revival design

suited to local Protestant idealism—namely, undecorated and spare. A main perpendicular-style window and modified wall buttresses are a few of the building's Gothic details. The parish house to the north was completed in 1953 and complements the church structure with its similar brick veneer and pointed recessed molding with modified corbel stops on the annex entrance.

In 1922, the Colored Workers of the Episcopal Church held their national convention at St. Andrew's. This particular meeting dealt with the issue of racism within the Episcopal sect and strengthened the congregation's commitment to civil rights, which continues to the present day.

51. FRIENDSHIP BAPTIST CHURCH
(Originally Temple Tifereth Israel, 1894)
Architects: Lehman and Schmidt
Location: 5600 Central Avenue

The imposing, foreboding dark-stone structure of Friendship Baptist Church looms over the southeast corner of Central Avenue and East 55th Street. This religious facility, originally housing the Temple Tifereth Israel congregation, was designed by Lehman and Schmidt, the architects of the Cuyahoga County Courthouse.

Temple Tifereth Israel was founded in 1848 when forty-seven members of the earlier established Israelitic Anshe Chesed Society left that group because of religious disputes. In 1854, the newly formed congregation received enough funds from New Orleans philanthropist Judah Touro to build a new synagogue at the corner of Huron and Miami streets.[14] Completed in 1855, this building served the congregation until a new temple was built on Central Avenue at present-day East 55th Street. This synagogue soon established itself as a local leader of Reform Judaism and began to be referred to as The Temple.

The gradual movement of members from the neighborhood surrounding The

Temple to Wade Park and Cleveland Heights encouraged the congregation to move again. First, the congregation moved to Ansel Road at East 105th Street and dedicated their Charles Greco–designed structure in 1924.[15] The congregation then established a branch in Pepper Pike in 1969. The religious structure on Central Avenue thus became the home of the Friendship Baptist Church.

Constructed with coarsed ashlar offset by contrasting trim, the Central Avenue building represents a combination of Byzantine and Romanesque designs common to late nineteenth-century Jewish synagogues. Since Jewish tradition does not spell out the specifics for constructing a synagogue, the actual interior and exterior designs were left to the congregation and the architect. Like so many other synagogues in Cleveland, this temple represented the decisions and religious interpretations of the congregation. This building, thus, is in the fashion of its time with a huge, curved mansardlike dome, rugged masonry, and picturesque towers topped with conical roofs.[16]

The classical dome of Shiloh Baptist Church, built as Temple B'nai Jeshuran, can be seen from I-77 and throughout the community. Established by a group of Hungarian Jews in 1866 under the leadership of Orthodox Rabbi Sigmund Dreschler, the original members met in Herman Sampliner's house until the growing congregation began to hold services at the German Theater and at Halle's Hall in the 1870s.[17] In 1886, B'nai Jeshuran bought the Eagle Street synagogue from the Anshe Chesed congregation and remained at this location for twenty years.

The gradual movement eastward of the members of B'nai Jeshuran prompted the leaders of the synagogue to authorize the construction of a new religious facility at East 55th Street and Scovill Avenue in 1906. The congregation remained at this site until a new structure, Temple on the Heights, was dedicated on Mayfield Road in Cleveland Heights in 1922. The congregation again moved east in 1980 when a fourth synagogue was erected in Beechwood.[18]

The Shiloh Baptist congregation bought the Scovill Avenue temple in 1922 and

52. Shiloh Baptist Church

(Originally Temple B'nai Jeshuran, 1906)
Architect: Harry Cone
Location: 5500 Scovill Avenue

have occupied the structure ever since.[19] Founded as a Protestant mission in 1850 on East 14th Street, Shiloh was the first African-American Baptist Church in the city, and it enjoyed a significant growth immediately following the Civil War. Under the guidance of the Reverend W. P. Brown, the church moved from its original location to a more suitable site on Central Avenue in 1865. In 1869, the church relocated to East 30th Street near Scovill Avenue. Continued growth of the congregation led the church to buy the large Temple B'nai Jeshuran building on Scovill. Congregations that grew out of Shiloh's membership include Mt. Zion Congregational, Messiah Baptist, Antioch Baptist, and Mt. Herman Baptist.[20]

The overall symmetrical design of the main rectangular block and transepts, the large portico with unadorned entablature, and the low-slung triangular gables are neoclassic details. Indeed, the building, with its high central dome and cruciform style, is similar in form to the Pantheon in Paris, the stylistically transitional structure that set the stage for the neoclassical movement.[21]

53. HOLY TRINITY AND ST. EDWARD ROMAN CATHOLIC CHURCH (1906)

Architect: William Guenther
Location: 7211 Woodland Avenue

Holy Trinity and St. Edward Roman Catholic Church is located on the eastern edge of Woodland Cemetery. Virtually alone, it is the only significant old building in the area.

Holy Trinity and St. Edward Roman Catholic Church is the result of two merging parishes. Holy Trinity began as part of the Holy Family parish and was organized by a number of Germans who wanted their own ethnic church; Father Peter Becker helped them establish Holy Trinity in 1880. After the German members left to form Holy Trinity, Holy Family reorganized and was renamed St. Edward. The two remained as separate entities until merging in 1975 as Holy Trinity and St. Edward Roman Catholic Church.[22]

Holy Trinity parish constructed its first church building in 1881. This was quickly followed by a larger stone structure at the corner of Woodland and East 69th Street in 1886. Subsequently, in 1906, the present building was built by master-builder William Tausch based on the plans of William Guenther. The dimensions of this structure are 119 feet by 65 feet; it has a seating capacity of 700. Rounded arches, squared-off towers with corner buttresses, and a corbel table below the front gable are reminiscent of Romanesque styling. The building's rough-cut stone was a common feature of the Romanesque churches in America at the turn of the century. The basic proportions of the structure, however, feel more Gothic. Thus, this church, like many in Cleveland, borrows elements from various styles and puts them together in new and interesting ways.

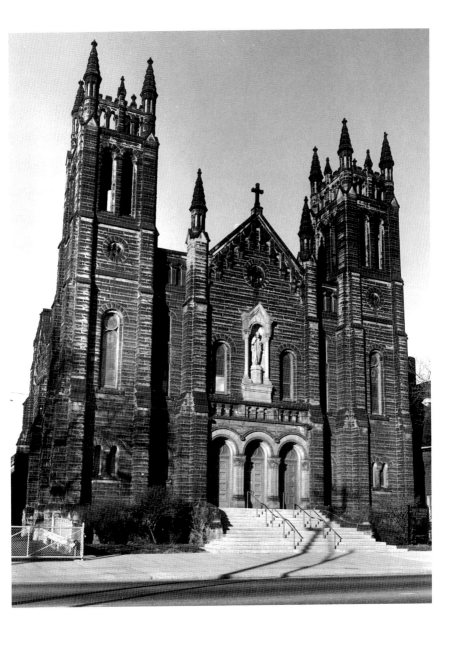

54. St. Adalbert Roman Catholic Church (1911)
Architect: William P. Ginther
Location: 2347 East 83d Street

Founded in 1883 under the guidance of Father Anthony Hynek, the Bohemian parish of St. Adalbert was an outgrowth of the earlier established St. Wenceslas congregation. Property was purchased in 1883 for a combination church-and-school and the facility was opened in 1884. This initial structure served the congregation until the present light-brown brick church was constructed in 1911.[23]

To celebrate the parish's sixty-fifth anniversary, the interior of the church was refurbished in 1948 under the guidance of Father Joseph Andel. In 1958, corresponding with the parish's seventy-fifth anniversary, the north belfry and the relics of the St. Adalbert and St. Gerard churches were restored. In 1961, the parishes of the Church of Our Lady of the Blessed Sacrament merged with this congregation and St. Adalbert to become the first Roman Catholic African-American congregation in Cleveland.[24]

Details such as symmetrically balanced open bell towers with copper crowns; a large, two-story central pavilion topped by a decorative gable; and a tripartite entrance flanked by classic columns that support a niche containing a statue of St. Adalbert make this neoclassical structure an impressive neighborhood landmark. The church's design seems to have been influenced by the cathedral in Salzburg, Austria.

55. St. James African Methodist Episcopal Church

(Originally Trinity Congregational Church, 1894)
Architects: Knox and Elliot
Location: 8401 Cedar Avenue

Built as Trinity Congregational Church, St. James A.M.E. Church is located on one of the neighborhood's major roads, Cedar Avenue. St. James's is the direct outgrowth of the East End Prayer Meeting organized by James and Rose Johnson at their Frank Street home in 1894. Initially containing sixteen members, the group quickly developed into the East End Mission of St. John A.M.E. Church. The congregation first held services at the Republican meeting hall called the Wigwam at Cedar Avenue and East 110th Street until 1899, when the new Hudson Avenue church building was completed.

The congregation continued to expand, and by 1925 St. James's had 516 members with over 460 people enrolled in the Sunday school. Under the guidance of the Reverend Joseph M. Evans, the congregation purchased the former Trinity Congregational Church at 8401 Cedar Avenue in 1926 and has remained at that site to the present day. The old Trinity Congregational building remained in good shape until a major fire ruined much of the edifice in 1938. Under the leadership of the Reverend Joseph Gomez, the congregation was able to refurbish the church

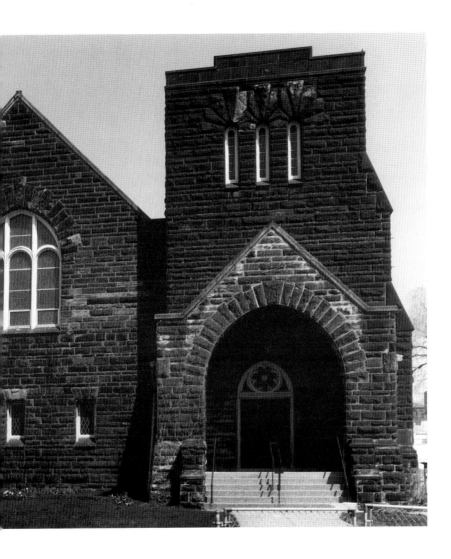

by 1941. This rebuilt structure was destroyed again by fire in 1950, but was rebuilt and rededicated in April of 1953. An education wing was added later that decade.[25]

Rock-faced coarsed ashlar, pronounced Syrian arches in the extended front portico and side entrance, and the short, squat squared-off towers emphasize the building's Richardsonian Romanesque influence.

St. James A.M.E. has taken an active role in promoting civil rights within the Cleveland community since the time of the Reverend D. Ormonde Walker in the 1920s. Reverend Walker was the founder of the St. James Literary Forum, a platform for the discussion of pertinent public issues which gained national recognition. In more recent times, the Reverends Donald G. Jacobs and Alvia A. Shaw have led the 1200-member congregation through the uncertainties associated with the civil rights movement by encouraging the church's involvement in solving the problems of the inner city and by providing a meeting place for discussing community issues.[26]

Antioch Baptist Church, with its prominent corner tower, was originally erected in 1892 to serve the Bolton Avenue Presbyterian congregation. It remained the home of the Presbyterian congregation until 1934, when the Bolton congregation joined with the congregation of Calvary Presbyterian Church at East 79th Street and Euclid Avenue.[27] The Cedar Avenue church was then purchased by the Antioch Baptist congregation.

Antioch Baptist traces its origins to Shiloh Baptist Church, one of the oldest African-American churches in Cleveland. Not fully in accord with Shiloh church leadership, a number of church members began holding their own church services in the late 1880s at the home of Henry Meyers on what is now known as East 29th Street. Officially organized in 1893 by the Reverend Alexander Moore, the church first met at the Odd Fellow's Hall on Ontario Avenue and then at a remodeled house on Central Avenue. In 1905, John D. Rockefeller donated funds to relocate

56. ANTIOCH BAPTIST CHURCH
(Originally Bolton Avenue Presbyterian Church, 1892)
Architect: William Warren Sabin
Location: 8869 Cedar Avenue

the congregation to the corner of Central Avenue and East 24th Street. The church remained at that site until the federally sponsored Cedar-Central Housing Project forced the congregation to move to its present building in 1934.[28]

The church building reflects the Romanesque design popular in America during the 1880s and 1890s. The overall asymmetrical design combined with such specific features as the massive bell tower, rusticated Syrian arches, and deep-set rounded window headers give the church its Romanesque styling. The combination of rectilinear and curved forms and the tall corner tower make it an interesting composition.

Antioch Baptist is a leading African-American institution in Cleveland, and its current minister, the Reverend Mervin McMichel, is a respected leader in the city.[29]

57. OLIVET INSTITUTIONAL BAPTIST (1954)
Architect: Unknown
Location: 8712 Quincy Avenue

Olivet Institutional Baptist Church traces its roots to the Old Third Baptist Church Mission. Established in 1884 by the Reverend C. H. Prescott, Olivet Baptist Church joined the Baptist Association in 1893. Olivet Institutional grew out of Olivet Baptist in 1931; and under the leadership of the Reverend Odie Millard Hoover, the present church was erected in 1954.[30] In 1966, the congregation built the O. M. Hoover Christian Community Center, which contains a gymnasium and religious school.

This church is essentially a modern structure with some historic ornamentation. The smooth-planed walls form a simple modern massing, while details such as the wide front gable with parapet, modified buttresses, and use of stone trim to offset the red brick veneer reflect religious tradition.

Olivet Institutional has long been recognized for its leadership in the African-American community. Under the auspices of the Reverend Otis Moss, the congregation has championed civil rights causes in Cleveland. The group also provides assistance to the neighborhood through various special programs for the elderly and others in need.

58. St. Elizabeth Roman Catholic Church (1918)
Architect: Emile Uhlrich
Location: 9016 Buckeye Road

St. Elizabeth Roman Catholic Church, an important architectural landmark, served the Hungarian Catholics who first arrived in the old Hungarian neighborhood along Buckeye Road. Established by Father Charles Boehm in 1892 to serve the local Magyar community, St. Elizabeth's has the distinction of being the oldest Hungarian Catholic parish in America. Prior to the creation of St. Elizabeth's, Cleveland's Hungarian immigrants worshiped in the Slovak parish of St. Ladislas. The original Gothic-style brick church-and-school, located at the corner of Buckeye Road and present-day East 90th Street, was completed in 1896. This building served the congregation until the parish built a social hall in 1917 and the present church structure in 1918 under the guidance of Father Julius Szepessy.[31]

The 1,344-seat church is 200 feet by 65 feet and was designed by Emile Uhlrich. Uhlrich's use of a smooth ashlar finish is reminiscent of Italian Renaissance designs. The two-story central pavilion flanked by open bell towers and a pedimented gable with side scrolls on the front facade complete the neoclassical structure. The interior space breaks away from the traditions suggested by the exterior; the interior is a large auditorium rather than the anticipated traditional nave form with central and side aisles.

Southeast Cleveland is composed of six neighborhoods: Buckeye-Woodland, Shaker, Mt. Pleasant, Lee-Miles, Corlett, and Union.

The Buckeye-Woodland area is bound on the north by Fairhill Road, on the east by East 116th Street, on the south by Kinsman, and on the west by the railroad paralleling Woodhill Road. Woodland Avenue, Shaker Boulevard, and Buckeye Road are major east-west roads; Woodhill Road, MLK Boulevard, East 110th Street, and Woodhill Road are major north-south roads.

Known as Cleveland's Little Hungary at the end of the nineteenth century, the composition of the Buckeye-Woodland neighborhood had shifted considerably, with, by 1972, African-Americans making up over 43 percent of the population. During the civil unrest of the 1960s and 1970s, the neighborhood's crime rate increased alarmingly, and many of the Hungarian immigrants, as well as other residents, left the area. In the 1980s, some of the remaining Hungarians joined forces with the newer African-American residents to establish the Buckeye-Woodland Community Development Congress with the primary goal of rejuvenating and stabilizing the neighborhood. Since then, the congress has merged with other community-oriented organizations, and the Buckeye-Woodland neighborhood is slowly being revitalized.[1]

Tour

After coming off Fairhill Road from University Circle, on Woodhill Road, begin this tour traveling south on MLK Boulevard. At the first traffic light, look to the west and note **Werner United Methodist Church**. Continue on MLK Boulevard for one more block and then turn west (right) onto Carmel Avenue.

After one block on Carmel, look to the north and note **Blessed Virgin of Mt. Carmel Roman Catholic Church**. On the northeast corner of the Carmel–Notre Dame intersection, this church stands unobtrusively in a quiet residential area. Stay on Carmel for two more blocks and then turn south (left) onto East 110th Street.

Travel on East 110th past Shaker Boulevard and proceed on MLK Boulevard. At the top of Buckeye Hill notice how FIRST HUNGARIAN LUTHERAN CHURCH (59) and the FIRST HUNGARIAN REFORMED CHURCH (60) frame Buckeye Road to form a visual portal to the downtown. Immediately following First Hungarian Reformed, turn west (right) onto a drive that runs along the edge of St. Benedictine High School. This drive leads to the small, parklike enclosure that is the setting for ST. ANDREW ABBEY (61). Its interior is one of the most moving modern sacred landmarks in the city. After visiting the abbey, turn around in the drive and head back to MLK Boulevard.

Turn south (right) onto MLK Boulevard and continue on it for one block. Turn west (right) at Lamontier. When turning, note the imposing, gray-stone ST. BENEDICT ROMAN CATHOLIC CHURCH (62), a modern interpretation of the

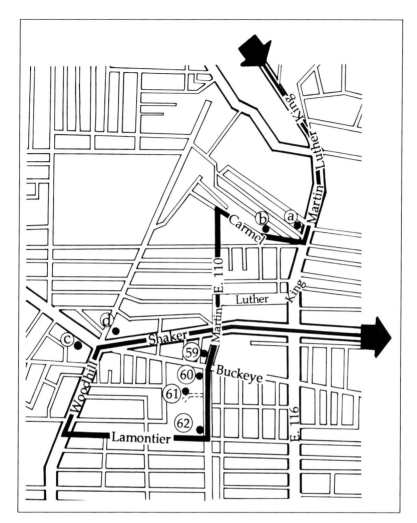

WOODLAND HILLS

59. First Hungarian Lutheran Church
60. First Hungarian Reformed Church
61. St. Andrew Abbey
62. St. Benedict Roman Catholic Church
a. Werner United Methodist Church

b. Blessed Virgin of Mt. Carmel Roman Catholic Church
c. Calvary Apostolic Assembly
d. Calvary Hill Church of God

classical style, holding down the northwest corner of the intersection. Continue on Lamontier until it ends at Woodhill Road.

Turn north (right) at Woodhill and take it until the five-point intersection. Turn northeast (right, but not hard right) onto Shaker Boulevard. When turning, look to the west and note **Calvary Apostolic Assembly;** look north and see **Calvary Hill Church of God**. Continue on Shaker Boulevard. Cross East 116th Street and enter the Shaker neighborhood. Shaker is bound on the north and east by city limits, on the south by Abell and Imperial streets, and on the west by East 116th

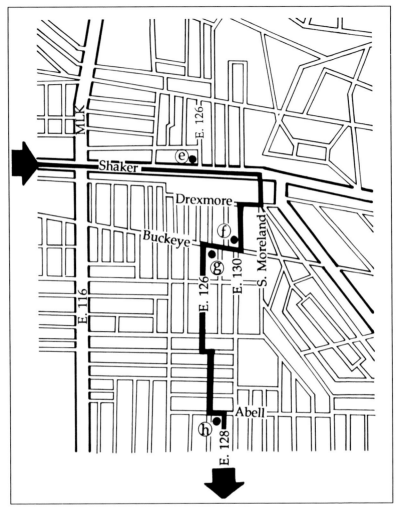

BUCKEYE-SHAKER

e. Our Lady of Peace Roman Catholic
   Church
f. Holy Grove Baptist Church

g. Grace Fundamental Baptist Church
h. Mt. Pleasant United Methodist Church

Street. Shaker Boulevard and Buckeye Road are major east-west streets; Moreland is a major north-south road.

Stay on Shaker Boulevard. At its intersection with East 127th Street, note **Our Lady of Peace Roman Catholic Church**. Located on the north side of the Shaker Rapid Transit tracks, this church is in a neighborhood of apartment houses and institutions.

Continue to move east on Shaker Boulevard, entering Shaker Square, built as an early shopping center in conjunction with the development of Shaker Heights to the east. Transformed from a traffic circle laid out in the teens, architects Philip

Small and Carl Rowley created an octagonally enclosed space based on Amalienborg Square in Copenhagen. Central pavilions flanked by lower wings can be seen in each quadrant.[2]

Exit from the southwestern quadrant of the square onto South Moreland. Travel on South Moreland for one block and then turn west (right) onto Drexmore. Stay on Drexmore for only a block and then turn south (left) onto East 130th Street. Midway down the street, look to the west and note **Holy Grove Baptist Church**. Built in 1930, it was originally Shaker Square Baptist Church.

After one block on East 130th, turn west (right) onto Buckeye Road. Stay on Buckeye until East 126th Street and then turn south (left). When turning, note the elegant proportions of the small, brick **Grace Fundamental Baptist Church** at the southeastern corner of the intersection. Designed by the Cleveland architectural firm of Hamilton and Waterson, it was built as First Hungarian Baptist in 1918.

Travel on East 126th for seven blocks and then turn east (left) onto Abell. Stay on Abell for one block and then turn south (right) onto East 128th Street. When turning, notice **Mt. Pleasant United Methodist Church** located on the northern edge of the Mt. Pleasant neighborhood. This neighborhood is bound on the north by Imperial and Abell roads and city limits, on the east by city limits, on the south by Glendale, Bartlett, and Farringdon roads, and on the west by MLK Boulevard and East 116th Street. Kinsman and Union are major east-west roads; East 140th Street is the major north-south road.

Take East 128th for two blocks and then turn west (right) onto Kinsman Road. After one block, look north and notice **Providence Baptist Church**. Stay on Kinsman for seven blocks and then turn south (left) at East 116th Street.

Travel on East 116th for one block and then turn west (right) onto Regalia. Stay on Regalia for two blocks, then turn north (right) onto East 113th Street. At this intersection, notice the contemporary church of **St. Philip Lutheran** settled into a residential neighborhood. Take East 113th back to Kinsman and then turn west (left). After one block on Kinsman, look north and see **Zion Hill Missionary Baptist Church** located just east of Luke Easter Park.

Travel on Kinsman for one more block and then turn north (right) onto MLK Boulevard. Stay on MLK for only a block and then bear west to follow the line of the park on Ramona Boulevard. Travel on Ramona for two blocks and then look north. There on the northwest corner of the intersection is **Incarnation Episcopal Church**. This little building fits in beautifully with this residential setting overlooking the park.

Follow Ramona for another block and at the northwest corner of Ramona and East 94th Street notice the large brick building of **Hayes Temple Church of God in Christ** that dominates the intersection. Bear left on the intersection to follow the curve to East 93d Street. Take East 93d for eight blocks and then look to the southeast corner of the Heath–East 93d intersection. Located in the center of the Union neighborhood just north of the library on the commercial strip is **St. Catherine Roman Catholic Church (63)**. The Union neighborhood is bound on the north by Kinsman Road, on the east by MLK Boulevard, on the south by Erie Railroad tracks, and on the west by the old Pennsylvania Railroad.

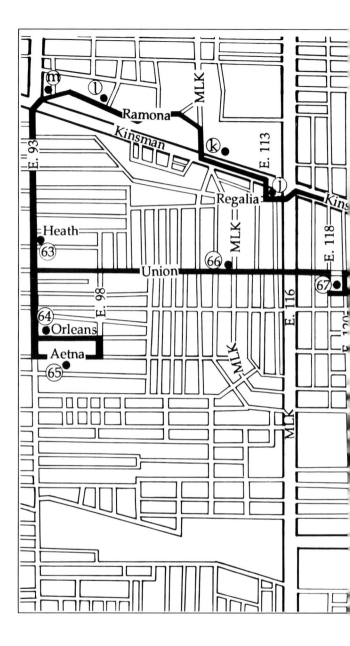

Union/Mt. Pleasant/Corlett ⚏

63. St. Catherine Roman Catholic Church
64. Greater Zion Hill Baptist Church
65. Nativity of the Blessed Virgin Mary
66. Mt. Haven Baptist Church
67. Epiphany Roman Catholic Church
68. St. Cecilia Roman Catholic Church
69. Mt. Pleasant Catholic Elementary
    School
70. St. Mary of Czestochowa Roman
    Catholic Church

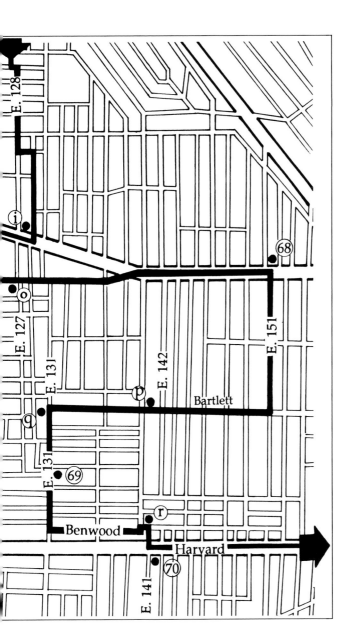

i. Providence Baptist Church
j. St. Philip Lutheran
k. Zion Hill Missionary Baptist Church
l. Incarnation Episcopal Church
m. Hayes Temple Church of God in Christ
n. Second Tabernacle Church
o. Christian Missionary Alliance
p. St. Mark A.M.E.
q. Holy Trinity Baptist Church
r. Fifth Christian Church

71. Lutheran Church of the Good Shepherd
s. St. Henry Roman Catholic Church
t. Harvard Avenue Church of God in Christ
u. Lee Heights Community Church
v. Southeast Seventh Day Adventist
w. St. Paul United Methodist Church
x. Lee Seville Baptist Church

Take East 93d for six more blocks and then turn east (left) at Orleans. Look to the north and notice the dominant structure of **GREATER ZION HILL BAPTIST CHURCH (64)**, originally constructed for the St. Joseph Byzantine Catholic parish. Take Orleans for one block and turn south (right) onto East 98th Street. Stay on East 98th for one block and turn west (right) onto Aetna. Midway down the block look to the south and see **NATIVITY OF THE BLESSED VIRGIN MARY (65)**, a rather large neoclassical-style neighborhood church. Take Aetna one block and turn north (right) at East 93d Street.

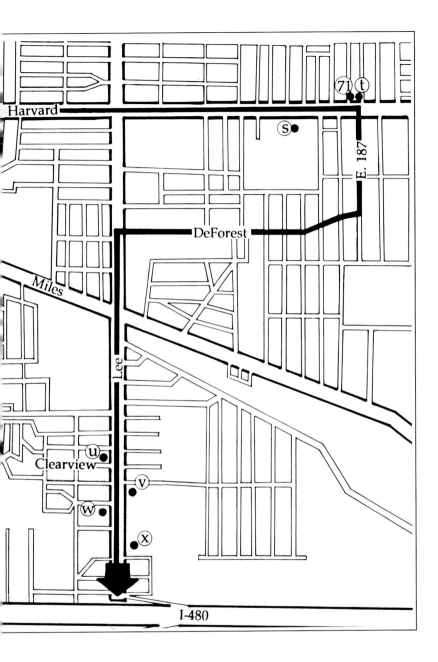

Backtrack on East 93d for six blocks and then turn east (right) at Union Avenue. At Union's intersection with MLK Boulevard, note the elegant, gray-stone building of **MT. HAVEN BAPTIST CHURCH (66)** on the northwestern corner, originally constructed by the congregation of Concordia Evangelical Lutheran Church.

Continue on Union until East 118th Street. Turn south (right) at East 118th and travel on it for one block. Turn east (left) onto Oakfield and travel on it for only a block. Turn north (left) onto East 120th. When turning, note **EPIPHANY**

ROMAN CATHOLIC CHURCH (67) with its unique combination of modern and Gothic styling.

Take East 120th for only a block and then turn east (right) back onto Union. Look to the north and note **Second Tabernacle Church** on the northwestern corner of Union's intersection with East 121st Street.

Take Union for four more blocks and then look to the east to note **Christian Missionary Alliance** on the southwestern corner of Union's intersection with East 127th. Continue on Union until its three-point intersection with Kinsman.

Travel east on Kinsman until East 150th Street. Here at the northeast corner of the intersection notice St. CECILIA ROMAN CATHOLIC CHURCH (68), a modern interpretation of the Georgian style. Take Kinsman for one block and turn south (right) at East 151st Street.

Stay on East 151st for two long blocks and turn west (right) at Bartlett. Continue on Bartlett for seven blocks. At the northwest corner of Bartlett's intersection with East 140th Street, in a tidy residential neighborhood, is **St. Mark A.M.E.** Stay on Bartlett for two more blocks and then turn south (left) onto East 131st Street to enter the Corlett neighborhood. Corlett is bound on the north by Farringdon and Bartlett, on the east by Judson Road and East 154th Street, on the south by Cleveland city limits and Erie Railroad tracks, and on the west by MLK Boulevard. Harvard and Corlett are major east-west roads; East 131st is the major north-south street.

Immediately after turning, look west and note **Holy Trinity Baptist Church**. With the next two churches, the elementary school, library, and surrounding stores, this church helps define the center of the Corlett neighborhood. Keep on East 131st for five more blocks. Look east and note the MT. PLEASANT CATHOLIC ELEMENTARY SCHOOL property (69), formerly Holy Family Roman Catholic Church, now used as a school only. Stay on East 131st for three more blocks and turn east (left) onto Benwood.

Stay on Benwood for three blocks. Here, opposite East 141st Street in a totally residential neighborhood, is **Fifth Christian Church**. Turn south (right) onto East 141st and stay on it for one block. Turn east (left) on Harvard Avenue. When turning note St. MARY OF CZESTOCHOWA ROMAN CATHOLIC CHURCH (70) diagonally opposite Jamison Intermediate School. Proceed east on Harvard Avenue and enter the Lee-Miles neighborhood at East 154th Street. After crossing Lee Road, opposite East 183d Street, look south and note **St. Henry Roman Catholic Church** just east of the Whitney Junior High School playing field. Stay on Harvard for two more blocks. Opposite East 187th Street are two churches that share the same facility, LUTHERAN CHURCH OF THE GOOD SHEPHERD (71) and **Harvard Avenue Church of God in Christ**.

Turn south (right) onto East 187th Street. After two blocks, turn west (right) onto De Forest and take it until Lee Road. At Lee Road turn south (left) and follow it for six blocks. Here, look to the northwestern corner of Lee's intersection with Clearview and note **Lee Heights Community Church**.

Travel two more blocks on Lee. Look to the southeast corner of the intersection and observe **Southeast Seventh Day Adventist**. Stay on Lee for another block and look to the west to see the octagonal **St. Paul United Methodist**

Church. Continue one more block on Lee and note **Lee Seville Baptist Church** to the east.

This ends the tour of the Southeast neighborhoods. Lee Road intersects with Interstate-480 a few blocks south of Lee Seville Baptist Church.

59. First Hungarian Lutheran Church (1940)
Architect: R. Orr
Location: 2830 MLK Boulevard

Located at the top of the Buckeye Road hill in a predominantly residential neighborhood, First Hungarian Lutheran Church and First Hungarian Reformed Church located across the street frame a magnificent western view of downtown. Founded in 1906 to serve the Hungarian community, the First Hungarian Lutheran congregation bought its first religious structure on Rawlings Avenue in 1907. First Hungarian Lutheran remained at that location until its present Gothic-style facility at the corner of Buckeye Road and MLK Boulevard was constructed in 1940. The church exhibits such Gothic details as pointed arches and wall buttresses. Louvers in the belfry give it a more universal architectural flair. Kossuth Hall, built in

1953, was designed to complement the earlier church structure. The lightly colored brick veneer and its height help the building to blend in well with the original sanctuary.

The First Hungarian Lutheran congregation has had a long tradition of helping others, including homeless in the United States and in Europe. In 1913, the church sponsored the first Hungarian orphanage in America, and in the 1940s the congregation assisted over 200 immigrants in finding employment and homes in the Cleveland area. After the Hungarian uprising in 1956, the church helped 100 freedom-fighters relocate to the United States.[3]

60. First Hungarian Reformed Church (1948)
   Architect: H. W. Maurer
   Location: 2856 MLK Boulevard

First Hungarian Reformed Church was founded by the Reverend Gustav Juranyi in 1891. The congregation authorized the erection of a frame church on what is today East 79th Street in 1894. The congregation's growth necessitated the construction of a larger facility, and under the leadership of the Reverend Alexander Csutoros a stone facility was constructed on the East 79th Street site in 1899.[4] In 1948 the congregation moved to a new Romanesque-style structure located on what is now MLK Boulevard. This new religious center was designed by H. W. Maurer to complement and connect with Bethlehem Hall and an educational facility already located on the site.

Since the building's proportions and overall styling are far more formal than many other comparably sized contemporary churches, First Hungarian Reformed has been called a miniature cathedral.[5] A twin arcade effect in the nave windows, rounded arches, and a corbel table suggest Romanesque detailing.

61. St. Andrew Abbey (1986)
Architect: Evans Woolen
Location: 2900 MLK Boulevard

Nestled into a parklike setting behind St. Benedictine High School is a newer chapel that is much more visually stimulating than the school. The modern St. Andrew Abbey, a Benedictine monastery, represents the oldest Roman Catholic monastic community in the world.[6]

The Benedictines came to Cleveland in 1922 when two monks assumed the pastorate at the Slovak parish of St. Andrew on Superior Avenue. In 1929, the Benedictines were given charge of the St. Benedict parish on what is now MLK Boulevard; in the same year, the newly relocated monastery gained recognition as an independent community.[7]

In 1952, a new abbey was constructed, and it served the Benedictines until the present abbey was built in 1986. In the new structure designed by architect Evans

Woolen, traditional architectural forms, such as the classical portico, are amalgamated with more modern spaces, such as the soaring, skylit chapel, to create a distinctive design. The hexagonal shape of the chapel, the centralized altar (though slightly off center), and the face-to-face seating arrangement emphasize the concepts of Vatican II: God among the people. However, there is also the suggestion of procession created by the central axis which runs through the Romanesque-style portico, exterior entry, altar, and scalloped rear wall, alluding to the energy of the early church. Perhaps more than any other sacred landmark, this abbey church successfully combines the tradition of procession while encouraging participation among its worshipers.[8]

62. St. Benedict Roman Catholic Church (1952)
Architect: J. Ellsworth Potter
Location: 2940 MLK Boulevard

The severe-looking gray-stone building of St. Benedict Roman Catholic Church anchors the northwest corner of a well-kept residential neighborhood at MLK Boulevard and Lamontier Avenue. Originating from the Slovak parish of St. Ladislas, the first church was constructed in 1922 as a parish hall and school. In 1928 the bishop transferred the church and school to the Benedictine fathers to serve parishioners who were moving east of the parent parish located on East 92d Street.

The plan of the church is unusual. The main part of the congregational space is square at the ground level but octagonal above. To maintain the traditional cruciform shape, a portion of the nave is extended east to the narthex; the transepts serve as side chapels and side aisles rather than seating space. The sanctuary and

apse at the western end are aligned with the narrower eastern part of the nave completing the Latin cross within the larger form. Overall, the church measures 117 feet by 181 feet and seats 1,300 people. The dome over the central space is 53 feet in diameter and 60 feet above the floor.

Made of smooth Indiana limestone, the church is classical in style. The central entry doors are flanked first by slender columns with Corinthian capitals and then by massive walls that support a large gable. Between the gable end and the entry doors is a rose window depicting St. Benedict surrounded by palms and garlands made of stone. To the southwest is the bell tower designed in the baroque style. The bells are from the former parish hall and school. Nearby, a white Italian-marble statue of Our Lady of Fatima faces Lamontier Avenue.

63. St. Catherine Roman Catholic Church (1917)

Architect: Edward J. Schneider
Location: 9412 Heath Avenue

St. Catherine Roman Catholic Church is located across from the Union neighborhood library on a busy commercial street. Founded in 1898 by Father John T. Carroll, St. Catherine's parish served the people formerly living within the northeast section of the Holy Name parish. Shortly after the congregation created its first structure, the building was destroyed by fire; a second frame church was built in 1899. In 1900, Father James J. Quinn became pastor of the congregation. Father Quinn authorized the construction of a new rectory in 1908 and the erection of a classical-style sanctuary in 1917. This new religious facility was designed to fit the growing congregation and can seat up to 800 worshipers.[9]

The building's dark-colored, rough-textured brick offset by lighter-colored, smooth stone ornamentation is characteristic of early twentieth-century classical-style churches. The corbel stone detail evident in the gables and the pyramidal shape of the bell tower roof are modified Romanesque detailing. Butticini marble altars and reredos, statues of St. Anne and the Sacred Heart, windows with representations of the four evangelists, and an oak pulpit and communion rail grace the interior.

64. GREATER ZION HILL BAPTIST CHURCH

(Originally St. Joseph Byzantine Catholic Church, 1933)
Architect: Joseph Franczak
Location: 9411 Orleans Avenue

Located in an area of small houses, Greater Zion Hill Baptist, built as St. Joseph Byzantine Catholic Church, is one of the neighborhood's dominant forms. St. Joseph Byzantine Catholic, one of eleven Ruthenian Byzantine Rite congregations in Cleveland that traces its origins to St. John the Baptist Byzantine Rite Catholic Church on Scovill Avenue, was founded in 1898 and became a cathedral in the late 1960s.

Built in 1933, this Orleans Avenue religious complex was sold to the Greater Zion Hill Baptist congregation when the original congregation moved to Brecksville. The basic form is traditional, but the yellow brick and simplified details give the church a more modern feeling. The narthex facing Orleans Avenue contains three doors topped by three windows that are proportional to the doors, thus creating a sense of verticality. All are framed in a singular Romanesque arch that is flanked by two towers capped by copper semidomes which convey the church's Byzantine character.

65. NATIVITY OF THE BLESSED VIRGIN MARY (1927)
Architect: William Jansen
Location: 9614 Aetna Road

Not only the size, but also the distinctive classical detailing of Nativity of the Blessed Virgin Mary set it apart from the predominantly small-scale, vernacular residential neighborhood. Established as a Slovak parish by Father Joseph Ptasinski as an outgrowth of St. Ladislas, the congregation of the Nativity of the Blessed Virgin Mother built its first church-and-school on Aetna Road in 1903. The original church was a two-story frame structure that served the parish until the present brick building was erected in 1927.[10]

The church's twin bell towers with oculi, open belfries, and quoins provide a rather elaborate frame for the tripartite entrance. The center portal, framed by classical columns and capped by a triangular pediment, creates an elaborate gateway for the church's processional. The overall composition, system of proportions, and contrasting materials make the church a good example of neoclassical styling. On the interior, the glass-covered stations of the cross are from the former church, and a wood figure of the Blessed Virgin is housed within a chamber to the right of the vestibule.

66. Mt. Haven Baptist Church

(Originally Concordia
Evangelical Lutheran
Church, 1937)
Architect: H. W. Maurer
Location: 3484 MLK
Boulevard

Located at the crossing of MLK Boulevard and Union Avenue, the elegant stone Mt. Haven Baptist Church rests on the intersection's northwest corner. Built as Concordia Evangelical Lutheran Church, this structure marks the eastern edge of the Union neighborhood.

Concordia Evangelical Lutheran was founded in 1914 by Pastors M. Ilse, Sr., P. Kleinhaus, and G. Goetsch to serve the Lutheran community located within the greater Union Avenue area. The Cleveland City Mission Society assisted the new congregation in the erection of a combination church-and-school at the corner of Union Avenue and what is now Martin Luther King, Jr., Boulevard in 1916. Growth of the congregation in the 1930s led church officials to approve the construction of a new church facility in 1937. The limited size of the parcel (85 feet by 40 feet) forced architect H. W. Maurer to link the old to the new by placing

halls on either side to serve both structures. This arrangement allowed seating for 700 people. Concordia Lutheran remained at this site until merging with St. John Lutheran in Independence in 1967.[11] The structure was then sold to Mt. Haven Baptist Church.

Established in 1905 by the Reverend I. A. Lawson, the congregation soon relocated from East 22d Street near Central Avenue to a former residential structure on East 33d Street.[12] In 1911, the congregation moved to Cedar Avenue and remained there until purchasing the Concordia Lutheran building in 1967. The interior was refurbished in 1980. Lancet windows, modified crenelation, and a squared-off open belfry give this rough-stone structure an English Gothic flair. Stained-glass windows by Howard G. Wilbert and Albert W. Weitershausen of Pittsburgh and the pulpit's handcarved tracery add grace to the church's interior.

67. Epiphany Roman Catholic Church (1948)

Architect: George W. Stickle
Location: 11901 Oakfield Avenue

Epiphany Roman Catholic Church is located in a residential neighborhood one block south of Union Avenue. The parish was established in 1944 to serve the Catholic community residing within the greater Union-Miles neighborhood. The present structure was built in 1948 under the direction of Father John Dunn, formerly of the St. Anne parish in Youngstown.[13]

The building is essentially a simple ashlar-stone meetinghouse with a more elaborate facade facing East 120th Street. Here the rough stone is complemented by smoother stone trim at the roofline and around the door. The recessed entry is the most unique feature of the structure and is quite a bit more modern than the rest of the church. In place of the typical entry door and rose or perpendicular window, the architect has combined the entry door and window into a singular recessed form. In place of the typical round or pointed arch, the designer has placed large corbel stones at the top of the recessed opening to create a jagged effect, and the entire recessed space is filled with glass block, with the exception of the church sign and door.

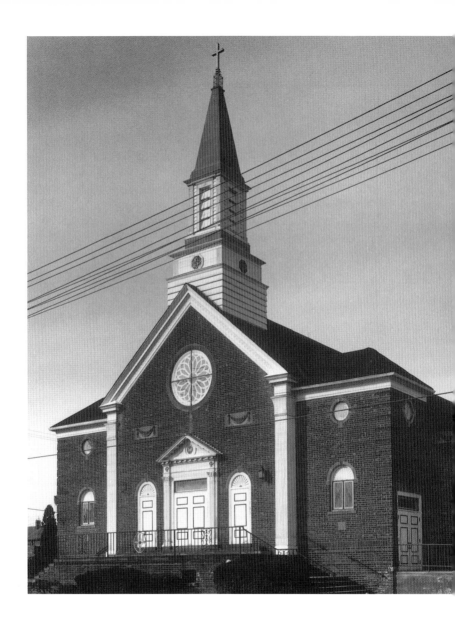

68. St. Cecilia Roman Catholic Church (1916)

Architects: Schneider and Potter
Location: 3476 East 152d Street

Location on the northwest corner of the East 152d–Kinsman intersection, St. Cecilia Roman Catholic Church is on the edge of one of the neighborhood's busiest commercial streets. St. Cecilia's was established by Father John T. Farrell in 1915 to serve the various nationalities residing within the greater East 152d–Kinsman area. Religious services were held in a store on Kinsman Avenue until a frame church was erected on the corner of Kinsman and East 152d in 1916.[14] In the 1940s, Bishop James A. McFadden permitted the structure to be enlarged and modernized; seating was increased from 475 to 950, and the exterior was given a new brick veneer with contrasting trim. The symmetrical composition, central gable, and rose window topped by plain square bell tower with belfry louvers and simple spire create a modified Georgian-style structure.

Along with Grace Missionary Baptist and Holy Trinity Baptist, what used to be Holy Family Church and School forms a physical center of the Corlett neighborhood. Mt. Pleasant Elementary School, a library, and stores create this local hub.

The Holy Family congregation began as a division of the much-larger Our Lady of Lourdes parish. A Bohemian parish, the Holy Family congregation, under the guidance of Father Stephen Furdek, erected their first church on East 131st Street in 1911. Under the leadership of Father Kresina, the congregation built the existing combination church-and-school in 1920. In 1988, Holy Family Church was closed and the property was given to Mt. Pleasant Catholic Elementary School.[15]

69. Mt. Pleasant Catholic Elementary School
(Originally Holy Family Church and School, 1920)
Architect: William Koehl
Location: 13205 Chapelside Avenue

Built in an "L" shape, the building was designed on a human scale by featuring the low-profile extended eaves generally associated with the Prairie School style made popular by architect Frank Lloyd Wright. Its jerkin-head roof with projecting eaves and slightly projected central block helps create a residential scale and silhouette. The grouped windows below the roofline, the tripartite entrance, and the protruding waterlines establish a layered effect in the facade. The bottom layer of the facade then extends out from the structure to form steps.

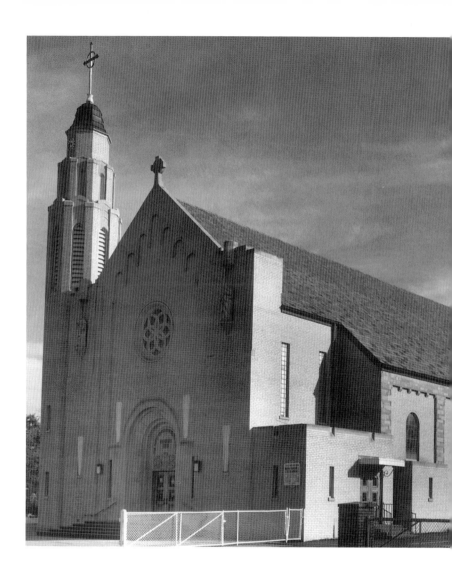

70. St. Mary of Czestochowa Roman Catholic Church (1952)
Architect: Stickle and Associates
Location: Harvard Avenue at East 141st Street

St. Mary of Czestochowa Roman Catholic Church is located diagonally across from Jamison Intermediate School in the midst of a predominantly residential neighborhood. Organized in 1913 by Father Victor Szyrocki out of the larger Polish parish of the Sacred Heart of Jesus, St. Mary of Czestochowa first held services in a house remodeled as a church at the corner of Harvard and East 141st in 1914.[16] The original church was enlarged in the early 1920s and then replaced by a more modern brick facility in 1930. This building, which acted as both a church and school, served the congregation until growth of the parish after World War II necessitated the construction of a new sanctuary in 1952.

Corbeling below the roofline, a recessed double-door main entrance below a modified compound arch, and a modern rose window help define this church's smooth planar facade and give it Romanesque characteristics. The octagonal bell tower with its arched louvered belfry topped by a multilayered cupola placed next to the main volume appears more detailed than the rest of the church.

71. Lutheran Church of the Good Shepherd (1945, 1959)

Architect: T. A. Badowski
Location: 18615 Harvard Avenue

The Lutheran Church of the Good Shepherd is located in the heart of a residential neighborhood near the eastern city limit. It was organized in 1945 as the Lee-Harvard Mission by the Reverend Paul Dergdall to serve the Lutheran community located along the southeast border of Cleveland.[17] The first church was constructed in 1945 and was renovated to serve as the educational center for the congregation when the present structure was erected in 1959. More recently, the original structure, which is attached to the new church, has been used by another, growing congregation, Harvard Avenue Church of God in Christ.

Built of light-colored brick with dark-brown brick accents, this modern structure with its high ridge and low eaves lacks much of the historic detail often associated with more traditional religious facilities. Wall surfaces are plain and serve as a backdrop for the large, white cross that is the focus of the entire structure. The bell and steeple above the chancel seem small and delicate in contrast to the heavy masses of masonry below.

CHAPTER SIX

The Broadway Corridor

The Broadway Corridor is made up of two neighborhoods situated along State Route 14, Broadway to the northwest and Miles Park to the south and east.

The Broadway neighborhood is bound on the north by Rapid Transit tracks, on the east by Garden Valley Avenue and Erie Railroad tracks, on the south by old New York Central Railroad tracks, and on the west by the Willow Freeway and Cleveland city limits. Union, Aetna, Fleet, and Harvard are major east-west roads; East 65th and 55th are major north-south streets. Broadway Avenue cuts through the neighborhood from the northwest corner to the southeastern edge. In contrast to other areas, Broadway maintains its strong ethnic character to the present day. This is due, in part, to the solid ethnic base of the local parishes.

TOUR

Begin the tour at the intersection of I-77 and Fleet Avenue, traveling east on Fleet. At the southeast corner of the Fleet–East 50th intersection, note **St. John Nepomuceine Roman Catholic Church**. Visible from I-77 and the Fleet Avenue exit, this church, with its tall tower and dark brick exterior, acts as a gateway to Slavic Village, the old Warszawa neighborhood.

Continue east on Fleet for four more blocks and then turn north (left) onto East 55th Street. Take East 55th north past the tracks and pause at the corner of Hamm to note **OUR LADY OF LOURDES ROMAN CATHOLIC CHURCH (72)** to the west. Stay on East 55th until Broadway Avenue. Turn northwest (left) at Broadway and continue on it for two blocks.

At the southern corner of the McBride-Broadway intersection, note the **KOREAN AMERICAN UNITED METHODIST CHURCH (73)**. Turn northeast (right) onto McBride. Continue on McBride past St. Alexis Hospital until East 55th Street. Turn north (left) onto East 55th, cross the tracks, and continue for four blocks.

Turn east (right) on Francis and pass three blocks. Look to the south and note the old and new **St. Hyacinth Roman Catholic Church**. Located in an older, secluded neighborhood off Broadway and separated by railroad tracks, these two structures demonstrate how this institution has been an integral part of this community throughout the years.

Continue on Francis for a block and then turn south (right) onto East 65th Street. Travel on East 65th until it ends at Union Avenue. Turn east (left) onto Union and stay on it for seven blocks. Turn south (right) on East 80th Street and stay on it for one short block. Turn east (left) onto Mansfield. After one block turn south (right) onto East 81st Street and note **ST. LAWRENCE ROMAN CATHOLIC CHURCH (74)** to the west.

Travel south on East 81st for two blocks. Turn west (right) onto Aetna and continue on it until East 65th Street. Turn south (left) at East 65th. After three blocks look to the east and note **ST. STANISLAUS ROMAN CATHOLIC CHURCH (75)**, one of the largest churches in Cleveland.

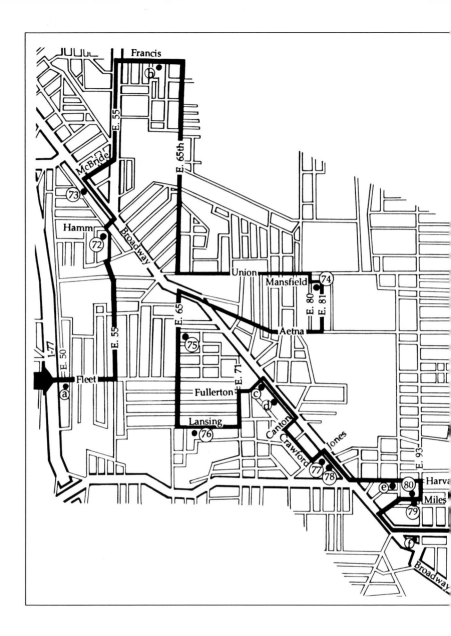

Continue on East 65th for seven more blocks and then turn east (left) at Lansing. Look to the south and note **THE IMMACULATE HEART OF MARY ROMAN CATHOLIC CHURCH (76)**. Stay on Lansing until it ends at East 71st Street. Turn north (left) onto East 71st and stay on it for two blocks.

Turn east (right) at Fullerton and stay on it until Broadway. Turn northwest (right) onto Broadway. When turning note the Gothic **Church of the Holy Transfiguration**. Following this is the small brick **Holy Trinity National Polish Cathedral**.

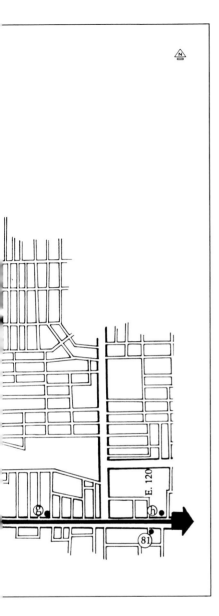

72. Our Lady of Lourdes Roman Catholic Church
73. Korean American United Methodist Church
74. St. Lawrence Roman Catholic Church
75. St. Stanislaus Roman Catholic Church
76. The Immaculate Heart of Mary Roman Catholic Church
77. Jones Road Congregational Church
78. Holy Name Roman Catholic Church
79. Miles Park Presbyterian Church
80. Allen Chapel-Missionary Baptist Church
81. Shaffer Memorial Methodist Church
  a. St. John Nepomuceine Roman Catholic Church
  b. St. Hyacinth Roman Catholic Church
  c. Church of the Holy Transfiguration
  d. Holy Trinity National Polish Cathedral
  e. Calvary Episcopal Church
  f. Triumph the Church and Kingdom of God in Christ
  g. Apostolic House of God
  h. East Mt. Vernon Baptist Church

Stay on Broadway only to Canton Avenue and then turn southwest (right) onto Canton. Continue on Canton for one block and then southeast (left) onto Crawford. Stay on Crawford until it ends at Jones Road. Turn northeast (left) onto Jones. Look to the east and note **JONES ROAD CONGREGATIONAL CHURCH (77)**. Stay on Jones until it intersects with Broadway.

Turn southeast (right) at Broadway. After passing under the railroad tracks, look to the southwest and see **HOLY NAME ROMAN CATHOLIC CHURCH (78)**. Continue on Broadway until it intersects Harvard Avenue.

Turn east (left) and proceed on Harvard for three blocks. Note **Calvary Episcopal Church**, formally Grace Episcopal, in the southwest corner of the intersection. Stay on Harvard for one more block and then turn south (right) onto East 93d Street. Stay on East 93d until its intersection with Miles Park Avenue.

Turn west (right) onto Miles Park and enter Miles Park proper, the heart of what used to be the Village of Newburgh. Created when the village was plotted in 1850, the park and commons at what are now East 93d and Sawyer streets were the site of a town hall in 1860. Annexed to Cleveland in 1873, the site was named Miles Park in honor of Theodore Miles, who donated the land to Newburgh.[1]

The Miles Park neighborhood is bound on the north by New York Central Railroad and Erie Railroad tracks, on the east by East 124th Street, on the south by city limits, and on the west by city limits and New York Central Railroad tracks. Harvard and Miles Park are major east-west avenues; Broadway Avenue runs diagonally through the neighborhood from northwest to southeast.

After turning, look to the south and notice **MILES PARK PRESBYTERIAN CHURCH (79)**. After one block, look to the north and note **ALLEN CHAPEL-MISSIONARY BAPTIST CHURCH (80)** on the northeast corner of the intersection.

Follow the curve of Miles Park Avenue to Broadway and turn southeast. After one block, bear east (left) onto Miles Avenue. Shortly after this intersection, look to the south and note **Triumph the Church and Kingdom of God in Christ**. Lovingly restored by its congregation, it is located at the southeastern edge of the neighborhood's commercial district.

Continue east on Miles Avenue. At the northwest corner of East 110th Street note the **Apostolic House of God**. Continue on Miles Avenue until it intersects with East 120th. On the south is **SHAFFER MEMORIAL METHODIST CHURCH (81)**. Travel on Miles Avenue one block farther east and note **East Mt. Vernon Baptist Church** on the northwest corner of East 124th Street and Miles Avenue. This ends the tour of the Broadway Corridor. Continue east on Miles to Warrensville Center Road. Turn right (south). After a few blocks there is an interchange with Interstate-480. Take I-480 west to I-77 north to get to the West Side, where the next tour commences.

72. OUR LADY OF LOURDES ROMAN CATHOLIC CHURCH (1891)
Architects: Emile Uhlrich and J. Vandervelde
Location: 3395 East 53d Street

Our Lady of Lourdes Roman Catholic Church is tucked away one block south of the busy commercial intersection of Broadway Avenue and East 55th Street. The congregation traces its origins to the St. Wenceslas parish, a Bohemian parish established by Father Anthony Krasney on East 35th Place near Woodland Avenue in 1867. The growth of the St. Wenceslas congregation during the 1870s necessitated the creation of a second Bohemian parish in the district; in 1883 Our

Lady of Lourdes was organized under the guidance of Father Stephen Furdek. During its first year, the parish built a frame church-and-school. The rapid growth of the parish led to the construction of a larger church building in 1891. This late-nineteenth-century Victorian structure is still used by parishioners.

Designed by architects Emile Uhlrich and J. Vandervelde, this brick building trimmed in stone contains details typical of Victorian Gothic structures, such as the tripartite entrance with double points, the large rose window, and the wall buttresses. More unique features include the statue of Our Lady of Lourdes above the rose window, the oculus windows on the south tower, and the clock beneath the steeple on the north tower.

73. KOREAN AMERICAN UNITED METHODIST CHURCH

(Originally Broadway Methodist Church, 1918)
Architect: Unknown
Location: 5246 Broadway Avenue

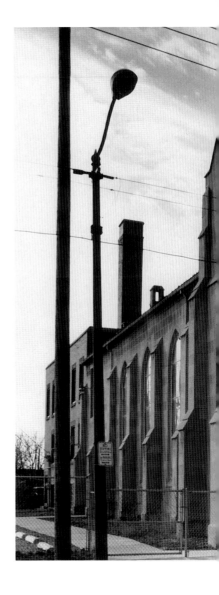

Located diagonally across the street from St. Alexis Hospital is the Korean American United Methodist Church, built as Broadway Methodist Church in 1918. Established as a nondenominational religious institution in 1872, Broadway Church served the Bohemian community centered in the Broadway–East 55th neighborhood. The Gothic-style frame church originally located on this site was often referred to as "the wigwam" and was home to the congregation until 1917, when the Methodists unveiled plans to erect the current complex.[2] Finished in 1918, the new complex includes a church with a 600-seat sanctuary, a school with a 2,000-seat auditorium, and a community center.

In the early twentieth century, the Methodists attempted many missions aimed at serving newly arrived immigrants. Of these missions, Broadway Methodist Church was the most successful. The church offered a wealth of activities in ad-

dition to worship, including employment services, health care, and English language instruction in addition to theater performances, recreational activities, and social activities for area residents. Services were conducted in a number of languages and religious education was offered in seventeen different languages.[3] In 1985 the Korean American United Methodist Congregation purchased the facility.

Built out of Indiana limestone, this church has pointed arches, wall buttresses, and a recessed main entrance, all of which suggest Gothic styling. A large square bell tower with crenelation and pinnacles is one of this building's most noteworthy features. The interior, according to Cleveland historian Clay Herrick, has one of the best copies of Leonardo da Vinci's *The Last Supper.* When the original was being restored in Milan, Italy, the artists who were doing the restoration and preservation traveled to Cleveland to examine this church's reproduction.

74. St. Lawrence Roman Catholic Church (1924, 1939)
Architect: George S. Voinovich, Sr.
Location: 3547 East 81st Street

St. Lawrence Roman Catholic Church serves a small, well-kept residential neighborhood located in the northeast corner of the larger North Broadway neighborhood. Located between Union and Aetna on East 81st, the church must be approached via Mansfield and East 80th Street due to the Union Street bridge over the Erie Railroad line.

Organized as a Slovenian parish in 1901 by Father Francis Kerze, the congregation attended services in the basement of Holy Name Roman Catholic Church until St. Lawrence's combination church-and-school on East 81st Street was completed in 1902. This facility was greatly enlarged in 1924 by Cleveland architect William Jansen. The church was converted into a school when the new church was constructed in 1940. A newer, modern entry to the school covers the facade of the earlier church. The present brick church structure with stone trim was designed by George S. Voinovich, Sr., and can seat 700.[4] The church's rounded arches and squared-off bell tower give the smooth, plain building a Romanesque character.

75. St. Stanislaus Roman Catholic Church (1886)
Architect: William H. Dunn
Location: 3649 East 65th Street

St. Stanislaus Roman Catholic Church is one of the largest Gothic-style churches in the United States. Located in the heart of Slavic Village, this red-brick building has served Cleveland's Polish community since 1886, and has the distinction of being the oldest Polish parish in Cleveland. Established by Father Victor Zareczny in 1873, the St. Stanislaus congregation held their first services at St. Mary of the Flats.[5] The congregation continued to use the St. Mary church until Father Wolfgang Janietz moved the parish to the former Franciscan monastery on Hazen Street in 1879.

A two-story structure was erected at the corner of Forman Avenue and East 65th Street in 1881, and this combination church-and-school served the parish for nearly ten years. Additions to the church between 1881 and 1885 included a rectory and an enlarged main sanctuary. By 1884 it was already apparent that these alterations were temporary, and plans were unveiled for the present, larger church in 1886. Under the auspices of Father Anthony Kolazewski, the brick, Gothic-style structure was completed in 1892. Because the cost of construction was considered too extravagant, Father Kolazewski was removed as pastor in 1892 and was initially replaced by Father Benedict Rosinski. The parish was returned to the administration of the Franciscan community in 1906.[6]

Built of brick with contrasting white trim, the original church contained two 232-foot towers, which were destroyed by a tornado in 1909; the replacement towers are 122 feet high. The main door of the tripartite entrance is crowned by a large stained-glass window over which a statue of St. Stanislaus is placed. Vaulted ceilings, pronounced ribs, stained glass, and polychromatic figures within the various niches at the side and in the altar add to the medieval flavor of the interior.

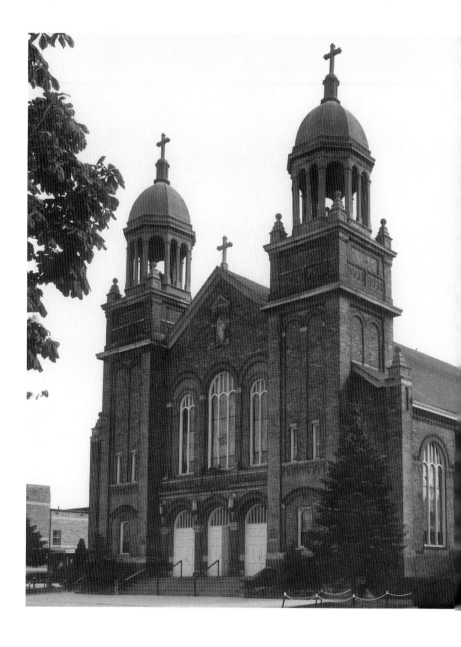

Located in a tree-lined residential neighborhood on the south side of Lansing Avenue, the large, imposing Immaculate Heart of Mary Roman Catholic Church serves the Polish Catholic community located south of Fleet Avenue. The Immaculate Heart of Mary was founded in 1894 under the leadership of Father Anthony Francis Kolazewski, the former pastor of St. Stanislaus. Originally this parish served the Polish immigrants living within the Warszawa district of Cleveland who were not affiliated with the St. Stanislaus congregation. The congregation first erected a frame structure that was used as a combination church-and-school. Under the leadership of Father M. Pawloski, the parishioners built the structure

76. The Immaculate Heart of Mary Roman Catholic Church (1914)
Architect: A. F. Wasilewski
Location: 6700 Lansing

with donated materials; blueprints from a similar church in Tulsa, Oklahoma, were used to guide the construction process. The church is 152 feet by 85 feet and has a seating capacity of 1,250.[7] Under the direction of Father Aloysius Dombrowski, the sanctuary was remodeled consistent with the recommendations of the Second Vatican Council (1962–65).

The classical-style church has such Romanesque elements as rounded arches, modified compound arches around the main entrance, and corbeling. However, the open belfries in the symmetrical twin towers surrounded by copper finials and topped by copper cupolas are associated with the Italian Renaissance style.

77. Jones Road Congregational Church (1876)
Architect: A. D. Kent
Location: 8000 Jones Road

This little church, which abuts the railroad tracks just south of Broadway, is one of the oldest in the city. Established in 1857 to serve the religious needs of Welsh immigrants settling within what was then the Village of Newburgh, the congregation met at the home of William Jones on Harvard Avenue until they built their first small church on Wales Street in 1860.[8] Referred to as the Wales Street Congregational Church, this congregation did not hire a full-time minister until 1865.

The growth of the congregation after the Civil War prompted church leaders to authorize the construction of a main sanctuary on Jones Street in 1876. Dedicated on July 4, 1876, this religious facility was originally called the Centennial Church. Pointed stone arches, engaged buttresses, and elongated stained-glass windows with tracery give this modest building a Gothic character. The Jones Road Congregational church is still an active part of the Welsh community in Cleveland, even though most of its parishioners no longer reside in the neighborhood.[9]

78. HOLY NAME ROMAN CATHOLIC CHURCH (1881)
Architect: E. Malone
Location: 8328 Broadway Avenue

The Most Holy Name of Jesus Church, commonly known as Holy Name, stands nearly alone between the railroad tracks and Harvard Avenue on Broadway. The tall church with its slender spire serves as a neighborhood landmark. The Holy Name parish originated in the Village of Newburgh in 1854 under the guidance of Father Eugene O'Callaghan. Initially called Holy Rosary, the congregation erected its first church at the corner of Woodland Hills and Miles Park avenues in 1862. Completed in 1867, the church was expanded in 1872 to include a new frame sanctuary.[10]

The large number of Eastern and Southern Europeans migrating to the Broadway-Harvard neighborhood after the Civil War encouraged Father Joseph F. Gallagher and the congregation to relocate to a larger, more central site on Broadway Avenue in 1874. The present church was erected at the new site in 1881. In the early 1880s, the congregation adopted its current name as a result of the establishment of the Holy Name Society. Holy Name is the mother church for a number of parishes, including St. Catherine, St. Therese, St. Timothy, Immaculate Conception (Bedford), and Epiphany.[11]

The building measures 160 feet by 65 feet. Detailing based on several different architectural styles decorates the exterior. Side buttresses, elongated pointed windows with tracery on the north and south facade, and the recessed main door with jamb shafts are reminiscent of the Gothic style, while the corbel effect is more Romanesque. The church's louvered belfry topped by four gables, each with an oculus, is Victorian. Similarly, the interior is a beautiful example of Victorian design. Light and playful, it contrasts with the church's dark, somber exterior.

79. MILES PARK PRESBYTERIAN CHURCH (1872)
Architect: Walker and Company
Location: 9114 Miles Park Avenue

Miles Park Presbyterian Church faces what was once the public square of the Village of Newburgh. The Miles Park congregation was initially organized as the First Congregational Church of Newburgh in 1832. This link between the Congregational and Presbyterian denominations was common in the early years of the Western Reserve. Based on an agreement called the Plan of Union (1801), participating churches were to be served by Congregational ministers while being administered by the Presbyterian General Assembly and its synods. Many of these congregations changed or modified their original affiliation once they were well enough established to assume their own religious aims.[12] The Miles Park Presbyterian Church is a direct outgrowth of this religious arrangement.

Constructed of brick and trimmed in stone with Romanesque detailing, this religious facility's massing is dominated by a single large tower at the north entry. Windows with round arched mullions surround the sanctuary. On the interior, oak paneling and ceiling trusses complement the wooden pews.

80. ALLEN CHAPEL-MISSIONARY BAPTIST CHURCH

(Originally Miles Park United
Methodist Church, 1872)
Architect: Unknown
Location: 9105 Miles Park Avenue

Allen Chapel-Missionary Baptist Church, like Miles Park Presbyterian across the street, also faces Newburgh Village's original public square. Established by Lyman Ferris in 1832 as the Miles Park United Methodist Church, the congregation originally met in a farmhouse near present-day Harvard Avenue and East 71st Street. However, the congregation soon relocated to Newburgh's town hall.[13]

In 1841, the church received a parcel of land from the estate of Theodore Miles. This site became the home for a new frame church in 1850. With wood contributed by Lyman Ferris, the congregation built its own structure. The growth of local steel mills nearby contributed to the expansion of the congregation, which outgrew its initial frame facility within twenty years. Allen Chapel-Missionary Baptist Church, an African-American congregation, has occupied the building since 1979.

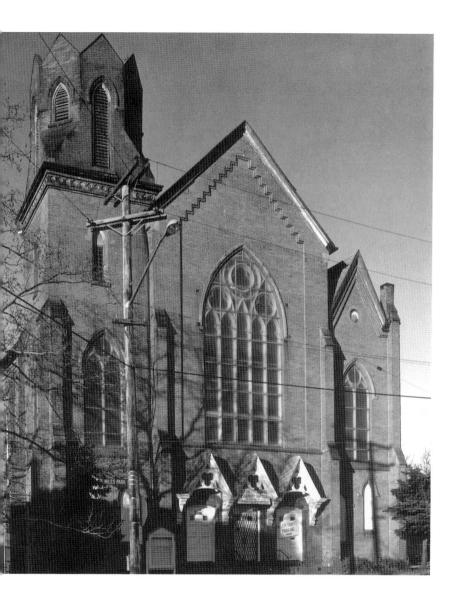

In 1872, the frame structure was moved to the corner of Walker Avenue and East 91st Street while the Reverend A. S. Dobbs supervised the construction of the present church. The first-floor meeting hall was dedicated in 1873, but due to a depressed regional economy the 1,000-seat sanctuary was not completed until 1883. Originally the church's interior was quite plain, but more ornate additions, such as ceiling beams and pointed archways, were added in the 1930s. The exterior has a combination of styles—Victorian gables over the doors, perpendicular Gothic windows and Romanesque corbeling. The belfry on the tower, with its pointed crown, is the church's most unique architectural element.

81. Shaffer Memorial Methodist Church (1914)

Architects: Maurer and Mills
Location: 12002 Miles Avenue

In conjunction with the more contemporary East Mt. Vernon Baptist Church one block further east, Shaffer Memorial Methodist Church anchors the east end of the Miles Park neighborhood. Shaffer Memorial was organized in 1899 by the Reverend J. F. Fisher, then the presiding officer of the Cleveland Methodist district.[14] Known initially as the Mars Hill Methodist Episcopal Church, the congregation moved from its original location to its present address in 1914.

This Georgian-style religious structure on Miles Avenue can accommodate up to 425 people. The well-proportioned brick building, trimmed with light stone waterlines and quoins, is situated high off the ground, providing ample light to the club rooms and dining facilities on the lower level.[15] Wide stairs rise to the beautifully detailed portico supported by Doric columns. The actual entrances are lo-

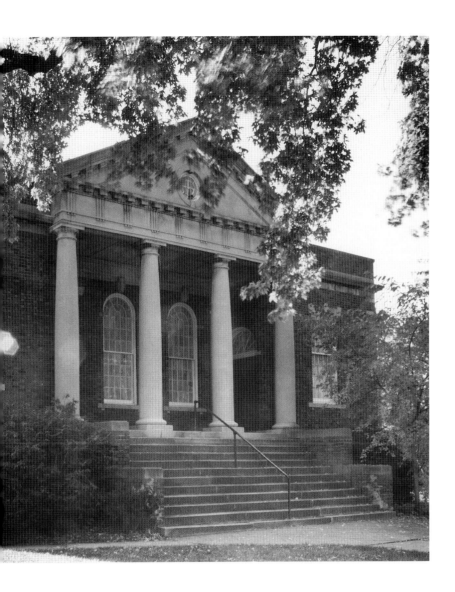

cated at the east and west wings of the building on either side of the portico. As a result, the double doors face each other on the porch rather than the street. The gable end above the dentilated entablature contains a single oculus.

In 1949 a fire destroyed much of the interior, and the congregation responded by providing funds and energy to refurbish the structure. Parishioners helped to restore the sanctuary, including the orchid-tinted windows and the floors, pews, pulpit, and choir loft.[16] In 1957, an education building was added and the sanctuary was further remodeled. Consistent with the church's history of community service, the Union-Miles Development Corporation now operates out of this facility.

CHAPTER SEVEN

The Near West Side

The Near West Side community is comprised of two neighborhoods, Ohio City and Tremont.

Ohio City is bound on the north by Lake Erie, on the east by the Cuyahoga River and Interstate routes 71 and 90, on the south by I-90, and on the west by West 45th Street. Major north-south roads are West 25th Street and Fulton Road; major east-west roads are Detroit and Lorain. The Ohio City neighborhood is one of Cleveland's oldest neighborhoods, and until 1854 it was an independent municipality that extended from the Cuyahoga River west to West 58th Street. After its annexation to the city of Cleveland, the area became home to many German, Hungarian, and Irish immigrants. By the 1980s, Ohio City was home to over fifteen ethnic groups; among the newer immigrant and migrant groups today, Hispanic-Americans and Asian-Americans are two of the largest.[1]

TOUR

Begin this tour at the west end of the Detroit-Superior Bridge heading west. At the first intersection, Detroit and West 25th Street, look north (right) and notice **ST. MALACHI ROMAN CATHOLIC CHURCH (82),** which is topped by a Celtic cross that is occasionally lighted at night. At the intersection, turn south (left) onto West 25th Street. After the first block, turn west (right) onto Church. Go one block. At the corner of West 26th Street and Church note the city's oldest existing sacred structure, **ST. JOHN EPISCOPAL CHURCH (83).**

Continue to move west on Church for another block and then turn south (left) on West 28th Street. As West 28th intersects Franklin Boulevard, note **FRANKLIN CIRCLE CHRISTIAN CHURCH (84)** at the southwestern corner. Bear to the right past the church and move southwest on Fulton Road until its intersection with Bridge. Turn west (right) onto Bridge and notice **ST. PATRICK ROMAN CATHOLIC CHURCH (85)** opposite the park and a branch of the Cleveland Public Library.

Continue to move west on Bridge. At its intersection with West 38th Street, note the **West Side United Church of Christ.** Travel on Bridge until it intersects with West 44th Street. At the southeast corner of this intersection, note the **First Hispanic Methodist Church.** Built as St. Mark's German Methodist in 1916, its change to a Hispanic church represents the social change in this ethnic neighborhood. Turn south (left) onto West 44th Street and travel on it past the intersection with Lorain until its intersection with Bailey Road. At the southwest corner of this intersection notice **Independent Evangelical Lutheran Church** with its asymmetrical entrance tower and Gothic revival details.

Turn east (left) onto Bailey Road and continue to move east until it ends at Fulton Road. At Fulton turn north (left) and continue on Fulton until its intersection with Chatham. At the northwest corner of this intersection note **Iglesia Hispana Pentecostal Church.** Turn east (right) onto Chatham and continue on it for three blocks. Turn north (left) at Chatham's intersection with West 30th Street.

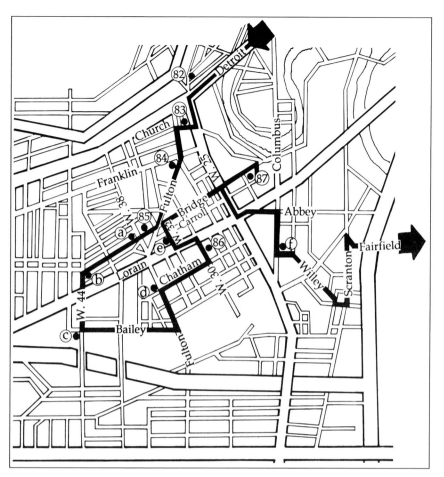

Ohio City

82. St. Malachi Roman Catholic Church
83. St. John Episcopal Church
84. Franklin Circle Christian Church
85. St. Patrick Roman Catholic Church
86. Trinity Evangelical Lutheran Church
87. St. Emeric Roman Catholic Church
a. West Side United Church of Christ
b. First Hispanic Methodist Church
c. Independent Evangelical Lutheran Church
d. Iglesia Hispana Pentecostal Church
e. Iglesia Católica Parroquía San Juan Bautista
f. St. Wendelin Roman Catholic Church

On the east side of the street prior to its intersection with Lorain is **TRINITY EVANGELICAL LUTHERAN CHURCH (86).** At West 30th Street's intersection with Lorain, note St. Ignatius High School on the north side of Lorain. Turn west on Lorain and travel on it for one block. At West 32d Street turn north (right) and travel on it for one block. At its intersection with Carroll, note **Iglesia Católica Parroquía San Juan Bautista,** with its copper-capped tower, that formerly housed the West Side Hungarian Reformed Congregation. Continue to move north on West 32d Street until its intersection with Bridge. At Bridge, turn east (right) and

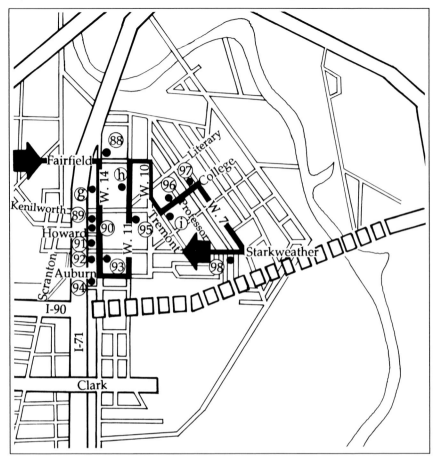

TREMONT

88. Greek Orthodox Church of
    Annunciation
89. Holy Ghost Byzantine Catholic
    Church
90. St. Augustine Roman Catholic
    Church
91. Cleveland Baptist Temple
92. Pilgrim Congregational Church
93. St. George Antiochian Orthodox
    Church
94. Zion United Church of Christ
95. Our Lady of Mercy Roman Catholic
    Church

96. St. John Cantius Roman Catholic
    Church
97. Saints Peter and Paul Ukrainian
    Greek Catholic Church
98. St. Theodosius Russian Orthodox
    Cathedral
g. St. Andrew Kim Korean Catholic
    Church
h. Spanish Assembly of God
i. Iglesia di Dios Pentecostal

travel on it until it curves along the high west bank of the Cuyahoga River and ends at **ST. EMERIC ROMAN CATHOLIC CHURCH (87).** When entering the church's turnaround, notice the magnificent view of downtown Cleveland to the northeast. Backtrack west on Bridge for one block and then turn south (left) onto

West 25th Street. At its intersection with Lorain, turn east (left) onto Lorain and then immediately bear right onto Abbey Road. Travel on Abbey Road for a block and then turn south (right) onto Columbus. Travel south on Columbus for two blocks and then turn east (left) onto Willey. At the southeast corner of the Willey-Columbus intersection, note **St. Wendelin Roman Catholic Church.** Continue on Willey until its intersection with Scranton Road. At Scranton turn north and travel on it for one block. Turn east (right) onto Fairfield and enter the Tremont neighborhood, which is bound on the north and northeast by the Cuyahoga River, on the southeast and south by Quigley Road and Holmden Avenue, and on the west by Interstate routes 71 and 90. The major north-south street is West 14th.

Tremont is an industrial and residential neighborhood that was originally part of Ohio City. In 1850, Cleveland University was founded in what was to become Tremont. Closed just five years later, the university left a legacy of once-fashionable streets, such as College Avenue, Literary Road, Professor Street, and University Road. Tremont's location on the western edge of Cuyahoga's industrial valley offered a home to many immigrants who settled in the area. Ethnic groups included Irish and Germans in the 1860s, Poles in the 1890s, Greeks and Syrians in the 1900s, Ukrainians in the 1950s, and Hispanics in the 1960s. By 1985 there was a total of thirty nationalities represented in Tremont.[2]

Entering on Fairfield Road, notice the bright blue domes of the **Greek Orthodox Church of Annunciation (88)** on the corner of Fairfield and West 14th Street. Turn south (right) onto West 14th Street and notice **St. Andrew Kim Korean Catholic Church** located on the west side directly across from Grace Hospital. At the next intersection, note **Holy Ghost Byzantine Catholic Church (89)** on the southwest corner.

Continue to move south on West 14th Street. Where 14th intersects with Howard, note **St. Augustine Roman Catholic Church (90).** One block further south on the corner of West 14th Street and Starkweather are three churches which work together to frame the green-space of the southwest corner of Lincoln Park: **Cleveland Baptist Temple (91)** to the northwest, **Pilgrim Congregational Church (92)** to the southwest, and **St. George Antiochian Orthodox Church (93)** to the southeast.

Continue to drive south on West 14th Street until Auburn Avenue. At Auburn look to the west side of West 14th directly before the bridge and note **Zion United Church of Christ (94)** with its tall steeple.

Turn east (left) onto Auburn and travel on it for one block. At the corner of Auburn and West 11th, turn north (left). Travel on West 11th Street past its intersection with Starkweather and notice the newest church in the neighborhood, **Our Lady of Mercy Roman Catholic Church (95),** located on the east side facing Lincoln Park. Drive north on West Eleventh through the Kenilworth intersection and notice the yellow-brick **Spanish Assembly of God,** formerly St. Vladimir Ukrainian Orthodox Church, located on the west side of the street behind Grace Hospital. Travel north until West 11th intersects with Fairfield.

At Fairfield, turn east (right) and travel on it for one block. At West 10th Street turn south (right) and travel on it past Literary until Tremont intersects with it to the east. Travel southeast on Tremont for one short block. Turn northeast onto

College Avenue and note **Iglesia di Dios Pentecostal.** Continue to move in a northeasterly direction on College. At the intersection of College and Professor, notice the large, yellow-brick ST. JOHN CANTIUS ROMAN CATHOLIC CHURCH (96) on the northwest corner. Travel on College until it intersects with West Seventh Street. On the northwest corner note SAINTS PETER AND PAUL UKRAINIAN GREEK CATHOLIC CHURCH (97).

At West Seventh turn southeast (right) and travel three blocks until Starkweather. At Starkweather look west and notice the multiple domes of ST. THEODOSIUS RUSSIAN ORTHODOX CATHEDRAL (98) on top of the hill. Turn west (right) onto Starkweather and look at St. Theodosius and its surrounding neighborhood, which was featured in the 1978 film *The Deer Hunter.* Continue west on Starkweather to West 14th Street. Turn right on West 14th and proceed to I-71. This route leads to downtown Cleveland.

82. ST. MALACHI ROMAN CATHOLIC CHURCH (1945)
Architect: George W. Stickle
Location: 2459 Washington Avenue

Before the buildings grew up around it and before the construction of the Shoreway, old St. Malachi Roman Catholic Church had a fine view to Lake Erie. Because of its prominent position on the hill and because it was visible from the lake, St. Malachi's cross was lighted at night to act as a beacon. Now that the old church is gone and the lake is no longer as visible, due to the location of the Shoreway bridge, a green Celtic cross is sometimes lighted at night on the new St. Malachi spire to commemorate those earlier times. Although neither the neighborhood nor the parish are as populous as they once were, St. Malachi still plays a leading role in the Ohio City neighborhood.[3]

St. Malachi's parish was organized by Father James P. Molony in 1865 to serve the needs of the Near West Side Irish community located near the lake. Many of these new St. Malachi parishioners formerly belonged to St. Patrick Roman Catholic Church on Bridge Avenue. One of the first actions taken by the congregation in 1866 was to buy several lots on West 25th Street for their new church. However, construction delays prevented the completion of the new church until 1871. As a result, the parish held its services at St. Mary on the Flats for nearly five years.[4]

The original Gothic-style brick building was noted for its beautiful statues and for the tall spire topped by the lighted cross. This spire was destroyed by a storm

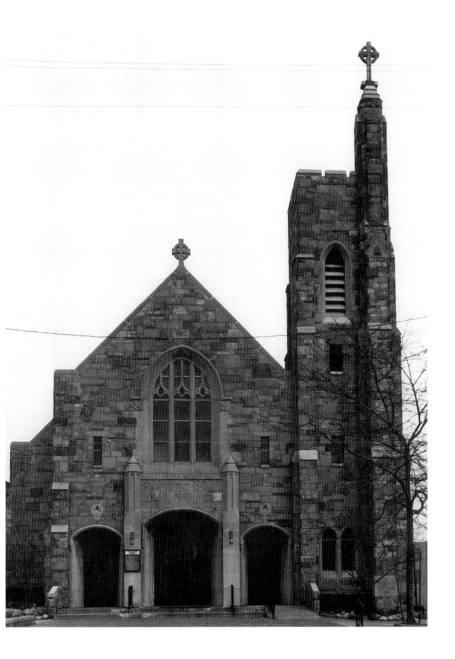

in the 1870s and was never rebuilt. A devastating fire destroyed much of the original church structure in 1943. Under the guidance of Father George F. Martin, the parish was able to build a new religious facility in 1945 southwest of the original building. Designed in the traditional cruciform plan with a long nave and shorter transepts, the church can seat up to 524 worshipers. Details such as decorative buttresses, lancet windows, and the prominent square tower topped by modified battlements suggest an English Gothic tradition. What helps to distinguish this building and its attached eighteen-room convent for the Sisters of St. Ursula is its multicolor Tennessee crab-orchard stone.[5]

83. St. John Episcopal Church (1836)

Architect: Hezekiah Eldredge
Location: 2600 Church Avenue

As the oldest standing church in Cleveland, St. John Episcopal Church is rich in history.[6] St. John Episcopal grew out of Trinity parish, begun at the home of Phineas Shepherd in the village of Brooklyn, Ohio, in 1816. The Trinity congregation met in Cleveland until 1820 when it moved to Brooklyn. Trinity's relocation back to Cleveland in 1825 split the congregation. A number of parishioners were unhappy with this move, so they decided to establish their own congregation in Ohio City in 1834. The new church met in the Columbus block until the completion of the new structure in 1836 at the corner of Church Avenue and the present-day West 26th Street.

This church was designed and constructed by local builder and parishioner Hezekiah Eldredge. It is likely that Eldredge was familiar with John Henry Hopkins's *Essay on Gothic Architecture,* the first book on Gothic ecclesiastical architecture published in America, for the designer seems to have taken many cues from the book. Like many churches of the early Gothic period in America (1820–60), St. John's is essentially a simple meetinghouse with Gothic details. This gray stone edifice has buttresses, lancet windows with tracery, and a tower with a pointed enclosed belfry. The church is important because it predates Trinity Church in New York City by more than a decade, and it was only after Trinity's construction that Gothic-style church architecture became popular in the United States.

The interior of the church was totally destroyed by fire in 1866 and was renovated with a redesigned interior space that better conformed to the more traditional cruciform plan. The roof was also reconstructed at a higher pitch. A tornado in 1953 again destroyed much of the roof and parts of the interior.[7] This time the congregation decided to restore the interior to its original meetinghouse plan. More recently, the Gothic finials on the turrets and central tower were removed for safety reasons.

After World War II, in response to the changing membership, the church agreed to share its facility with a new interdenominational group called the Inner City Protestant Parish. During the early 1970s, these two congregations decided to unite to become the new and enlarged St. John parish. This church's age, history, and early Gothic revival style make it a significant landmark within the city of Cleveland.

84. FRANKLIN CIRCLE CHRISTIAN CHURCH (1874)
Architects: Cudell and Richardson
Location: 1688 Fulton Avenue

As the only example of circular planning on the West Side, Franklin Circle was once a unique urban hub and familiar gathering spot. Over the years the circle has lost its strong geometric pattern, but remnants of the circular street can still be seen directly in front of the Franklin Circle Christian Church.

The Franklin Circle Christian Church was established at the Apollo Hall north of Superior Avenue in Cleveland in 1842 by the Disciple of Christ minister John Henry.[8] The group did not have a permanent home until 1848, when a large frame church—often referred to as God's Barn—was built on Franklin Avenue near the present site of the Masonic Hall. It was in God's Barn that James A. Garfield served as pastor in 1857 before entering politics. The growth of the congregation after the Civil War necessitated the building of a new church facility in 1875. Completed in 1883, this new building, along with the religious school added in 1916, continues to serve the congregation.

This Gothic-influenced church is well suited to the physical limitations imposed by the truncated triangular site. Gothic details found on the exterior of this historic church include pointed windows and a squared-off side bell tower with Yorkshire battlements. The eastern tower with its pitched roof facing Franklin Circle, however, is an anomaly. Designed by important local architects Cudell and Richardson, the sanctuary's interior features unique decorated metal tie rods to keep the exterior walls from spreading and soft-colored American-style glass windows with foliated tracery.

In recent years the church has dedicated much of its efforts to helping the poor in the Ohio City neighborhood by providing special low-cost meals to local residents as well as organizing summer recreational programs.[9] The church also offers preschool activities and a Chinese Sunday school. As in the past, Franklin Circle Christian Church continues to be a social, as well as an architectural, landmark.

85. St. Patrick Roman Catholic Church (1871)
Architect: Unknown
Location: 3602 Bridge Avenue

St. Patrick Roman Catholic Church is sited to face onto a triangular green-space that is punctuated in the middle by the Carnegie West Library. Within the surrounding urban fabric, St. Patrick's takes on landmark proportions because of its size and distinctive style.

One of the earliest Catholic parishes in the city, St. Patrick's was founded by Father James Conlan in 1853 to serve the needs of the Irish community located in Ohio City. St. Patrick's first church was erected on Whitman Avenue in 1854. This Gothic-style brick structure was capable of seating 650 people and remained the home of the parish until the early 1870s, when the congregation built the present religious structure on Bridge Avenue under the auspices of Bishop Richard Gilmour.[10]

The cornerstone for the present church was laid in 1871; however, the exterior of this church was not completed until 1877, and the interior was not finished until 1881. A depressed economy was responsible for the church's slow construction. Indeed, if it were not for the innovative leadership of Father Eugene O'Callaghan, the construction process may have taken even longer. O'Callaghan was able to secure free material from the stone quarry in Sandusky by arranging to have it cut and hauled to the site. He organized the parish into work crews that transported the stone from Sandusky to Cleveland.

Additions to the church in the 1880s included new altars, new stations of the cross, and new stained-glass windows. This was followed in 1913 by a 55-foot addition to the north side of the facility, which provided more space for the sanctuary and apse. The church, divided into three aisles, has a steeply pitched roof and quadripartite vaulting that give the interior a lofty appearance. Details such as its rough ashlar surfaces, pointed openings, and square-shaped bell tower with parapet and finials give the church a Gothic air.

86. TRINITY EVANGELICAL LUTHERAN CHURCH (1873)
Architects: Griese and Weile
Location: 2057 West 30th Street

Located on a street that is terminated to the north by St. Ignatius High School, Trinity Evangelical Lutheran Church makes a distinctive statement in this neighborhood of little homes and tiny lots. The church traces its origins to Zion Evangelical Lutheran Church, which began in 1843 at the Cleveland Concert Hall on Superior Avenue.[11] In 1853, under the leadership of the Reverend Henry C. Schwan, a mission to serve the twenty Lutheran families of the Zion congregation who lived in Ohio City was established. The mission remained under the direct control of Zion Evangelical Lutheran until 1858. At that time Trinity Evangelical Lutheran Church was founded, and the original church was constructed on Chatham Street.

The present masonry church was erected in 1873 to serve 1,500 West Side parishioners. The prominent Victorian-Gothic central tower with its 175-foot hipped steeple makes this church a visible neighborhood landmark. Described by Mary-Peale Schofield as a lovely version of a Gothic meetinghouse, the sanctuary is a simple rectangle divided into three parts by tall, thin, clustered iron columns with foliated capitals supporting Tudor arches.[12] The interior of the building has been remodeled several times. Originally, the balcony encompassed three sides of the auditorium and the decoration was more elaborate. The supporting wall between the narthex and sanctuary was constructed when the first organ was installed in the rear balcony; it is now graced by a mechanical action (tracker) organ from Rudolph von Beckerath of Hamburg, Germany, purchased by the congregation in 1957. Containing approximately 3,500 pipes, it was the first large modern organ in North America designed and built on historic principles.

Located high above the banks of the Cuyahoga River, St. Emeric Roman Catholic Church offers a splendid view of downtown Cleveland. St. Emeric's was established by Father Stephen Soltesz in 1904 to serve the West Side's Hungarian immigrants; it was over five miles to the nearest Hungarian parish, St. Elizabeth's on Buckeye Road.[13] The original church and school consisted of a few frame buildings on West 24th Street at Bridge Avenue; these structures served the parish until they were destroyed by fire in 1915.

Instead of building a new church, the parish decided to occupy the nearby Church of Annunciation facility that formerly had served a French immigrant congregation. The newly acquired church-and-school facility was modernized by the congregation and used until 1921, when another fire severely damaged this build-

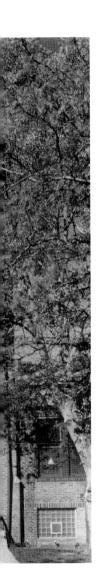

ing. In 1925 the parish built the present church. The old rectory was subsequently moved to the south side of the new structure and a new convent was built on the north side of the site. During the early 1970s the parish modernized the entire facility.[14]

This 450-seat building serves as a combination church-and-school. The basement has a social hall, a stage, and a series of club rooms. Many of the furnishings in the church—the altars, confessionals, stained-glass windows, and communion rails—were originally part of the Church of Annunciation. On the exterior, details such as pointed arch openings, perpendicular-style front windows, and a squared-off bell tower topped by large finials suggest a Gothic influence.

88. GREEK ORTHODOX CHURCH OF ANNUNCIATION (1918)
Architect: Unknown
Location: 2187 West 14th Street

Located on the edge of the Tremont neighborhood, the blue-topped towers of the Greek Orthodox Church of Annunciation are easily visible from I-90 as well as West 14th Street. The Greek Orthodox Church of Annunciation is an outgrowth of the Pan Hellenic Society. Established in Cleveland during the first decade of the twentieth century, this society brought Greek immigrants together on a regular basis by offering them familiar cultural, social, and religious activities and events. In terms of religious needs, the society, in 1910, prevailed upon Father George Scarpas of Pittsburgh to conduct services for them once a month. These religious services were held in a public hall at the corner of Bolivar and Ontario Street in downtown Cleveland until 1912, when the group bought a residence on Fairfield Avenue near West 14th Street. The society remained at that site until 1914 when they moved back downtown to Arch Hall on Ontario at East Fourth Street.[15] However, the steady growth of the congregation at the time of World War I necessitated further expansion.

The society decided to shed its earlier name to become the Greek Orthodox Church of Annunciation, and it began to build the present sanctuary on the Fairfield Avenue property in 1918. Later, Annunciation served as the mother church for St. Constantine's and St. Helen's in Cleveland Heights (1956) and St. Demetrios's in Rocky River (1962). All three religious institutions are known collectively as the American-Hellenic Community of Greater Cleveland. Annunciation has retained its importance as the mother church for the local Greek Orthodox community.[16]

Built of yellow brick with louvered bell towers topped by blue domes and Greek crosses, this church is clearly influenced by Middle Eastern design. The interior contains many frescoes and paintings, and between 1924 and 1928 Father John Zografos added more than eighty icons. The church's heritage and the manifestation of Greek culture in both the interior and exterior design make this building unique.

89. Holy Ghost Byzantine Catholic Church (1910)
Architects: M. E. Wells and Joseph Fuvalaski
Location: 2420 West 14th Street

Located just west of Lincoln Park and facing Kenilworth Avenue, Holy Ghost Byzantine Catholic Church marks what was once the Ruthenian community located within the Tremont neighborhood.[17] Ruthenia is in the western Ukrainian republic south of the Carpathian mountains. Before World War I it was a part of Hungary and between World Wars I and II it was a province of Czechoslovakia. At the turn of the century thousands of Ruthenian immigrants emigrated to Cleveland. Their Catholic faith and native culture dear to their hearts, they soon established the Holy Ghost Byzantine Catholic Church. In 1910, under the leadership of Father Emil Burik, the present church was constructed in Tremont because many of the parishioners had migrated to that neighborhood from the larger Ruthenian district on Bolivar Avenue between Ontario and East 9th streets in downtown Cleveland.

The yellow-brick facade facing Kenilworth Avenue is more grand than the re-

mainder of the church. The recessed tripartite entry seems small because it is sandwiched between a wide stairway below it and an oversized rose window above it. The playful line of the stone turns capping the gable end takes a shape resembling San Spirito in Florence, Italy, while the domes and crosses over the altar and atop the three stage towers are definitely Middle Eastern in character. The church's interior is able to accommodate 1,100 parishioners; a new marble altar and a lighter color scheme were introduced in 1955.[18] The *ikonostas,* the icon screen that is the dominant feature of the church's interior, was also retouched at that time. This screen that separates the altar from the nave is one of the most elaborate in the city and was made in Budapest in 1924. The screen contains forty-eight icons and three doors. The central door, or royal door, is used only by the priest, while the two side doors, deacons doors, may be used by lay people.

90. St. Augustine Roman Catholic Church
(Originally Pilgrim Congregational Church, 1864)
Architect: Antonio
Di Nardo
Location: 2486 West 14th
Street

Since 1896 this structure has faced Tremont's main open space, Lincoln Park. Between 1864 and 1896 this edifice housed the Pilgrim Congregational Church, now located one block south. The present Catholic congregation was organized in 1860 by Bishop Amadeus Rappe to serve the growing needs of Catholic parishioners living in the greater Tremont area. A frame church was constructed on Jefferson Avenue near Tremont Avenue later that same year. This initial frame building was expanded in 1868 to include a brick rectory and was used by the St. Augustine congregation until 1896, when the parish relocated to its present facility at 2486 West 14th Street.[19]

This 600-seat structure constructed by the Pilgrim congregation in 1864 measures 120 feet by 40 feet with transepts extending to 80 feet. The interior is a cruciform design with a raised altar at the end of a very wide nave. At the opposite end, a pipe organ is located in a loft above the narthex. This church includes such Romanesque traits as a corbel table below the roofline, large extended gables, and pilasters. However, pointed arches above the side entrance and other openings are more suggestive of Gothic detailing. At St. Augustine's, the subtleties of Gothic and Romanesque styles blend together to create a humanly scaled, eclectic structure typical of the time in which it was built.

91. CLEVELAND BAPTIST TEMPLE

(Originally Emmanuel Evangelical United Brethren
Church, 1910)
Architect: Unknown
Location: 2536 West 14th Street

Situated on the northwest corner of West 14th and Starkweather, the Cleveland
Baptist Temple, built as the Emmanuel Evangelical United Brethren Church,
faces Lincoln Park and helps frame the park together with Pilgrim Congregational
Church and St. George Antiochian Orthodox Church.

Emmanuel Evangelical United Brethren Church was founded in 1865 by newly
settled German immigrants in the Tremont neighborhood. Services were conducted in German there until World War I. The present church was built by the
German congregation in 1910 to replace an existing wood-frame structure.[20]

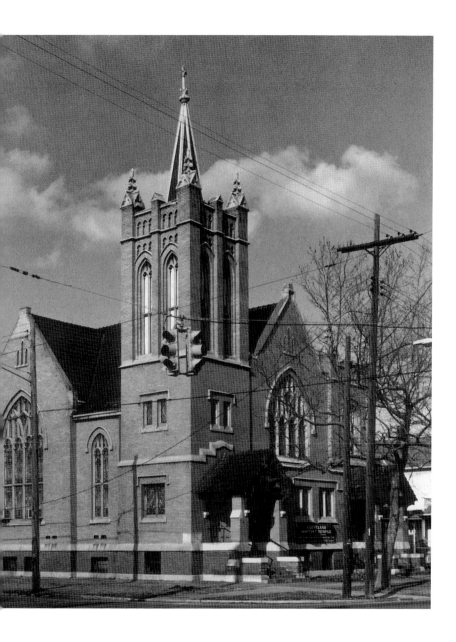

Emmanuel Evangelical had more than 300 members in the mid-1930s and was known for its missionary work in the Far East.

The Cleveland Baptist Temple, founded in 1958 by the Reverend Cecil Simmons, bought the church facility in 1968. The building has since been occupied and maintained by the Temple. Elements such as the large pointed windows with hood moldings and corbel stops on the front and side facade convey a Gothic feeling. The east entry porches and short steeple atop the corner tower are more in the English vernacular.

92. PILGRIM CONGREGATIONAL CHURCH (1893)

Architect: Sidney R. Badgley

Location: 2453 West 14th Street

Located opposite the southwest corner of Lincoln Park is Pilgrim Congregational, the largest of the three churches on this corner. Pilgrim Congregational Church was organized in 1859 as the University Heights Congregational Church and originally met in the assembly hall of the Humiston Institute. At that time the Tremont area was known as University Heights and was home to Cleveland University from 1850 to 1855. From the outset, the congregation was ecumenical, with Congregational, Methodist, Wesleyan Methodist, and Presbyterian members.[21] Various German, Evangelical, and Jewish religious groups have also held joint religious services and social gatherings at the church.

Pilgrim has a long tradition of helping the less fortunate in the community. As early as 1895, the church sponsored a number of recreational and educational programs for the neighborhood. It also has the distinction of opening the first library on the West Side and providing the first kindergarten and cooking school in the city.[22] The establishment of the Jones Home for Children (1886), now located on West 25th Street at I-71, is a direct outgrowth of the Congregationalists' social commitment to the Cleveland community.

The original Pilgrim Congregational Church building dates back to 1865 when the group built what is today St. Augustine Roman Catholic Church on West 14th Street at Howard Avenue. The present structure was built under the auspices of the Reverend Charles Mills in 1893 on what was then called Jennings Road. The interior of the church is noted for its very spacious sanctuary and adjoining classrooms; large doors serve to delineate these two major functional areas. A design that has classrooms opening directly onto the main sanctuary, as in this church, is referred to as an Akron Plan, so named because it was first used in the First Methodist Church in Akron in 1867. The plan provides for flexible seating and enables larger groups to hear special speakers or participate in special programs.

The central leaded-glass dome, the main visual focus of the entire auditorium, is supported by four massive semicircular arches, eliminating the need for additional supporting columns below.[23] The seating is thus able to fan out from the pulpit in an unimpeded sweep. The church's main tower is reminiscent of Henry H. Richardson's Brattle Street Church tower in Boston. Other Richardsonian Romanesque characteristics found on the exterior of this structure include a rough ashlar finish, a prominent round arch at the front entrance, and pyramidal roofs atop square-based towers.

The Paris Exposition of 1900 featured the design of Pilgrim Congregational Church as a way to illustrate how a religious facility might coordinate a sanctuary, kitchen, library, art museum, and gymnasium into a series of well-planned attached buildings. Such recognition helped place this structure in the forefront of Cleveland ecclesiastical architecture.

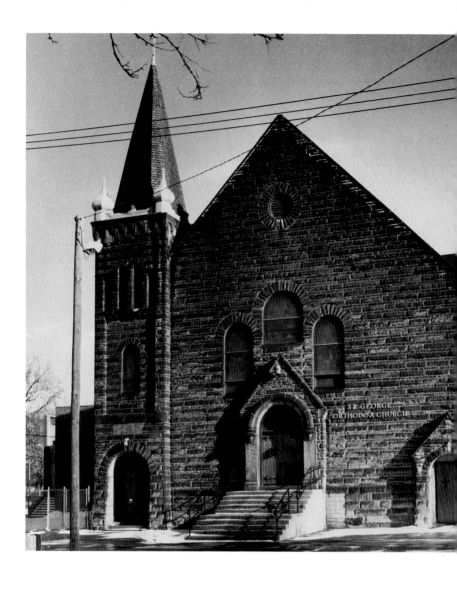

St. George Antiochian Orthodox Church, built as the Lincoln Park Methodist Episcopal Church, is located directly west of the old Lincoln Park Bath House and helps to frame Lincoln Park's southwest corner. As one of several Syrian Christian societies which existed in Cleveland by the turn of the century, the Antiochian Orthodox Society formed its own congregation in 1926. Soon known as St. George Antiochian Orthodox Church, this congregation held its first services in a variety of locations, including Gray's Armory in downtown Cleveland. The group purchased the former Lincoln Park Methodist Episcopal Church at 2587 West 14th Street in 1933 and refurbished it to serve the needs of its new parishioners.[24] However, a fire destroyed most of the interior of the structure shortly after the refurbishing efforts were completed.

Under Father Elias Meena, the congregation contributed enough money to rebuild the gutted structure, and the sanctuary was reopened in 1935. Featured was

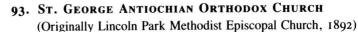

93. St. George Antiochian Orthodox Church
(Originally Lincoln Park Methodist Episcopal Church, 1892)
Architect: Sidney R. Badgley
Location: 2587 West 14th Street

a handcut crystal chandelier designed by Father Meena and a handmade altar screen crafted by the Syrian artist David Deeb. In 1964, an educational and cultural facility was added to the main church as a way to attract younger members to St. George's. By the late 1980s, there were more than 450 families in the congregation.[25]

Details such as a wide front gable, rounded arches above the window openings, and a relatively short, squared-off tower with a conical roof suggest a Richardsonian Romanesque style. The overall heavy effect of the structure, created in part by the minimal use of windows and massive exterior walls, is also associated with Richardsonian Romanesque. But the onion-shaped finials at the top of the bell tower are unique and are indicative of the congregation's cultural and religious heritage.

94. ZION UNITED CHURCH OF CHRIST

(Originally United German Evangelical Protestant Church, 1884)
Architect: Unknown
Location: 2716 West 14th Street

Overlooking I-490 is Zion United Church of Christ, known initially as the United German Evangelical Protestant Church. Long active in the Tremont community, Zion has often offered assistance to the less fortunate through various charitable and outreach programs.

Founded in 1867 by the Reverend P. Stempel to serve the German immigrants settling within the greater Tremont neighborhood, Zion built its first sanctuary on College Avenue in 1867. The original church structure was refurbished and moved to the site of the present church in 1872. The congregation worshiped in this facility until the present church structure was completed in 1884. A parsonage was built adjacent to the church in 1897 and a religious school was constructed in 1906; in 1957 a new kitchen was built and the main auditorium was renovated. Extensive steeple and roof repairs were made in 1959.[26]

While the architect of the church is not known, the exterior strongly resembles St. Joseph Franciscan Catholic Church by Cudell and Richardson. In both instances the exterior form of the narthex takes on a transept-like appearance. On the other hand, the interior, with its clustered columns and Tudor arches, is similar to that found in Trinity Evangelical Lutheran Church by Griese and Weile. Pointed arches over window and door openings and above the open belfry and an octagonal spire atop the squared-off bell tower suggest a Gothic-inspired design. The soaring height of the steeple above the central bell tower makes the church visible for miles.

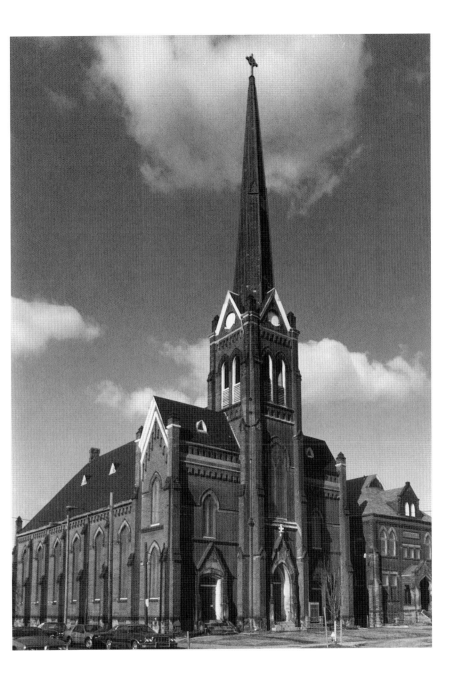

95. OUR LADY OF MERCY ROMAN CATHOLIC CHURCH (1948)
Architects: Stickle, Kelly and Stickle
Location: 2421 West 11th Street

Among the many churches in the Lincoln Park–Tremont area, Our Lady of Mercy Roman Catholic Church is the newest. Established by Father Francis Dubosh as a Slovak parish in 1922, a small frame church on West 11th Street held the parishioners' first services until 1926 when a new combination eight-room brick school-and-hall was completed.[27] Because of its substantial growth through to the 1940s, Father John W. Krispinsky announced plans to erect a new church in 1945.

Construction of the crab-orchard stone structure began in 1948 immediately following the demolition of the earlier frame church. Completed in 1949, the sanctuary can accommodate more than 500 worshipers. The interior is noted for its carved wooden statues and its shrines to St. Joseph, St. Cyril, and St. Methodius.[28] Interior walls are painted coral and serve as a backdrop to the marble altars and the mosaic of the Blessed Virgin.

The church's semicircular entrance portal and corbel table in the large central gable are reminiscent of Romanesque design. However, the octagonal bell tower with copper cupola is more indicative of later Renaissance designs. Here, both styles work together to form a simple, well-proportioned structure. The church is nicely scaled to its setting and can be enjoyed close up or from the far side of Lincoln Park.

96. St. John Cantius Roman Catholic Church (1925)
Architects: Potter and Gabele
Location: 906 College Avenue

Located on the corner of Professor and College streets in what was once intended to be a university neighborhood, St. John Cantius marks what was originally the Polish section of Tremont. The congregation was organized in 1898 in response to the growing number of Polish Catholic immigrants settling in the area.

Early on, a car barn on the same site was renovated under the authorization of Father Hippolit Orlowski and used as a temporary parish church. The rear portion of the refurbished structure was used as the school and residence quarters for the pastors and for the Sisters of St. Joseph. Under the guidance of Father Francis Doppke, the parish built a new combination church-and-school in 1913. This new brick structure was soon followed by a new parish house and a new convent. In the early 1920s, Father Joseph Kocinski initiated a building fund drive with the intention of erecting a larger church. Designed by Potter and Gabele, the new facility, seating 1,000, was completed in 1925.[29]

Cruciform in plan, this church is 184 feet long by 67 feet wide. The width at the transepts is 97 feet. Built of yellow brick and offset by stone trim, the building shows a Romanesque influence with round arches over doors and windows. The building's mass and detailing, nevertheless, are more modern than most of the churches in the Tremont neighborhood. Large and imposing, St. John Cantius Roman Catholic Church is a significant architectural landmark amid the smaller homes and shops of eastern Tremont.

97. Saints Peter and Paul Ukrainian Greek Catholic Church (1910)

Architect: Stephen Paliwoda
Location: 2280 West Seventh Street

The Brotherhood of Saints Peter and Paul was founded in 1902 as a branch of the Ruthenian National Association when the twenty-six members of the association petitioned the bishop in Philadelphia to organize a new parish. The bishop celebrated the first Holy Liturgy with the group in the hall of the German Association at Jefferson and West 10th Street in the fall of 1909, and a new brick church was begun under the tenure of the first pastor, Wolodymyr Dowhowycz, in the spring of 1910.[30]

The parish grew quickly and began providing members with various services. For example, in 1915 the Ruthenian Savings and Loan was established to facilitate home ownership among parishioners. Following the influenza epidemic of 1918, when many mothers and fathers lost their lives, a Ukrainian orphanage was established. Following World War II, under the leadership of Mitred Monsignor Dmytro Gresko, two all-day parish schools were constructed and a new convent for the Sisters of St. Basil was built. In 1956 the church was remodeled. At that time the original Byzantine-style cupolas were removed and the iconostasis was

refurbished. Extensive improvements were also made in 1978. Stained-glass windows commemorating the Millennium of Ukrainian Christianity were added at that time.[31]

Such architectural elements as semicircular arches over the window and door openings, a parapet screen located above the roofline in the gable, and a front rose window express the church's modified Romanesque influence. Similarly, both the meeting room and the tower are buttressed in the Romanesque tradition. However, the bell tower, which is topped by a semicircular form and Greek-style cross, alludes to the Ukrainian culture, thus reflecting the congregation's religious heritage. Known as the "Mother Parish" of Ukrainian in the greater Cleveland area, the members of the parish assisted in the establishment of three other parishes in the county: St. Mary Ukrainian Catholic Church at E. 105th and Kinsman, St. Andrew Ukrainian Catholic Church on Hoerty Road in Parma, and St. Josaphat Ukrainian Catholic Cathedral on State Road in Parma.

98. St. Theodosius Russian Orthodox Cathedral (1911)
Architect: Frederick C. Baird
Location: 733 Starkweather Avenue

When approaching from the east, St. Theodosius Russian Orthodox Cathedral rises from the crest of the hill. This building's tremendous visual strength landed a role for St. Theodosius and the surrounding neighborhood in the 1978 film *The Deer Hunter*.[32] A visual focal point for the neighborhood, the church is also central to local Russian cultural activities.

St. Theodosius traces its origins to a group of Russian immigrants who settled in the Tremont area in the mid-1890s. These immigrants first worshiped at another Russian church, but internal religious conflicts between the new arrivals and their established counterparts caused twenty-three individuals to found their own religious group in 1896. Called the St. Nicholas Society, this group was the predecessor of the St. Theodosius parish. Their first church was a frame building located at the corner of Literary Road and present-day West Sixth Street. This religious structure served the congregation until 1902 when the parish relocated to the former St. John Convent. The parish bought the convent and surrounding territory and divided it into individual lots that were sold to parishioners. The proceeds generated from these sales helped finance the cathedral.[33]

The growth of the parish during the first decade of the twentieth century necessitated further expansion, and in 1911 the congregation decided to build. Czar Nicholas II is reported to have sent funds for the construction of this newly recognized cathedral. Under the direction of Cleveland architect Frederick Baird, this church was built in a Greek cross plan with the central onion dome representing Jesus and the twelve surrounding smaller cupolas symbolizing the Apostles. Renovations to the church include religious murals done by Yugoslavian artist Andrei Bicenko, developer of the neo-Byzantine style. Older paintings and decorations made in Russia prior to World War I were also refurbished as part of the renovation.

St. Theodosius contains architectural elements associated with both Byzantine and Romanesque designs, reminiscent of the Church of Our Savior in Moscow. The central onion dome and surrounding cupolas are derived directly from the Byzantine style as applied to earlier Orthodox churches in Russia. The barrel vaults in the transepts are also characteristic of Byzantine design. Such architectural elements as rounded arches with keystones over elongated main window openings, full-length pilaster strips, and exaggerated classic sills placed within the context of a smooth brick exterior are more closely associated with Western European Romanesque style. Here, the styles come together to create a unique and visually powerful religious structure that, because of its prominent location on the western ridge of the Cuyahoga Valley, can be seen from many parts of the city.

CHAPTER EIGHT

The West Side South

West Side South is composed of three neighborhoods: Old Brooklyn, Archwood-Denison, and Fulton-Clark.

The Old Brooklyn neighborhood is bound on the north by Big Creek Valley and on the east by the Cuyahoga Valley, on the south by I-480 and on the west by the city of Brooklyn. Major north-south roads are Pearl, State, and Broadview; major east-west roads are Memphis and Schaaf. Old Brooklyn was incorporated as the Village of Brighton in 1838, and until the twentieth century it was an important market for the surrounding agricultural community.[1] In 1905 the area was annexed to the city of Cleveland.

TOUR

Begin the tour of this neighborhood at the intersection of Broadview and Brookpark roads. Travel north on Broadview. Immediately after crossing the bridge over I-480, look to the west and notice the sweeping roof of **St. Leo the Great Roman Catholic Church** located opposite Broadview Gardens, a community of modest, well-maintained apartments.

Continue to travel north on Broadview for five blocks. At the intersection of Broadview and Alvin note **St. James Lutheran Church** at the southeast corner. This church's steeple is reminiscent of New England church steeples influenced by English architect James Gibb and is a bit of an anomaly on this commercial street.

Turn east (right) onto Alvin and drive on it for one short block. At the first block, turn north (left) onto West 20th Street. Continue on West 20th until it intersects with Schaaf Road. At the southwest corner of this intersection note the **Brooklyn Heights United Church of Christ**. Located in a neighborhood of pleasantly proportioned homes and tree-lined streets, Brooklyn Heights U.C.C. maintains some prominence yet fits nicely into the neighborhood.

Turn northwest (left) onto Schaaf. As Schaaf turns into Broadview, continue to move north on Broadview until it intersects with Saratoga. Turn west (left) and travel on Saratoga until it ends at State Road. At State turn south (left) and travel for three blocks. Here, at the crest of the hill on State Road and Biddulph opposite the Brooklyn Cemetery is **ST. MARY BYZANTINE CATHOLIC CHURCH (99)**, with its very large central window over the doors.

Continue south on State for two more blocks and then turn west (right) onto Germaine. Travel on Germaine for two blocks and then turn south (left) onto West 45th Street. Travel three blocks on West 45th and then turn west (right) onto Archmere. Continue on Archmere for one block until its intersection with Pearl Road. At the southeastern corner of this intersection note **Cleveland Korean Baptist Church** and **Corpus Christi Roman Catholic Church** located directly west of it across the street. Together they form a visual gateway that straddles Pearl Road.

Turn northeast (right) onto Pearl and continue on it past the Lutheran Cemetery on the west. Directly north of this cemetery is **Unity Lutheran Church**.

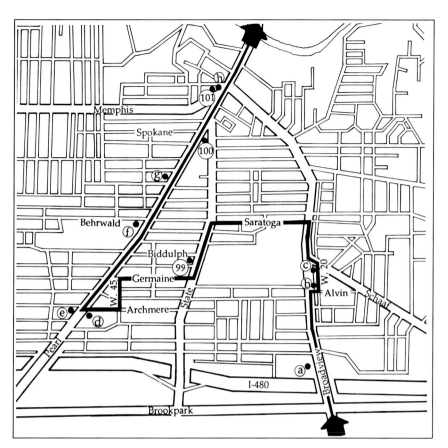

OLD BROOKLYN

99. St. Mary Byzantine Catholic Church
100. Our Lady of Good Counsel Roman Catholic Church
101. St. Luke United Church of Christ
  a. St. Leo the Great Roman Catholic Church
  b. St. James Lutheran Church
  c. Brooklyn Heights United Church of Christ
  d. Cleveland Korean Baptist Church
  e. Corpus Christi Roman Catholic Church
  f. Unity Lutheran Church
  g. St. Mark Lutheran Church
  h. Pearl Road United Methodist Church

Travel four more blocks on Pearl and then look to the west and note **St. Mark Lutheran Church.** Built in 1924, it abuts a neighborhood of well-kept duplex homes.

Continue on Pearl for three more blocks. At its intersection with Spokane, notice **OUR LADY OF GOOD COUNSEL ROMAN CATHOLIC CHURCH (100)** to the east. Continue to move northeast on Pearl. At the intersection of Memphis, look to the west and note **ST. LUKE UNITED CHURCH OF CHRIST (101)**. Just beyond and also to the west is **Pearl Road United Methodist Church**. It is a large church, but the portion facing Pearl Road is small. Continue to move northeast on Pearl. Cross over the bridge and enter Archwood-Denison, a triangular neighborhood bound on the north by I-71, on the east and southeast by the industrial valley, and on the southwest by the railway adjacent to the zoo in Big Creek Valley. The major north-south road is Pearl; the major east-west road is Denison.

The Archwood-Denison neighborhood is beginning to make a strong comeback. Owners' restorations of late-nineteenth- and early-twentieth-century houses and the construction of a new fire station designed in accord with the neighborhood's architecture characterize the potential of this neighborhood's rebirth.

Continue to move north on Pearl until its intersection with Denison Avenue. Turn east (right) onto Denison and continue until its intersection with West 15th Street. **St. Barbara Roman Catholic Church** is located on the south side on the rim above the valley. St. Barbara, thus, marks the end of the residential neighborhood.

Backtrack west on Denison through its busy intersection with Pearl. At West 33d Street note **St. Philip the Apostle Episcopal Church** and the St. Agnes Mission for the Deaf. Continue to travel west on Denison and then turn north (right) onto West 39th Street. After one block turn east (right) onto Archwood and enter the historic district with its many restored residences.

Continue to move east on Archwood for six blocks and then look to the north side of the street and note **ARCHWOOD UNITED CHURCH OF CHRIST (102)** with its Georgian detailing. Almost opposite, but a little further east, notice **BROOKLYN MEMORIAL UNITED METHODIST CHURCH (103)** with its high lantern that admits light to the sanctuary below. At the end of the Archwood Avenue vista is the neighborhood fire station. Designed with neighborhood input, the station reflects the community's architectural taste.

Turn north (left) onto Pearl. At the corner of Mapledale and Pearl is the **Third Church of Christ Scientist** with its Greek revival portico. Opposite is Riverside Cemetery, planned by landscape architect E. O. Schwagerl in 1875. Riverside attracts visitors because of its fine, recently renovated gatehouse, its view of the Cuyahoga Valley, and its Victorian chapel. Although its size has been limited by the construction of new expressways and its lakes have been drained, the cemetery remains an interesting place to visit because of its scenic beauty and because it is the burial place of the old West Side aristocracy, including the Brainards, the Lamsons, the Sessions, and the Rhodeses. It is also reported to be the burial site of Chief Blackhawk's mother.[2]

After visiting the cemetery, continue to move north on Pearl Road and enter the Fulton-Clark neighborhood. This neighborhood is bound on the north by I-90, on the east and south by I-71, on the west by Ridge Road to Denison, and on the northwest by the railroad to West 65th Street. Major north-south streets are Scranton Road, Fulton Road, West 25th, West 45th (north only), West 44th (south only), and West 65th streets. The major east-west avenues are Clark and Storer.

Fulton-Clark is a finely scaled, diverse neighborhood. Beginning as a predominantly German neighborhood, it is becoming a home to more and more Hispanic-Americans. In this mostly residential sector, moderate-income families are settled around the Clark Avenue and West 25th Street commercial spines.

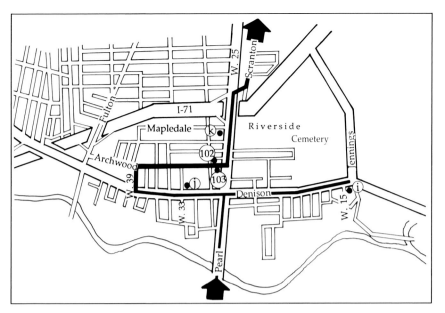

ARCHWOOD-DENISON

102. Archwood United Church of Christ
103. Brooklyn Memorial United
Methodist Church

i. St. Barbara Roman Catholic Church
j. St. Philip the Apostle Episcopal Church
k. Third Church of Christ Scientist

From the intersection of West 25th Street and Scranton Road just north of Pearl Road bridge over I-71, travel north on Scranton. The church on the left, directly opposite the Jones Home on West 25th, is **TRINITY UNITED CHURCH OF CHRIST (104)**; it also houses the offices of the Western Reserve Association of the United Church of Christ. Immediately following is the **MOTHER OF GOD OF ZYROVICY, BYELORUSSIAN AUTOCEPHALIC ORTHODOX CHURCH (105)** with its raised central entry framed by two huge blue spruce. After passing Metro General Hospital on the right, one can see the **Iglesia Sinai** on the left. Located at the intersection of Meyer and Scranton, Iglesia Sinai was constructed in 1900 as the St. Matthew German Evangelical Lutheran Church, mirroring the change in the identity of the neighborhood from German to Hispanic.

Continuing to move north on Scranton Road, pass the Holy Ghost Revival Assembly. This is quickly followed by Cleveland Central Catholic High School on the same side. This building's original buff-colored stone has darkened with age so that it now matches the exterior of **ST. MICHAEL ROMAN CATHOLIC CHURCH (106)**, which dominates the southwestern corner of Scranton Road and Clark Avenue. Following the Clark Avenue intersection is a gateway formed by the **SCRANTON ROAD BAPTIST CHURCH** on the right and the South Branch of the Cleveland Public Library on the left. Traveling through this gateway note **IMMANUEL EVANGELICAL LUTHERAN CHURCH (107)** on the Seymour–Scranton Road

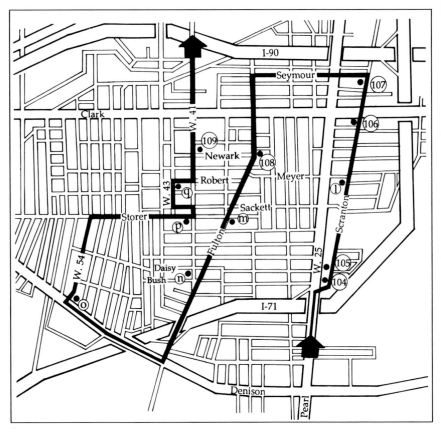

FULTON-CLARK 🔼

104. Trinity United Church of Christ
105. Mother of God of Zyrovicy,
     Byelorussian Autocephalic Orthodox
     Church
106. St. Michael Roman Catholic Church
107. Immanuel Evangelical Lutheran
     Church
108. St. Rocco Roman Catholic Church

109. St. Procop Roman Catholic Church
l. Iglesia Sinai
m. Church of the Blessed Sacrament
n. Faith United Methodist Church
o. St. Boniface Roman Catholic
   Church
p. Bethany United Church of Christ
q. Christ Lutheran Church

corner. Just beyond the church, turn west (left) on Seymour and continue to move west until Fulton Road.

At Fulton, turn south (left) and continue past the bustling intersection of Clark and Fulton Road. Three blocks south of this intersection, **ST. ROCCO ROMAN CATHOLIC CHURCH (108)** is located on the left. Continuing to move along Fulton, one will pass the **Church of the Blessed Sacrament** on the left at Storer Avenue. At this point, look back toward St. Rocco, sited to terminate this Fulton Avenue vista. Staying on Fulton, **Faith United Methodist Church**, built in 1909 as Evangelical Tabor Church, can be seen on the west side of West 41st Street between Daisy and Bush. Continue on Fulton.

After crossing the bridge over I-71, turn west (right) onto Denison Avenue. After another bridge over I-71, go five blocks and turn north at West 54th Street. On the right, located in a peaceful setting and designed on a small scale, is **St. Boniface Roman Catholic Church**.

Continue to travel north along West 54th Street until its intersection with Storer. At Storer turn east (right) and continue until West 41st Street. At the southwestern corner of the Storer–West 41st Street intersection is **Bethany United Church of Christ**. At this intersection turn north (left) onto the one-way West 41st Street. One block north at Sackett, turn west (left). One block west at West 43d, turn north (right). Two blocks north at the intersection of West 43d and Robert is **Christ Lutheran Church**, typical of neighborhood churches built around 1900.

Turn east (right) onto Robert. Travel one block and then turn north (left) again onto West 41st Street. Travel north for two blocks. At the intersection of Newark and West 41st Street is **ST. PROCOP ROMAN CATHOLIC CHURCH (109)**, a large stone church with twin bell towers flanking the central double entry. Continue to move north until the West 41st Street and Clark intersection. At the northeast corner of this intersection is a cemetery that provides quiet relief from the commercial uses along Clark Avenue. A few blocks north of the cemetery is an intersection with I-90. This ends the tour of the West Side South neighborhood. To get to the next tour, take I-90 west to the West 117th Street exit and then turn south (left) onto Lorain Avenue.

St. Mary Byzantine Catholic Church was established in 1938 under the auspices of Father Edmund Tabakovich and Father Stephen Petrick. The congregation's first religious services were held in a rented store at the corner of Stickney Avenue and West 35th Street. In 1939, the congregation purchased the site of the present church plus additional adjacent land for just over $2,000. Under the leadership of Father Daniel Ivancho, the parish built a rectory and planned a new religious facility for a site near the corner of Biddulph Avenue and State Road.[3] However, with the outbreak of World War II, plans for the new church were delayed. Father Ivancho left St. Mary's in 1946 to become a bishop. Father Ivancho's successor, Father Nicholas Elko, resumed the fundraising campaign for a new church. The new church on State Road was dedicated in 1950.

The original religious facility at 4119 Stickney Avenue was renovated in 1956 to serve as the parish school, and the former rectory became a convent for the teachers from the Sister Servants of Mary Immaculate. Increasing enrollments in the religious school prompted Father Joseph Bodnar, with the help of architect Nicholas Lesko, to plan the construction of a new school building in 1959. The

99. St. Mary Byzantine Catholic Church (1949)

Architect: Unknown
Location: 4600 State Road

growth of the school continued with the renovation of an adjacent building, the Crystal Chalet Catering Hall, in 1981. The parish also supports a day care, pre-school, and kindergarten.[4]

This church has a Romanesque flavor with traces of Byzantine, most evident in the octagonally shaped honeycombed copper cupolas located at the top of the twin bell towers. The most prominent Romanesque architectural element is the double-door entrance topped by a large window within the large semicircular two-story arch between these towers. Other Romanesque details include the semicircular arches above the louvered belfries and the semicircular arches above the double and triple side windows. Pronounced stone sills below all windows, the protruding stone waterlines defining the top of the raised basement, and the red-tile roof also add distinction to the structure. Unique features include prominent multicolored reliefs depicting religious scenes placed within specially lighted panels at the bases of the bell towers and brightly colored murals, symbols, and the name of the church around and above the main entrance.

100. OUR LADY OF GOOD COUNSEL ROMAN CATHOLIC CHURCH (1930)

Architects: Henry A. Walsh and Erwin O. Lauffer

Location: 4423 Pearl Road

Located on the crest of the hill at the southern edge of the center of Old Brooklyn on Pearl Road opposite the old Bucyrus Interurban streetcar barn, Our Lady of Good Counsel Roman Catholic Church dominates the neighborhood with its size and height. Established by Father Patrick Quigley in the early 1870s, the parish was originally referred to as The Sacred Heart of Mary. Services were held in a cooper shop until 1875 when a brick church was erected. Steady growth of the parish during the first two decades of the twentieth century led Father Luke Rath to build a new basement church in 1918. The original brick structure was then renovated to serve as classrooms for the religious school. These newly renovated classrooms were designed to complement the adjacent school completed in 1915.[5]

The present brick-and-stone church was built in 1930. It was one of the last buildings in Cleveland to be built in the classical eclectic tradition. This style was popular between Chicago's Columbian Exposition in 1893 and the rise of modernism in the 1930s. During this period architects, especially those trained in the tradition of the Ecole des Beaux Arts in Paris, borrowed from classical styles of all types. It was, thus, not unusual to see a Roman temple portico over an Italian Renaissance facade on a Georgian building placed on a modern base adjacent to a Palladian-style bell tower. Indeed, at Our Lady of Good Counsel these diverse elements come together comfortably. Its large sanctuary measures 168 feet by 69 feet. The two-story entrance portico is made of smooth-cut stone. Four monumental columns with composite capitals support the triangular pediment above. The plain, light stone frieze, dentilated cornice, stone cupola, and copper spire contrast nicely with the dark brick.

101. St. Luke United Church of Christ (1900)
Architect: Unknown
Location: 4216 Pearl Road

Located at the intersection of Memphis and Pearl roads, St. Luke United Church of Christ was organized by the Reverend C. Allard in 1843 to serve the German immigrants settling within the area. First referred to as St. Luke Evangelical Church, this congregation soon bought a small school building that was moved to the corner of Broadview and Schaaf roads where it was refurbished as a church. The congregation remained at that address until moving to its present site in 1853. In 1900 the present religious facility was erected, and the parish school was added in 1925.[6]

Elements such as the squared-off tower topped by a crenelated parapet, corner and side buttresses, and a wide central gable convey a Romanesque influence. However, the use of pointed arches above window and door openings is generally associated with Gothic styling. The adjacent school was designed to complement the church. Its use of similar brick and the pointed arches in the main window suggest that the church was looked to for design cues. Such repetition of elements lends an architectural unity to the complex.

102. ARCHWOOD UNITED CHURCH OF CHRIST (1929)
Architect: Daniel Farnham
Location: 2800 Archwood Avenue

Settled within the Archwood-Denison historic district, among late-nineteenth-century houses undergoing renovation, is the Archwood United Church of Christ, one of the oldest Protestant religious groups in Cleveland. Archwood U.C.C. continues to have a strong commitment to the welfare of the greater Archwood-Denison neighborhood and provides a wide variety of civic and social activities such as concerts, plays, social and political gatherings, and youth and senior citizen functions.[7]

Founded in 1819, the congregation moved to its present location in 1879.[8] Prior to that time, Archwood U.C.C. was located near Denison Avenue and West 33d Street. The continual growth of the congregation during the 1920s necessitated the construction of a new sanctuary on the Archwood Avenue site in 1929. At the same time the 1879 church was remodeled into a dining room and kitchen.

Modified Georgian designs became popular in America in the 1920s. Following this design trend, the Archwood congregation selected the Georgian style for this new building. A front portico with a centrally placed oculus, a tripartite entrance, and rounded six- and twelve-pane windows topped by keystones and fanlights exhibit this Georgian flavor. Many of the design elements in this church can be traced to eighteenth-century New England religious structures. Similarly, on the interior, features such as a stylized furniture rail, hurricane lamps, and a broken pediment design over the font are also reminiscent of eighteenth-century New England. The interior is noted for its special ornamentation, which includes alpha and omega symbols and dolphins, representing life, death, and life after the Resurrection. Archwood U.C.C.'s copper steeple and weathervane rise above the residential district to herald a church in the vanguard of neighborhood social concerns.

103. BROOKLYN MEMORIAL UNITED METHODIST CHURCH (1911)

Architect: Unknown
Location: 2607 Archwood Avenue

Brooklyn Memorial United Methodist Church is the oldest Methodist congregation in the greater Cleveland area. Founded as the Methodist Church Society by Oziah Brainard, Seth Brainard, Sylvanus Brainard, and Ebenezer Fish in 1818, Brooklyn Memorial held its first services in the Brooklyn Township Hall until 1827, when the congregation erected a log cabin–style church near Denison Avenue and West 25th Street. The original church was used by Methodists and Presbyterians and was noted for its long wood benches and the separate entrances for men and women. The original Sunday school was headed by Ebenezer Fish and served twenty children living in the area. Membership reached fifty-seven by the late 1820s.[9]

The continual growth of the congregation necessitated the construction of a larger, one-story frame sanctuary in 1849. Built on the northeast corner of Denison Avenue and West 25th Street, this church also contained separate entrances for men and women. This second facility served the congregation until a third, brick structure was erected under the leadership of the Reverend Samuel

Mower in 1881. The third church was located near the present site on Archwood Avenue at West 25th. It served the congregation until 1914 when the present church, located just west of the former church, was dedicated by the Reverend W. Arthur Smith. The sanctuary was renovated in 1942. The congregation currently maintains an active Sunday school, youth program, and senior citizen activity center.[10]

Of special interest architecturally is the hexagonal lantern tower with dormered windows above the sanctuary. The church's Akron Plan, with its sliding walls, enables the main sanctuary and adjacent Sunday school auditorium to be joined into one continuous space. Robust square towers with louvered belfries, lancet windows, and pointed arches above the doors frame the street facade. Other Gothic features include large perpendicular-style stained-glass windows and a crenelated parapet on the side tower.

The congregation's long history and the unique design of the building make this structure an important landmark.

Located on what was once part of millionaire Charles Brainard's estate, Trinity United Church of Christ has a prominent position in this diverse neighborhood that also contains Metro General Hospital and the Jones Home of Children's Services. Trinity United Church of Christ began as a mission church in 1911 and within a year opened its first Sunday school. The church erected its first religious facility in 1913 on a lot located between West 25th Street and Scranton Road. The original frame, accommodating 275 worshipers, served the congregation until 1923 when plans were made to construct a larger church on the same site.[11] Under the guidance of the Reverend August E. Kitterer, the congregation erected the new

104. Trinity United Church of Christ (1925)

Architect: Albert E. Skeel
Location: 3525 West 25th Street

church in 1925. This was followed by a new educational unit constructed in 1948. An addition in 1965 provided a new parlor and office space.

Classical in design, this structure uses many Gothic details, including pointed arches above the door and window openings, modified crenelations, tracery, and decorative finials above some windows. The structure is unique because of the small battlement details at the top of the bell tower. However, the structure is important also because it houses the Western Reserve Association offices of the United Church of Christ, the only major denomination founded and headquartered in northeastern Ohio.

105. MOTHER OF GOD OF ZYROVICY, BYELORUSSIAN AUTOCEPHALIC ORTHODOX CHURCH (1960)
Architect: Alexander Nazaretz
Location: 3517 West 25th Street

Mother of God of Zyrovicy marks what was once a Byelorussian immigrant neighborhood. The greater Tremont area is still considered to be the center for much of the religious and social activity for the Byelorussian community, and this church is still instrumental in these cultural and religious events.

The Mother of God of Zyrovicy, Byelorussian Autocephalic Orthodox Church was founded in 1951 to serve the Byelorussian immigrants who arrived in Cleveland following World War II. Since most of the immigrants lived in the neighborhood, the parish held its religious services and other activities in a variety of local private and public facilities prior to the completion of its present church in

1960. Over sixty families donated to the construction cost.[12]

The building components are symmetrically organized on an east-west axis. The paneled entrance door, stained-glass windows, and mosaics in the tower above the front entrance provide a decorative quality. The rounded arches above the windows and corbel detailing on the side wings suggest a Romanesque influence. Overall, the mass of the central entry form appears too large for the size of the church and the Cross of St. Euphosyria of Polatsk that caps it, but it is an interesting eclectic composition.

106. St. Michael Roman Catholic Church (1889)
Architect: Adolph Druiding
Location: 3114 Scranton Road

St. Michael Roman Catholic Church is the most impressive of the three magnificent edifices that tie down the Scranton and Clark Road intersection on the eastern edge of the Fulton-Clark neighborhood. Located diagonally across the street from the Scranton Road Baptist Church and opposite the South Branch of the Cleveland Public Library, the main bell tower of St. Michael's soars to a height of 232 feet, making the church a neighborhood landmark and orientation point visible for miles.[13]

Founded in 1882 by Father J. M. Koudelka to serve the then-German neighborhood, St. Michael's began as a frame church-and-school with dimensions measuring a modest 62 by 32 feet. The new church, now a century old, more than doubles the original church's size and provides seating for 1,500 parishioners; for many years it was the largest church in Cleveland.[14]

Dedicated in 1892, the church's exterior was finished with buff-colored rubble stone, which has since darkened with age. Two bell towers housing four tons of bells flank the church's tripartite entrance. Pointed openings, pointed towers, and pointed corner turrets give the building a Victorian Gothic appearance. As a tribute to St. Michael, two large archangels crown the central portal. On the interior, the vestibule, nave, and side aisles are groin-vaulted with a multiplicity of ribs. The nave columns are clustered colonettes with naturalistic foliated capitals. The church is furnished with over fifty polychrome statues, many of them imported from Germany. The altar is modeled after the altar of the Church of St. Francis in Borgo, Italy.[15]

107. IMMANUEL EVANGELICAL LUTHERAN CHURCH (1879)
Architect: Charles Griese
Location: 2928 Scranton Road

Located approximately one block north of a "gateway" created by the Scranton Road Baptist Church and the South Branch of the Cleveland Public Library, Immanuel Evangelical Lutheran Church remains a point of stability in a transitional neighborhood. Founded in 1872 as a new parish school for the emerging Scranton Road neighborhood, what is now Immanuel Evangelical Lutheran Church was started as an outreach of Trinity Evangelical Lutheran Church. Under the guidance of the Reverend Henry Weseloh, this branch of Trinity became a separate parish in 1879.[16]

The cornerstone for the present church was laid in September of the same year, and the brick church, which measures 100 feet by 48 feet, was dedicated on July 18, 1880. By the mid-1880s, the congregation had expanded to more than 2,300 members, and 494 children were enrolled in the religious school. Indeed, growth was so great that in 1885 another new Lutheran Church, St. Matthew's (now Iglesia Sinai) was started on the corner of Scranton Road and Meyers, about a dozen blocks south.

After a 1909 tornado damaged the Immanuel church, parishioners rebuilt the school and church. The third floor was removed from the school and the spire was removed from the church tower. In 1911, a new social hall was constructed, and in 1953 the church was again modernized.[17] Due to declining enrollment, the school was removed in 1958 and a new parking lot was constructed.

This well-proportioned, simple, sturdy meetinghouse structure with its elegant, square segmented bell tower and open belfry and well-crafted Gothic-style detailing around windows and doors is an important neighborhood landmark. On the well-maintained interior, plain plaster walls contrast with the polished light and dark woodwork. The central focus at the chancel end is an altar with carved wooden statues of the Apostles. At the opposite end a Weissenborn tracker organ is displayed in the loft above the narthex.

Located opposite the Newark Avenue and Fulton Road intersection, the flat facade of St. Rocco's terminates the view from the southwestern approach on Fulton Road. In an eclectic neighborhood, St. Rocco maintains a position of prominence as the controlling visual element of Fulton Road from St. Rocco Court to Roehl Court.

St. Rocco Roman Catholic Church traces its origins to a group of West Side Italian immigrants who decided to form their own Catholic religious society just prior to World War I, first meeting in a small chapel on Trent Avenue.[18] In response to the need for more standard religious procedures, the diocese called for the establishment of a new parish in that neighborhood during the early 1920s.

Founded as the first Italian parish on the West Side in 1922, St. Rocco held

108. St. Rocco Roman Catholic Church (1949)

Architect: Michael G. Boccia
Location: 3205 Fulton Road

religious services under the guidance of Father Alphonse de Maria and Father John D. Davidson at the original chapel until 1926. Then, local architect Franz Warner designed the parish's first brick church-and-school, which remained the focal point of the parish until the late 1940s when plans for a larger facility were unveiled. The present church was designed by Michael Boccia in 1949 and can seat up to 750.[19]

Because of the starkness of the front facade, the church presents a modern appearance. Typical Romanesque details, such as the corbeling below the parapet, compound arches in the entrances, and a squared-off bell tower with arcading in the belfry, have all been abstracted into more simplified forms. A rose window and a tower with a pyramidal roof are also simple and without detail.

109. ST. PROCOP ROMAN CATHOLIC CHURCH (1902)
Architect: Emile Uhlrich
Location: 3182 West 41st Street

Anchoring down the intersection of West 41st Street and Newark Avenue, St. Procop Roman Catholic Church and its rectory lend a distinctive air to the neighborhood of modest but well-maintained homes. Nearby local grocery stores and shops provide this mainly residential sector with pedestrian activity.

St. Procop's was established by Father Anthony Hynek of the St. Wenceslas parish in 1872. This parish was designed to serve the religious needs of Bohemian Catholics living in the southwest part of Cleveland. During the first two years of its existence, the congregation met in St. Mary on the Flats. In 1874, the church built its own frame church-and-school on West 41st Street near Clark Avenue. Religious differences among parishioners, pastors, and the diocese stopped all further plans for building a larger facility until the first decade of the twentieth century. Under the leadership of Father Wenceslas A. Panuska and Father Peter Cerveny, the parish finally authorized the building of a new church in 1902.[20] This completed structure measures 144 feet by 88 feet and can seat up to 1,300 people. A fourteen-room brick-and-stone school was erected near the church in 1908, and a convent was added to this complex in 1925.

Two symmetrically balanced bell towers flank the entrance and give the structure a sense of strength and stability. The fluted pilasters, the unadorned wide frieze above the entrance, and the two-story pavilion above the entry topped by a triangular pediment take on the proportions of the Italian Renaissance style, but the rough ashlar-stone facing is an anomaly. The two flanking entrance towers with rounded openings, pediments, and octagonal cupolas made of rusticated stone are also a bit unusual. The interior of the church contains impressive marble altars and a wide assortment of frescoes and statues, including statues dedicated to the Blessed Virgin of the Suata Horn (Holy Mountain) and the Infant Jesus of Prague located above the two side altars.

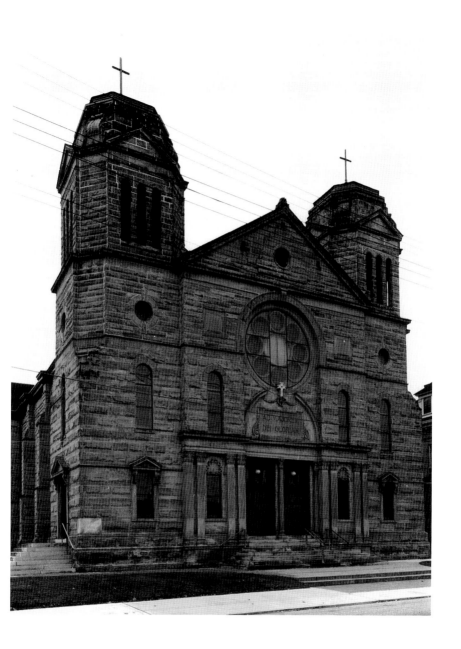

CHAPTER NINE

West Central Cleveland

The West Central community is comprised of three neighborhoods: West Boulevard–Lorain, Edgewater-Cudell, and Detroit Shoreway.

The West Boulevard–Lorain neighborhood is bound on the north by I-90, on the east by West 73d Street, on the south by the Rapid Transit tracks, and on the west by West 117th Street. Lorain is the major east-west road; West Boulevard is the major north-south road.

TOUR

Begin this tour at the intersection of West 117th Street and Lorain just south of the I-90–West 117th interchange. Travel east for one block and then turn south (right) onto Bosworth. Continue to move south on Bosworth for ten blocks. At the intersection of Bosworth and Flower notice the **Bosworth Road Presbyterian Church** to the east. Continue to move south on Bosworth for another two blocks. At the corner of Bosworth and Adeline note the imposing **Saints Philip and James Roman Catholic Church** on the northeast corner.

Continue south on Bosworth until it intersects with Bellaire, then turn left (east). Continue to move along Bellaire as it turns into West 105th Street. At the intersection of West 105th Street and West Boulevard bear right onto West Boulevard. Continue to move northeast on West Boulevard until its intersection with Lorain. At the corner of Lorain and West Boulevard note ST. IGNATIUS ROMAN CATHOLIC CHURCH (110) on the southwest corner.

Turn east onto Lorain and continue for one block. Turn southeast at Denison and proceed on Denison. At the intersection of Denison and West 99th Street is the **Denison United Church of Christ**. Go southeast on Denison for another block and then turn north (left) onto West 98th.

Continue north on West 98th and enter the Edgewater-Cudell neighborhood after passing under I-90. This neighborhood is bound on the north by Lake Erie, on the east by West 85th Street, on the south by I-90, and on the west by West 117th. Lake, Clifton, and Detroit are the major east-west roads; West Boulevard is the major north-south road. At the intersection of West 98th Street and Cudell is **Christ United Church of Christ**. Continue to move north on West 98th until it intersects with Madison. At Madison turn west (left) and proceed two blocks, noting on the right at West 98th the **Trinity United Methodist Church**. At the intersection of Madison and West Boulevard look south and note **West Boulevard Christian Church**. Tucked in a curve of West Boulevard and shaded by trees, this church completed its front addition in 1959.

Turn north onto West Boulevard and continue on it for one block. At the corner of Detroit and West Boulevard, turn west (left) onto Detroit. Continue on Detroit for six blocks. At the southwest corner of the West 114th Street and Detroit intersection note ST. ROSE ROMAN CATHOLIC CHURCH (111) and the statue of St. Rose against the blue background.

Continue to travel along Detroit until it intersects with West 117th Street. At West 117th Street turn north (right) and travel along this street which separates Cleveland and Lakewood. Continue on West 117th Street for three blocks. At the intersection of Lake and West 117th Street notice the commanding, domed **FIFTH CHURCH OF CHRIST SCIENTIST (112)** with its Palladian entry.

After viewing the church, turn right and proceed east on Lake Avenue past West Boulevard. Shortly past this intersection on the south side of the street is **St. Thomas Evangelical Lutheran Church**. This small church is located on a well-maintained residential street facing Edgewater Park and Lake Erie.

Keep on Lake. As you pass under the railroad, enter the Detroit Shoreway neighborhood, which is bound on the north by Lake Erie, on the east by West 45th Street, on the south by I-90, and on the west by West 85th Street. The major east-west streets are Detroit and Lorain; the major north-south road is West 65th Street.

At the northeast corner of Lake and West 78th Street, note the small, frame **St. Luke Episcopal Church**. Continue on Lake until it ends and then turn east on Detroit. Travel east on Detroit for three blocks until it intersects with West 70th Street. Here at the corner of West 70th and Detroit is **OUR LADY OF MT. CARMEL ROMAN CATHOLIC CHURCH (113)**, an important church in the Detroit Shoreway neighborhood.

Turn left on West 70th and note the housing for the elderly built by Mt. Carmel Roman Catholic Church. Stay on West 70th Street until it ends. Then follow it east (right) until it becomes West 65th Street. Travel south on West 65th. Just before the intersection with Detroit, note on the left **St. HELENA ROMANIAN CATHOLIC CHURCH (114)**, one of the sixteen Romanian parishes in the United States.

Turn east (left) at Detroit and notice **HOLY RESURRECTION RUSSIAN ORTHODOX CHURCH (115)** on the south side opposite West 61st Street. This was originally a Romanian Catholic church in what was at one time a predominantly Romanian neighborhood. At the intersection of West 58th and Detroit turn south onto West 58th Street and then turn west (right) onto Clinton one block later. At the southeast corner of Clinton and West 65th, note **Bethany Presbyterian Church**.

Turn south (left) onto West 65th Street and travel on it for one block. Turn east (left) onto Franklin and travel on it for one block. At the northeast corner of West 58th and Franklin note **Iglesia Adventis del Septimo Dia**. This little Hispanic church is evidence of the changing ethnic character of the neighborhood.

Turn south (right) onto West 58th Street. Travel on it for two blocks and then turn west (right) onto Bridge and proceed for one block. At the southwest corner of Bridge and West 65th Street is **People's Hope United Methodist Church**. Turn south (left) and proceed on West 65th Street. Between the intersections of Wakefield and Fir, note **Calvary Reformed Church**. Built in 1972, this modern building serves a congregation established in 1880.

Continue to move south on West 65th Street until it intersects with Lawn. On the east side of this intersection notice the imposing structure of **St. COLMAN ROMAN CATHOLIC CHURCH (116)**.

Turn west (right) on Lawn and travel on it for one full block and then turn south (left) onto West 73d Street. Travel one block south and then look west and see

110. St. Ignatius Roman Catholic Church
111. St. Rose Roman Catholic Church
112. Fifth Church of Christ Scientist
113. Our Lady of Mt. Carmel Roman Catholic Church
114. St. Helena Romanian Catholic Church
115. Holy Resurrection Russian Orthodox Church
116. St. Colman Roman Catholic Church
117. St. Stephen Roman Catholic Church
  a. Bosworth Road Presbyterian Church
  b. Sts. Phillip and James Roman Catholic Church
  c. Denison United Church of Christ
  d. Christ United Church of Christ
  e. Trinity United Methodist Church
  f. West Boulevard Christian Church
  g. St. Thomas Evangelical Lutheran Church
  h. St. Luke Episcopal Church
  i. Bethany Presbyterian Church
  j. Iglesia Adventis del Septimo Dia
  k. People's Hope United Methodist Church
  l. Calvary Reformed Church
  m. St. Paul Evangelical Lutheran Church
  n. Cleveland First Enterprise Baptist Church

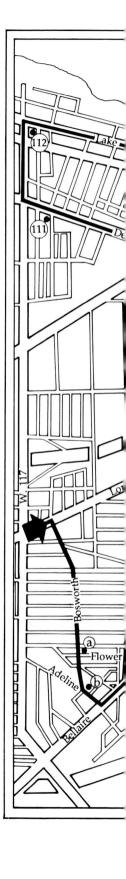

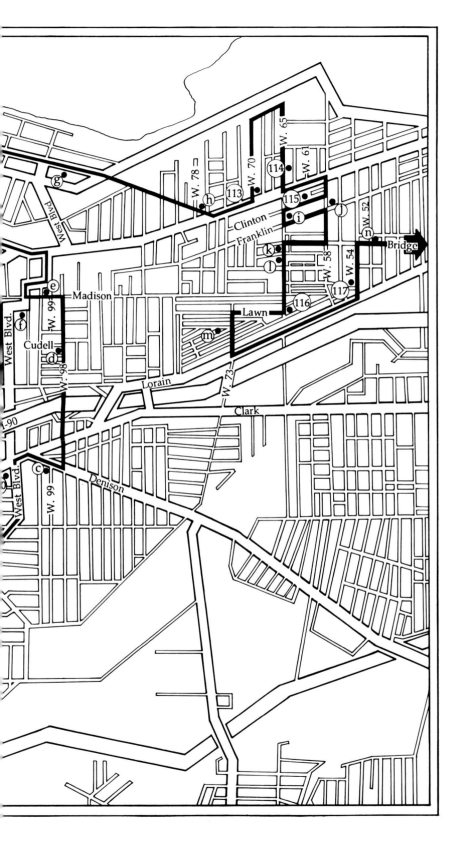

St. Paul Evangelical Lutheran Church. Located on a point of land, this small church is beautifully crafted and is scaled to suit the neighborhood of small residences. Continue to move south on West 73d Street until it intersects with Lorain.

At Lorain turn east (left) and travel in a northeast direction until Lorain intersects with West 54th Street. At West 54th turn north (left). On the left, midway up the block, is ST. STEPHEN ROMAN CATHOLIC CHURCH (117). Beautiful interiors make St. Stephen's an extremely significant landmark.

After one block on West 54th Street turn east (right) onto Bridge. At the northeast corner of Bridge and West 52d note **Cleveland First Enterprise Baptist Church**, an interesting little church that fits nicely into the neighborhood.

This ends the tour of the West Central neighborhoods. To gain access to the regional highway network, continue on East Bridge to West 45th and turn north (left) to get on the Shoreway, or take Bridge east to West 44th and turn south (right) to gain access to I-90.

110. ST. IGNATIUS ROMAN CATHOLIC CHURCH (1930)
Architects: Graham and Fish
Location: 10205 Lorain Avenue

Located on the southwest corner of Lorain and West Boulevard, St. Ignatius Roman Catholic Church commands a prominent position in its neighborhood. A minaret-like spire soars from the east transept of the church to create an urban landmark visible for miles.

Established by Ignatius F. Horstmann in response to the growing needs for a new parish in the southwest section of Cleveland, the initial combination church-and-school was built in 1902. A larger church was later erected on the same site, and a more modern brick school was added in 1917.[1] The congregation's continual growth throughout the 1920s necessitated Father Thomas Hanrahan to authorize the 1925 construction of an even larger structure, which still serves the parish.

Boston architects Edward T. P. Graham and F. Stillman Fish gave the church a Byzantine character by designing a minaret-like tower and a distinctive, recessed tripartite entrance supported by slender columns. The overall block shape of the building, the rounded arches over various door and window openings, and the modified blind arcade in the front facade are Romanesque.

III. St. Rose Roman Catholic Church (1957)
Architect: Anthony Ceresi
Location: 11411 Detroit Avenue

Located on the Edgewater-Cudell neighborhood's busiest commercial street, Detroit Avenue, St. Rose Roman Catholic Church is a transitional point between the working-class neighborhoods to the south and the more elegant homes found along the Lake Erie shore to the north. The church was established in the 1890s by Father Ignatius J. Wonderly to serve the neighborhood's growing population. Many of the parishioners formerly resided in the northern section of the St. Colman parish.

Initially, religious ceremonies were conducted in a local hall, but in 1900 a frame church was completed at the corner of Detroit Avenue and West 114th Street. Because of the congregation's growth under the leadership of Father Patrick J. O'Connell, the original church was demolished and replaced by another structure in 1930. This church, designed by Boston architects Graham and Fish, served the congregation until 1957 when the present building was constructed.[2]

Designed by Cleveland architect Anthony Ceresi, the new church can seat up to 1,000 people. The structure is composed of three simple elements—base, auditorium, and bell tower—which are all basically planar. The base plane is relieved by three glass-door openings with segmented arches above. The auditorium is relieved by a projecting entry portico topped by a monumental statue of St. Rose. A dark-blue screen mounted with early Christian symbols in cast aluminum serves as a backdrop for this statue of St. Rose. The plain, tall bell tower is capped by a simple cross mounted on a dark-blue base. Though historic detail is noticeably absent, the building maintains a human scale in spite of the plain surface and strong color contrasts. On the interior, there is a 24-foot aluminum altar screen framed in black. Adorned with religious symbols, the screen serves as a backdrop for the plain gray marble altar.[3]

112. FIFTH CHURCH OF CHRIST SCIENTIST (1928)
Architect: Frank W. Bail
Location: 11623 Lake Avenue

Located on the southeast corner of Lake Avenue and West 117th Street, the Fifth Church of Christ Scientist stands just east of the Cleveland-Lakewood border and has a visually significant position within its neighborhood. Begun in a public hall on Detroit Avenue at West 65th Street in 1915, the congregation of the Fifth Church of Christ Scientist grew enough to necessitate the construction of a larger religious center in 1928.[4]

Cleveland architect Frank W. Bail designed the church to seat 900. Acoustics, sight lines, and distance to the reader's desks were considerations which helped determine the octagonal shape of the central meeting room.[5] The placement of the pipe organ directly behind the reader's desk was also done for acoustical reasons. The interior is richly textured; the major materials are marble and walnut.

Birmingham buff sandstone trimmed by Nebo marble covers the church's exterior. Ludrivici tile laid in a fish-scale pattern forms the dome. Classical styling is often used in Christian Scientist churches because congregations believe that classical forms, like their religious beliefs, are quite rational. This church is no exception.

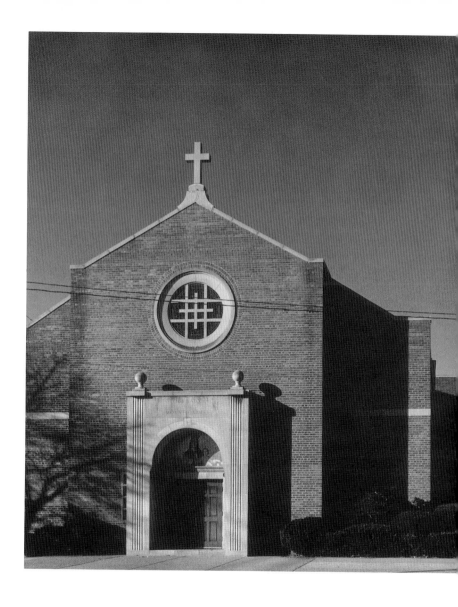

Our Lady of Mt. Carmel Roman Catholic Church was organized in 1926 by Father Sante Gattuso of the Order of Divine Mercy to serve the Italian community located along Detroit Avenue. Religious services and social events were held in a rented hall on West 69th Street from 1926 to 1933. In 1933 the parish relocated to a renovated house at 7104 Detroit Avenue.[6]

Following World War II, Father Gattuso authorized the erection of a new chapel on Detroit Avenue at West 70th Street. Dedicated in 1949, this chapel could accommodate 325 worshipers. A new parish house was erected in 1951, followed by the construction of the present church facility in 1952. The new church, 109 feet by 71 feet, was designed in a modified cruciform plan. The nave

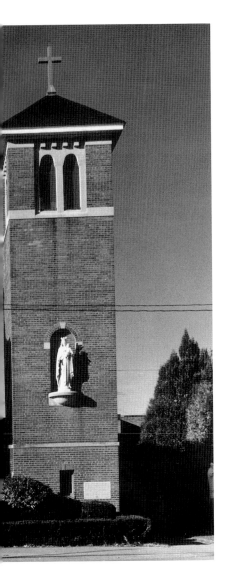

can hold 600 people.[7] This church is an example of simplified Romanesque design. The Romanesque architectural details found on this structure include round arches above the window and door openings, a recessed double door at the main entrance set in a plain portico, and buttressed side facades. The flared stone parapet front gable, modified rose window, and square bell tower with modified arcade and low hip roof also reveal the Romanesque influence. The statue of Our Lady of Mt. Carmel draws attention toward the tower, while the accentuated cut stone waterlines in the tower and on the main sanctuary provide a visual contrast to the building's plain brick veneer.

114. St. Helena Romanian Catholic Church (1906)
Architect: Unknown
Location: 1367 West 65th Street

St. Helena Romanian Catholic Church stands on the east side of West 65th Street near its intersection with northeast Detroit Avenue in what used to be a Romanian neighborhood. Founded in 1905 by Father Epaminonda S. Lucaciu, the first Romanian priest sent to America, this Byzantine rite church represents one of sixteen Romanian parishes in the United States. Initially this religious group held its services at St. Malachi Roman Catholic Church on Washington Avenue. In less than a year, however, the congregation had erected its own sanctuary on West 65th Street. The first frame church was completed in 1906; it was enlarged and resurfaced in brick just prior to World War II.[8] A further modernization effort undertaken in 1965 gave the building a contemporary flavor.

St. Helena's is a revitalized structure with minimal ornamentation, and its only recognizable historic ornamentation includes modified buttresses on the front facade, modified jamb shafts leading to a recessed front entrance, and stone moldings around the side windows. The brick school is directly attached to the sanctuary, while the parish house is connected to the church by a brick arch spanning the driveway.

115. HOLY RESURRECTION RUSSIAN ORTHODOX CHURCH
(Originally St. Mary Romanian Orthodox Church, 1905)
Architect: Unknown
Location: 6103 Detroit Avenue

Located in what was once the heart of Cleveland's large Romanian neighborhood, Holy Resurrection Russian Orthodox Church has a distinctive styling that makes this small building quite unique. Begun as St. Mary Romanian Orthodox Church by Father Moise Balea in 1904, the first church was erected on Detroit Avenue in 1905. The continued growth of the parish led the congregation to build an adjacent hall in 1927. Referred to as the National Home, this hall served both religious and social functions until 1960, when the 400-member congregation sold the church and hall to Holy Resurrection Russian Orthodox Church and moved to a larger complex on Warren Road.[9]

This eclectic building contains architectural elements associated with Byzantine, Romanesque, and Gothic styles. The Eastern-influenced steeples and belfry towers and the rounded transepts and apse areas are reminiscent of the Byzantine style. The rounded arches above the circular windows in the main body and tower are Romanesque, while elements such as the pointed gables are often associated with the Gothic style. An interesting feature is the building's entry, which is not perpendicular to the street, perhaps an effort to keep the altar at the east end of the processional aisle in accordance with ancient tradition.

116. St. Colman Roman Catholic Church (1914)
Architects: Count Lenore and Schneider and Potter
Location: 2027 West 65th Street

St. Colman Roman Catholic Church stands out among the residential and commercial structures located along West 65th Street because of its color, material, architectural quality, and size. The tall twin towers are even visible to motorists traveling along I-90 to the south.

St. Colman was established in 1880 by Father Eugene M. O'Callaghan to serve the needs of Irish parishioners in the area. The first religious services were held in an abandoned school on Pear Street. By 1882 the parish had moved to a new frame church on West 65th Street. In 1883 the church was expanded to accommodate 1,000 worshipers; this was followed by the erection of a new combination school-and-hall in 1885. This educational building was moved to another site in 1904 to make way for a larger brick school. A third parish school was built in 1923 and was located at the corner of Madison Avenue and West 65th Street.[10]

In 1914, Count Lenore of Rome, with the assistance of Cleveland architects Edwin Schneider and J. Ellsworth Potter, designed the present Indiana limestone church in the classical style. The structure is 192 feet by 97 feet and can accommodate 2,800 people. A two-story central pavilion supported by monumental paired fluted columns with Corinthian capitals dominates the central portion of the west entry facade. Symmetrically placed 130-foot bell towers frame the portico. The use of a smooth ashlar exterior accentuates the plain block form of the building. St. Procops has a similar form and mass, but it is made of rough rather than smooth stone and its central form does not include a portico.

On the interior, the narthex contains three bays. One might expect, therefore, that the nave would be similarly divided into the typical three-aisled arrangement; but this is not the case, for there are no interior columns. The space nevertheless alludes to the typical cruciform shape by providing a coffered ceiling in the shape of a cross; the long axis follows the central aisle, and the short axis projects over the side shrines. The altar, communion rail, free-standing pulpit, and stations of the cross were all made in Dublin, Ireland, under the direction of Father O'Leary, the pastor of St. Colman's at the time the church was built.

117. ST. STEPHEN ROMAN CATHOLIC CHURCH (1873)
Architects: Cudell and Richardson
Location: 1910 West 54th Street

Located on a quiet street in a residential neighborhood of modest homes, St. Stephen Roman Catholic Church possesses some of the most important ecclesiastical artwork in the United States. The contrast between the high-style artwork on the church's interior and the surrounding vernacular neighborhood is quite surprising.

The origins of St. Stephen's can be traced to the early 1850s when a group of German-speaking Catholics requested their own neighborhood parish. Established in 1854 by Father John J. Kramer of Alsace, France, the original congregation was placed under the patronage of the St. Mary of the Assumption parish, formerly located on West 30th Street. The continual growth of the new congregation after the Civil War led to the establishment of the St. Stephen parish in 1869.

Under the guidance of Father Stephen Falk, the parish built a brick church-and-school in 1869 on West 54th Street south of Bridge Avenue. It was used until Father Casimir Reichlin sanctioned the building of the present church structure in 1873. Financial constraints delayed completion of the church until 1881. After the completion of the church, the school building was enlarged and modernized in 1885 and again in 1890. An even more modern school was built in 1897 to serve the congregation's children. Ever-increasing school enrollments just prior to World War I encouraged Father Reichlin to erect a new brick school and auditorium in 1916.[11] The auditorium was refurbished as a social hall, and a ten-room addition to the original school was completed in 1952.

Architectural style elements on this church made of Amherst stone include lancet windows, decorative buttresses, and a square bell tower with corner finials. This gives the structure a Victorian Gothic–style appearance. Planned in the traditional cruciform shape, the building measures 165 feet by 74 feet. The church's interior was considered one of the finest in the world in the 1890s and was officially recognized in 1893 at the Columbian Exposition in Chicago, where the free-standing oak pulpit with its finely detailed canopy was displayed. The pulpit, altars, stations of the cross, statues, and shrines were all handcrafted in Germany. The wooden statuary is particularly unusual for the time, and the congregation's German heritage is evident in this statuary. (For example, in the Blessed Virgin's altar Mary's hair is blond.) In 1906, the beautiful stained-glass windows were commissioned through the Bavarian Institute of Art and imported from the Mayer Studios in Munich. In 1953, many of the windows were destroyed by a tornado, but they were replaced in 1954 by the same studio that produced them originally.

CHAPTER TEN

West Park

The West Park community is composed of the four Cleveland neighborhoods located west of West 117th Street and includes Jefferson, Kamms Corners, Riverside, and Puritas-Longmead.

The Jefferson neighborhood is bound on the west and north by Rapid Transit tracks, on the east by West 117th Street, and on the south by I-71. Triskett and Lorain are major east-west roads; West 140th Street, West 130th Street, and Berea Road are major north-south roads.

TOUR

Begin this tour at the eastern edge of the Jefferson neighborhood on Lorain Avenue just south of the West 117th and I-90 interchange. Move west on Lorain. At the intersection of West 128th notice the **Mt. Calvary Lutheran Church** on the northwest corner. The former church, now used as a school, is on the west while the new contemporary sanctuary is to the east.

A little farther west on the northwest corner of the intersection of Lorain and Berea Road is the church of **St. Vincent DePaul**, a modified Prairie School–style building of dark brown brick. Drive three more blocks and then turn south (left) onto West 138th, just after the shopping center on the south side of Lorain. The large gray-stone Gothic-style **CHRIST UNITED METHODIST CHURCH (118)** dominates the triangular intersection formed by West 138th and Fairwood just west of the shopping center.

Keeping to the right of the church, proceed south on West 138th one block. Then turn west (right) on San Diego. After two blocks, turn left (south) on West 140th. After two blocks turn west (right) on Carrydale and notice the small neighborhood church of **West Park Evangelical Friends** on the southwest corner.

At the end of Carrydale turn north (right) onto West 143d Street and return to Lorain Avenue. Turn west on Lorain and pass under the Rapid Transit bridge and enter the Kamms Corners neighborhood, an area of well-kept homes bordering the Rocky River Reservation of the Cleveland Metropolitan Park System. This neighborhood is bound on the north by I-90, on the east by Rapid Transit tracks, on the south by Melgrave Avenue, and on the west by the Rocky River. Rocky River Drive is the major north-south road; Lorain Avenue is the major east-west road.

A short distance beyond the intersection of West 150th Street and Lorain, make a very sharp right turn onto Triskett Road. Immediately on the left, at the intersection of Rockport, notice the traditional **Bethany English Lutheran Church**. It contrasts nicely with the modern edifice of **ST. MARK EPISCOPAL CHURCH (119)** located diagonally across the street.

Proceeding northeast on Triskett, notice another fine little contemporary church opposite the intersection of West 152d, the **West Park Christian Reformed Church**. Continuing on Triskett, the large, plain **St. Mel Roman**

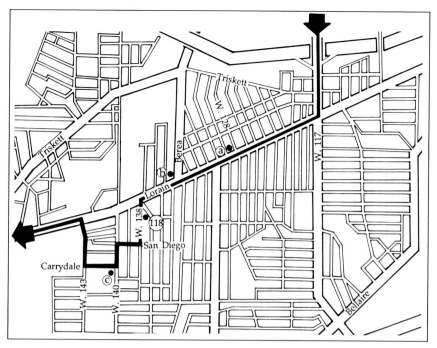

Jefferson ⬆N

118. Christ United Methodist Church
  a. Mt. Calvary Lutheran Church

  b. St. Vincent DePaul
  c. West Park Evangelical Friends

Catholic Church with its deeply recessed entry is located on the left side of Triskett just beyond the intersection of Orchard Park. Turn left onto Orchard Park and then bear right on Westland at the first intersection.

Terminating the vista at the end of Westland is **St. Mary Romanian Orthodox Church (120)**, formerly located in the Detroit Shoreway neighborhood. The church doors do not face Warren Road, as one might expect, so take the driveway on the north side of the church to see the church entryway. On the way, note the beautiful little outdoor shrine and carved wooden sculpture located on the north side of the entry drive. After viewing the church, return to the street and turn left (north) on Warren Road.

At the first intersection turn west (left) on Montrose and follow it to West 157th to where the modern brick **St. Mark Roman Catholic Church** was erected in 1959. The church-and-school adjoins a park and playground.

At the end of Montrose turn south (left) on West 159th Street. After two blocks bear right onto Alden Road. After one block turn left (south) on West 160th. After one block turn right (west) on Edgecliff and take it until it dead-ends at Rocky River Drive.

Turn left on Rocky River Drive and proceed south. In a few blocks notice **St. Joseph Academy and the Sisters of St. Joseph** set in an expansive campus on the

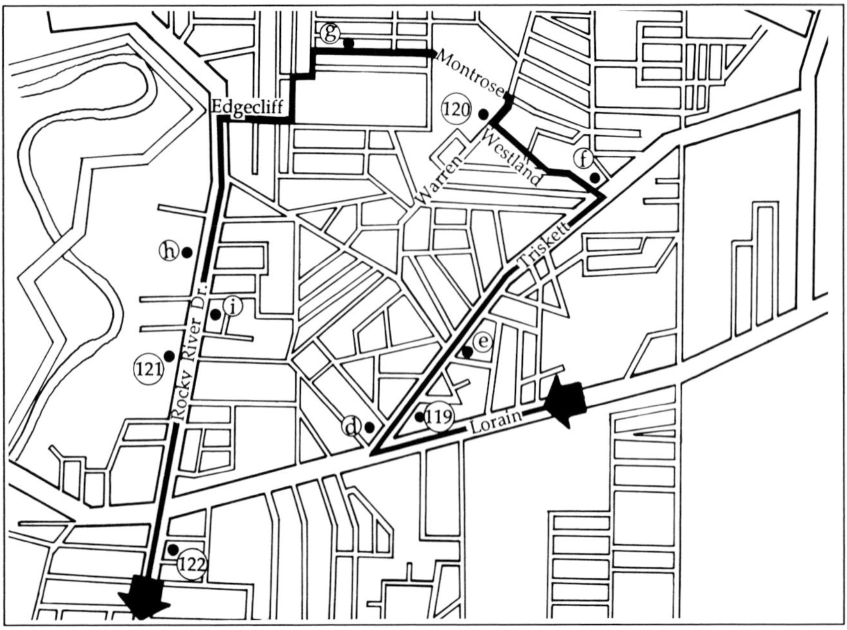

Kamms Corners

119. St. Mark Episcopal Church
120. St. Mary Romanian Orthodox Church
121. Our Lady of Angels Roman Catholic Church
122. West Park United Church of Christ

d. Bethany English Lutheran Church
e. West Park Christian Reformed Church
f. St. Mel Roman Catholic Church
g. St. Mark Roman Catholic Church
h. St. Joseph Academy and the Sisters of St. Joseph
i. Monastery of Poor Clares

right. The site borders the Rocky River Reservation to the west opposite Claire and Marquis.

Just a little farther south on the east side of Rocky River Drive is the **Monastery of Poor Clares**. Notice the beautiful little circular pavilion in the front yard. In just a short distance another institutional complex, including a church, school, hall, rectory, and housing for the elderly, appears on the right. The church of **Our Lady of Angels Roman Catholic Church (121)** anchors this beautiful complex and verdant setting.

Continue to move south on Rocky River Drive. Shortly after passing the Kamms Corners Shopping Center at the Lorain Avenue intersection, **West Park United Church of Christ (122)** appears on the left at the northeast corner of Truax and Rocky River. The older English Gothic–style building, formerly used as the sanctuary, now used as the educational unit, is attached to a newer modified-Georgian sanctuary in the Kamms Corners neighborhood.

Continuing south on Rocky River Drive, the Riverside neighborhood is entered after crossing Melgrave Avenue. Riverside is bound on the north by Melgrave, on

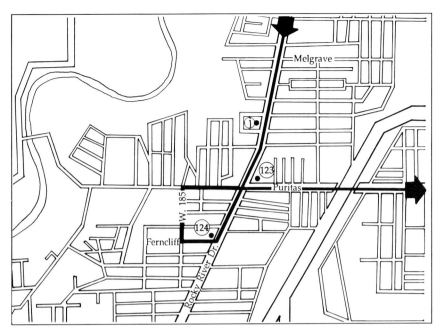

RIVERSIDE

123. St. Patrick West Park Roman   124. Riverside Community Church
     Catholic Church   j. Lutheran Church of the Holy Cross

the east by I-71, on the south by I-480, and on the west by the Rocky River. Rocky River Drive is the major north-south road; Puritas is the major east-west road. After a few blocks on Rocky River Drive, the long, low, contemporary **Lutheran Church of the Holy Cross** appears on the right. Built in 1957, this church has a porte cochere between the educational building to the south and the sanctuary to the north. Parking is located behind the building and hidden from the street.

On the northeast corner of the intersection of Puritas Road and Rocky River Drive is **St. Patrick West Park Roman Catholic Church (123)**, one of the oldest structures in the neighborhood. A few blocks south of this on the northwest corner of Ferncliff and Rocky River is **Riverside Community Church (124)**, which was remodeled in a modified Prairie School style after being moved here from another location. Across the street is Riverside Homes, the community that originally housed the NASA Lewis Research workers who created the first Riverside Community Church congregation. This is the last church in the Riverside area.

To get to the Puritas-Longmead neighborhood, turn right (west) on Ferncliff. After one block turn right again (north). In four short blocks turn right once more (east) onto Puritas Road. Drive east past Rocky River Drive and St. Patrick's church and under the I-71 and Rapid Transit bridges to enter the Puritas-Longmead residential neighborhood. This area is bound on the north by I-71, on

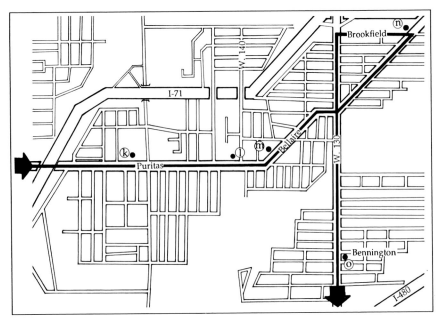

PURITAS-LONGMEAD

k. Hungarian Reformed Church
l. Ascension of Our Lord Church
m. Puritas Lutheran Church

n. Second Calvary Missionary Baptist Church
o. Annunciation Catholic Church

the east by West 117th, on the south by I-480, and on the west by Rapid Transit tracks. Puritas and Bellaire are the major east-west roads; West 150th and 130th are the major north-south streets. The western section of this neighborhood is characterized by newer houses, built in the 1950s, while smaller homes built circa 1920 are clustered around West 130th Street.

On the north side of Puritas between West 154th and West 152d is the **Hungarian Reformed Church** erected in 1977. Contemporary in design, it boasts a central bell tower and still has services in Hungarian. Continuing to move east on Puritas, the **Ascension of Our Lord Church** is located on the northeast corner of Puritas and West 140th. The Puritas Shopping Center is across the street to the south. Across the street to the east is the Rockport Branch of the Cleveland Public Library. Ascension is a large, plain, modern brick building that contrasts with an older, smaller frame antecedent that remains on the corner.

At West 139th, Puritas continues east and Bellaire Road intersects in a curve from the north. Bear left onto Bellaire and note to the north the very large, sprawling **Puritas Lutheran Church** built in a modified Georgian style in 1955.

Continue northeast on Bellaire to its intersection with West 130th Street. Here there are three options for ending the tour. The first is to continue on Bellaire to the **Second Calvary Missionary Baptist Church** located at the corner of Emery Road and Bellaire and then proceed downtown via West 105th and West Boulevard. The second is to turn right (south) onto West 130th Street and pass **Annunciation Roman Catholic Church** at West 130th and Bennington, gaining access to I-480 a few blocks farther south. The third alternative is to turn left on West 130th Street, which provides access to I-71 several blocks north of the intersection of Bellaire and West 130th.

Located on a point of land where Fairwood curves into the commercial intersection of Lorain and West 138th Street, Christ United Methodist Church's lawn provides a refreshing green-space. As an active participant in its community, the church sponsors craft fairs, charitable drives, social events, quilting shows, and self-help workshops.[1]

Christ United Methodist resulted from the merger of the Bethany German Methodist Episcopal Church and the West Park Church. The Bethany congregation traces its roots back to the 1850s when a German Methodist mission was founded on what is now West 130th Street. The continued growth of the congregation during the 1880s led to the 1893 construction of a religious facility at the corner of Williard Avenue and West 91st Street, which served the congregation until 1938 when the building was sold to the Immanuel Pentecostal Church.[2]

The West Park Church congregation was established in 1908 as a storefront mission by J. F. Hecker of Baldwin-Wallace College. In 1909 the congregation decided to relocate to a larger hall at the corner of Lorain Avenue at West 135th Street. Soon referred to as the Methodist Episcopal Society of West Park, the

118. CHRIST UNITED METHODIST CHURCH (1938)
Architect: Unknown
Location: 3578 West 138th Street

group constructed a main sanctuary on the same site in 1915. This was followed by a parsonage at 3670 West 138th Street in the early 1920s and a religious school in 1927.

During the Great Depression, the two congregations evaluated their economic needs, and in 1936 a joint committee authorized a merger of the two groups. The construction of the older portion of the present church during the late 1930s represented the first results of this union. The congregation continued to grow during the 1940s and 1950s, totaling more than 2,000 members by 1954. Responding to this growth, the church implemented a major building campaign in 1956, and those funds were used to enlarge the main sanctuary, the lounge area, the chapel, the religious school, and the main social hall.

Pointed arches above many of the window and door openings, window tracery, and plain ashlar wall surfaces give this church a Gothic flavor. An ornate, squared-off bell tower on the east side and a large, perpendicular-style bell tower on the west side add to this building's Gothic character.

119. ST. MARK EPISCOPAL CHURCH (1940, 1960)
Architects: Carr and Cunningham
Location: 15305 Triskett Road

St. Mark Episcopal Church was established in 1871 as a mission by the Reverend Lewis Burton, rector of St. John Episcopal Church, with the original chapel located on Vega Avenue near Scranton Road. In 1940 the congregation erected a new church facility at 15305 Triskett Road. The growth of the St. Mark Episcopal congregation during the 1950s led the group to build yet another new sanctuary in front of the older church in 1960. The new church facility is attached to the older structure; the earlier church was renovated to serve as the religious school.[3]

This congregation has always been interested in helping its neighbors in time of need. For example, in the mid-1880s Reverend Burton, with assistance from

his sister-in-law, provided a shelter for women that later became the Eliza Jennings Home. The home remained affiliated with the church until the mid-1920s when it became an independent organization.[4]

The present church is a modern structure. The low-pitched roof with bracketed eaves extends beyond the light-colored brick walls to create a strong horizontal effect. Windows are grouped into a horizontal band below the bracketed eaves permitting the sanctuary to receive much natural light while retaining privacy on the interior.

120. St. Mary Romanian Orthodox Church (1960)
Architect: Haralamb H. Georgescu
Location: 3256 Warren Road

St. Mary Romanian Orthodox Church was located at 6103 Detroit Avenue from its founding in 1904 until 1954, when the congregation relocated to its present site on Warren Road. The new church, built in 1960, was designed in the modern tradition of wood religious structures located in the Transylvanian Carpathian Mountains of Romania. This facility is noted for its high-pitched roof and steeple and its porcelain enamel figures of Jesus. The steeple, 176 feet tall and weighing 9 tons, is capped by a slender aluminum cross. The enameled figures, designed by Edward and Thelma Winter, consist of sixty-two distinct sections fused together by an intense heating process.[5]

Other special features found in this church include a conical-shaped entrance porch, a 24-foot mosaic of St. Mary, and many unique icons carved by Christo-Loveanu of New York. The church seats 600. The adjoining cultural center contains thirteen classrooms and also houses the art of Anisoara Stan, who willed her collection of Romanian art to St. Mary's in 1963. The original meeting hall on this site, located about 50 feet away from the new church-and-school, was destroyed by fire in 1973.[6] This meetinghouse had served as the main sanctuary from 1954 until 1960 when the new church structure was completed.

Our Lady of Angels Roman Catholic Church traces its origins to the adjacent monastery begun in 1904 by the Franciscan Fathers of the Province of the Sacred Heart of Jesus. The monastery contained a chapel that served the religious needs of the local Catholic community until after World War I. Known originally as the Church of the Stigmata of St. Francis, the chapel soon became known as Our Lady of Angels. The continued growth of the congregation immediately following World War I led Father Columbian Valentin to request parish status in 1922. With the assistance of Father Linus Koenemund, Our Lady of Angels was granted the rights and responsibilities of a parish in 1923. The new parish soon erected a brick school, which was enlarged by four rooms in 1931. The original frame chapel served the parish until, in 1928, Father Koenemund authorized the construction of an addition.[7] However, the continual growth of the parish necessitated a larger main church structure in 1941.

The new Romanesque-style structure measures 125 feet by 51 feet and can accommodate up to 1,000 parishioners. Built of gray brick with sandstone trim, this

121. OUR LADY OF ANGELS ROMAN CATHOLIC CHURCH (1941)
Architect: William Koehl
Location: 3644 Rocky River Drive

religious facility contains a 70-foot bell tower and stained-glass windows depicting the seven joys of the Virgin Mary, the Annunciation, the Visitation, and the Nativity. The stained-glass windows were designed by Oscar Zettler of New York City. A new gallery organ was built by Walter Holtkamp for the church in 1943. Other structures located immediately around the sanctuary include Linus Hall, completed in 1955, a one-story elementary school erected in 1964, the original senior elementary school, and a renovated house used as a special educational center since 1965.[8]

This church is a modified-Romanesque structure that contains semicircular arches above window and door openings, buttresses, and a wheel window. The church also has a square bell tower with a modified arcade and low hip roof. The compound arch around the double door entrance, the low-slung roof over the main sanctuary, the enlarged buttresses at the front facade, and the distinctive chapels flanking the front facade entrance give this church special character.

122. West Park United Church of Christ (1955)
Architect: Erwin O. Lauffer
Location: 3909 Rocky River Drive

Located on the southern edge of the Kamms Corners shopping district, West Park United Church of Christ rests on the corner of Rocky River Drive and the brick street of Truax. Established by the Reverend J. B. Allen in 1859, West Park United Church of Christ originated as the First Congregational Church of Rockport, Ohio. Although the church has always maintained basically the same religious beliefs through the years, it has undergone several name changes. In 1904, the church changed its name to the West Park Congregational Church to celebrate the establishment of the new village of West Park, and the present name was adopted in 1968 as a result of a merger between the Congregational Christian and Evangelical and Reformed churches a decade earlier.

Reverend Allen's religious group held its first services in a variety of private homes and public halls until, in 1861, the congregation erected its first church facility, which was graced with impressive straight-backed pews. The congregation retained its affiliation with the Cleveland Presbytery until 1869 when it joined the Congregational Conference. A second church, in the English Gothic style, was built on the same site in 1905, and a fellowship hall and kitchen were soon added.[9] This church served the congregation as a sanctuary until 1955 when a third church with attached office was erected on the southern half of the site. The second church is still used for educational activities and houses an upper-room chapel.

The newest church structure is symmetrically balanced. An extended entrance portico supported by four unadorned columns and topped by a large triangular pediment with an ornate lunette in the center together with brick quoins and a bell tower capped by a classic balustrade and copper urns give this church its modified-Georgian flair.

123. St. Patrick West Park Roman Catholic Church (1898)
Architect: Unknown
Location: 4427 Rocky River Drive

When St. Patrick West Park Roman Catholic Church was built, it was in the country; now the city has grown up around the church and cemetery. Established by Bishop Rappe in 1848 and entrusted to the care of Father Louis J. Filiere, pastor of the Olmsted Falls parish, the original frame church was built in a field on the site of the present graveyard and served as a sanctuary and school until 1875, when Father Patrick O'Brien founded a separate parish school.[10]

The initial frame building remained intact until the parish erected the present stone Gothic-style main sanctuary in 1898 under the supervision of Father Joseph Hoerstmann. A brick school designed to complement the existing church was constructed in 1916; it was replaced in 1930 by a larger ten-room school and an auditorium. Under the direction of Father William Thorpe, the parish renovated their church facility in 1938. The church was again refurbished in 1951 under the guidance of the Cleveland architectural firm of Ward and Conrad, and the sanctuary's seating capacity was increased to hold almost 900 worshipers.[11] The church's battlement tower with its pointed louvered belfry and the opposite tower with its rounded turrets frame the pointed arch entrance to create a Gothic effect.

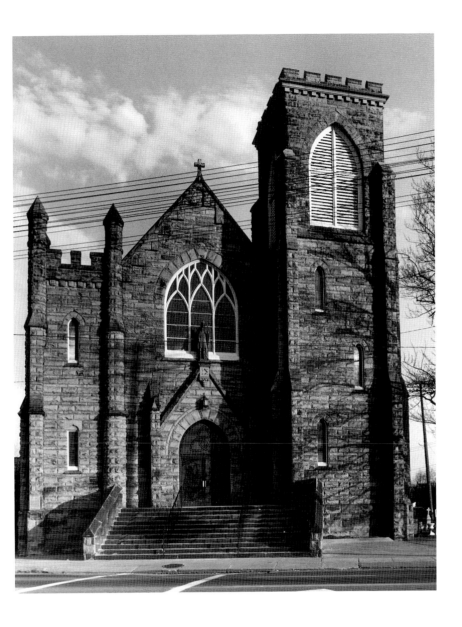

124. Riverside Community Church (1946)

Architect: Carl Droppers
Location: 4600 Rocky River Drive

Riverside Community Church is located on Rocky River Drive near the Cleveland Airport. The existing church structure was moved from Parma Heights to the present site in 1946 to serve the families of the newly settled NASA Lewis Research workers who organized a church in 1945. Most of the original members were NASA employees who lived in the Riverside Estates across the street. The church now serves a more varied congregation. The present religious structure was originally a frame building located at 6155 Pearl Road in Parma Heights. It served as a sanctuary for the Parma-South Presbyterian Church from 1893 until it was moved to its present site on Rocky River Drive in 1943.[12] Under the direction of Cleveland architect Carl Droppers, the church facility was subsequently reconstructed to meet the needs of the new congregation.

Of modified Prairie School design, an American style made popular by Frank Lloyd Wright, this church is composed of a series of horizontal planes that slide together to form the main mass of the sanctuary. The main entrance stairway slides out from this mass at different levels to separate into two stairways that lead down to the sidewalk. Low walls running alongside the stairway form a planter that embraces the entrance. Juxtaposed to the horizontal planes is the vertical, squared-off bell tower with open belfry located at the northeastern edge of the sanctuary. Extended eaves and a modified hip roof with gablet are Prairie School details that are not very common among Cleveland's public structures.

Notes

CHAPTER ONE
Sacred Landmarks in the Dual Hub Corridor

1. David D. Van Tassel and John J. Grabowski, eds., *The Encyclopedia of Cleveland History,* 379, 380; Jan Cigliano, *Showplace of America: Cleveland's Euclid Avenue, 1850–1910,* 346.

2. Van Tassel and Grabowski, 998.

3. Ibid., 638.

4. Ibid., 403; *Daily True Democrat,* Sept. 9, 1853; Eric Johannesen, *Cleveland Architecture, 1876–1976,* 5.

5. Van Tassel and Grabowski, 403; Johannesen, 18.

6. The Old Stone Church, brochure, 1988–89, unpaginated.

7. St. John the Evangelist, concert series program, May 3, 1987; Michael J. Hynes, *The History of the Diocese of Cleveland: Origin and Growth, 1847–1952,* 60.

8. Hynes, 469.

9. Timothy H. Barrett, architectural historian, conversation with Foster Armstrong, Nov. 1991; "St. Peter's, a Tree that Grew and Sent Roots Everywhere," *Cleveland News,* Oct. 24, 1959.

10. St. Peter Roman Catholic Church, "Jubilee Celebration" program, 1978; Julian Krawcheck, "New Steeple Placed Atop St. Peter Church," *Cleveland Plain Dealer,* Dec. 30, 1970.

11. "Unto Cleveland a Cathedral was Born," *Cleveland Press,* Dec. 1, 1964.

12. William G. Rose, *Cleveland: The Making of a City,* 663; Van Tassel and Grabowski, 981.

13. James Whitney and Thomas Hallet, "Notable Stained Glass in Cleveland," 36–37.

14. *Trinity Cathedral, Cleveland: Historical and Architectural Guide,* 27–29.

15. Ibid., 30.

16. Ibid., 3.

17. Van Tassel and Grabowski, 1080.

18. *Plain Dealer,* May 6, 1927.

19. *Cleveland Press,* Jan. 6, 1934.

20. Ella Grant Wilson, *Famous Old Euclid Avenue of Cleveland, at One Time Called the Most Beautiful Street in the World.*

21. *Plain Dealer,* Sept. 10, 1988; *Cleveland News,* Apr. 27, 1946.

22. Papers of St. Paul Shrine parish, Archives, Catholic Diocese of Cleveland.

23. Rose, 192; "Members are Moving Out but Cling to St. Timothy's," *Plain Dealer,* Jan. 8, 1972.

24. Cleveland Landmarks Commission, file 74, St. Timothy Missionary Baptist Church.

25. "Science Church on Euclid Sold for $65,000," *Cleveland News,* June 3, 1946; *Cleveland News,* Jan. 20, 1949.

26. Johannesen, 127.

27. Calvary Presbyterian Church, "25 Years, 1892–1917" brochure, 1917, 9–10.

28. Van Tassel and Grabowski, 151.

29. Mary Peale Schofield, *Landmark Architecture of Cleveland,* 145.

30. Cleveland Landmarks Commission, file 52, Liberty Hill Baptist Church; *Cleveland Press,* June 6, 1978; "Two Hough Churches Cited as Historical Landmarks," *The Call and Post,* Mar. 30, 1974.

31. Van Tassel and Grabowski, 375.

32. Ibid.

33. Euclid Avenue Congregational Church U.C.C., "Celebration of the 100th Anniversary of the Building" program, May 17, 1987.

34. Euclid Avenue Congregational Church U.C.C., "125th Anniversary" brochure, 1968; Euclid Ave. Cong. Church, "Celebration."

35. Euclid Ave. Cong. Church, "125th Anniversary," 6; Euclid Ave. Cong. Church, "Celebration"; Van Tassel and Grabowski, 381.

36. Van Tassel and Grabowski, 380.

37. Judy Gammon, "The Glory of Their Times," *Plain Dealer*, Oct. 19, 1980; Mary Hooper, "These Hallowed Halls," 10–11, 14–15.

38. William Dinwoodie, "Nine Christian Churches Stand in Tribute to General Bates," *Cleveland News*, May 9, 1942.

39. Johannesen, 159; Van Tassel and Grabowski, 961.

40. Van Tassel and Grabowski, 377.

41. Ibid.

42. Ibid., 22.

43. Ibid., 183; Johannesen, 100.

44. Van Tassel and Grabowski, 184.

45. Johannesen, 59, 60.

46. "New Congregational Church Is Dedicated," *Plain Dealer*, Oct. 1, 1956; Van Tassel and Grabowski, 697; Rose, 325.

47. Rose, 818; "Mount Zion Sets Goal of $140,000," *Plain Dealer*, Nov. 20, 1954; "Members Begin $213,000 Church," *Plain Dealer*, Sept. 26, 1955.

48. Works Progress Administration (WPA), *Parishes of the Catholic Diocese of Cleveland, History and Records*, 51.

49. Dinwoodie, "Nine Christian Science Churches," *Cleveland News*, May 9, 1942; Frank Stewart, "Dedicate First Church Christ Scientist," *Cleveland Press*, Oct. 5, 1946; *Cleveland Press*, June 14, 1943; James G. Monnett, Jr., "Scientists Will Build Atop Hill," *Plain Dealer*, May 12, 1928.

50. Johannesen, 63; Van Tassel and Grabowski, 432.

51. Johannesen, 63.

52. Van Tassel and Grabowski, 91; Johannesen, 67.

53. Johannesen, 67.

CHAPTER TWO
North Central Cleveland

1. Van Tassel and Grabowski, 525, 526.

2. Ibid., 307, 146; *Plain Dealer*, Nov. 2, 1972.

3. Van Tassel and Grabowski, 723; *Cleveland Press*, Oct. 10, 1945.

4. *Cleveland Press*, Oct. 10, 1945.

5. Hynes, 256–57, 275.

6. Papers of St. Paul parish.

7. Papers of Immaculate Conception parish.

8. "Willson Methodist 110 Years Old," *Plain Dealer*, Dec. 2, 1967.

9. *Record of the Founding of St. James Church, August 18, 1857*, 11; "Rebuilt St. James Episcopal to Open," *Plain Dealer*, June 4, 1938; "St. James Holds 90th Birthday," *Plain Dealer*, July 28, 1947.

10. John Wyman, *Seventy-five Years of Grace: Grace Lutheran Church History*, 11, 12.

11. Ibid., 13; "Church Will Mark Building Program," *Plain Dealer*, Jan. 10, 1953; Cleveland Landmarks Commission, file 79, Fellowship Missionary Baptist Church of Christ.

12. Cleveland Landmarks Commission, file 332, Fidelity Baptist Church.

13. Hynes, 256; WPA, 186.

14. WPA, 186; Hynes, 317.

15. "St. Vitus Church Dedicated Today," *Plain Dealer*, Nov. 19, 1932; William C. Janson, "The New St. Vitus Church of Cleveland," 5–7, 15.

16. Van Tassel and Grabowski, 838.

17. Hynes, 95; Papers of St. Mary Seminary; Van Tassel and Grabowski, 860.

CHAPTER THREE
Northeast Cleveland

1. Van Tassel and Grabowski, 453.

2. Ibid., 417.

3. Ibid., 289.

4. Ibid.

5. "Name Moves on with Church," *Plain Dealer,* Nov. 21, 1951; "St. Mark's Presbyterian to Move to East Boulevard," *Plain Dealer,* Mar. 19, 1952.

6. Frank Stewart, *Cleveland Press,* Apr. 2, 1945.

7. Van Tassel and Grabowski, 300.

8. Johannesen, 159.

9. Papers of St. Aloysius parish; Hynes, 256, 316.

10. Rose, 140.

11. Ibid.; "Northeast Section of City Has Fine New Church," *Plain Dealer,* May 16, 1926; Van Tassel and Grabowski, 872.

12. Hynes, 155–56.

13. "Immanuel Presbyterian Will Dedicate Church," *Plain Dealer,* Sept. 5, 1925; Van Tassel and Grabowski, 540.

14. "Immanuel Presbyterian Will Dedicate Church," *Plain Dealer,* Sept. 5 1925; "Strives for 1,000 on Church Role, Immanuel Pastor Prepares for Climax of 5 Year Progress Campaign," *Plain Dealer,* June 10, 1935.

15. "Chapel is Dedicated to Young Hero Here," *Plain Dealer,* Sept. 18, 1961.

16. "Lutherans Rites Set on Building," *Plain Dealer,* Mar. 27, 1954; "Lutheran Church Holds First Rite," *Plain Dealer,* Sept. 13, 1954.

17. Hynes, 315; "$500 Award for Church Plan Goes to Lithuanian D.P.," *Plain Dealer,* May 1, 1950.

CHAPTER FOUR
South Central Cleveland

1. Hynes, 70.

2. Ibid., 71; Johannesen, 21.

3. Schofield, 155.

4. "St. Philip Church Reaches 16th," *Plain Dealer,* Sept. 5, 1970.

5. Mary Jayn Woge, "New Churches Here Reflect the Times," *Plain Dealer,* Dec. 24, 1973; Timothy H. Barrett, "Faith, Form, and Function: Ecclesiastical Architecture in Cuyahoga County," 18.

6. Van Tassel and Grabowski, 734.

7. "Pick 10 Trustees of Euclid Temple," *Plain Dealer,* Dec. 29, 1952.

8. Van Tassel and Grabowski, 76.

9. Gordon H. Simpson, "Bishop Guest of St. John's Today," *Plain Dealer,* Nov. 16, 1930; Johannesen, 201.

10. Van Tassel and Grabowski, 857.

11. Ibid., 183.

12. Johannesen, 201; Van Tassel and Grabowski, 484.

13. "Negroes to Observe Church's 60 Years," *Plain Dealer,* June 23, 1951; "Church Will Observe Fiftieth Anniversary," *Cleveland News,* Nov. 30, 1940.

14. Temple Tifereth Israel, brochure, 1975; Van Tassel and Grabowski, 960.

15. Van Tassel and Grabowski, 960.

16. Schofield, 16.

17. Van Tassel and Grabowski, 108.

18. Rose, 477, 646; Van Tassel and Grabowski, 108.

19. Rose, 810.

20. Ibid., 217–18; Van Tassel and Grabowski, 890.

21. Henry Russell Hitchcock, *Architecture: 19th and 20th Centuries,* xxiii.

22. "Two East Side Parishes Merge," *The Catholic Universe Bulletin,* June 20, 1975, 1.

23. Hynes, 152, 275.

24. Van Tassel and Grabowski, 748; Papers of St. Adalbert parish.

25. Van Tassel and Grabowski, 855.

26. Ibid.

27. Ibid., 37.

28. Ibid., 38.

29. Ibid.

30. "Olivet Church, 50 Years Old, Celebrates," *Cleveland News,* Dec. 25, 1934; Mormon Chapel Dedicated Here," *Plain Dealer,* May 3, 1954.

31. *Plain Dealer*, June 26, 1975; WPA, 114.

CHAPTER FIVE
Southeast Cleveland

1. Van Tassel and Grabowski, 134; The Urban Design Center of Northeast Ohio, *Buckeye-Woodland: A Housing Design Portfolio*, 5.
2. Van Tassel and Grabowski, 886.
3. Ibid., 402.
4. Ibid.
5. *Plain Dealer*, Aug. 26, 1964.
6. Van Tassel and Grabowski, 852.
7. Ibid.
8. Foster Armstrong, "The Forms of Cleveland's Sacred Structures," 14.
9. Hynes, 255; Papers of St. Catherine parish.
10. WPA, 59, 60.
11. Concordia Lutheran Church, dedication program, 1938; "New Lutheran Church Holds Opening Services," *Cleveland Press*, Mar. 5, 1938; "Lutheran Church Ediface Dedicated," *Plain Dealer*, Mar. 7, 1938.
12. Jack Hume, "Two Lutheran Churches Will Merge," *Cleveland Press*, Sept. 8, 1965; *150 Years of Mission to Greater Cleveland, 1832–1982*, 76.
13. Papers of Epiphany parish; "Epiphany Church Dedicated by Bishop in Solemn Rite," *Plain Dealer*, Apr. 5, 1948.
14. "New Church Building Will Be Blessed," *Cleveland News*, June 6, 1942.
15. Hynes, 274; Papers of Holy Family parish/Mt. Pleasant Elementary School.
16. Hynes, 274.
17. Information provided by the Reverend Marcus Miller, pastor of Lutheran Church of the Good Shepherd.

CHAPTER SIX
The Broadway Corridor

1. Van Tassel and Grabowski, 683.
2. " 'Melting Pot' Church to Replace 'Old Broadway,' " *Plain Dealer*, Mar. 4, 1917; *Plain Dealer*, Mar. 22, 1919.
3. Van Tassel and Grabowski, 678–79.
4. Hynes, 256; "New St. Lawrence's Church Is Dedicated," *Plain Dealer*, Aug. 12, 1940.
5. Van Tassel and Grabowski, 863.
6. WPA, 176; Van Tassel and Grabowski, 863.
7. Hynes, 255; Van Tassel and Grabowski, 540; Papers of Immaculate Heart of Mary parish.
8. *Plain Dealer*, May 5, 1958.
9. Van Tassel and Grabowski, 581.
10. Hynes, 71.
11. Papers of Holy Name parish.
12. "Miles Park Presbyterian Will Observe Centennial," *Plain Dealer*, Jan. 13, 1933; Van Tassel and Grabowski, 790.
13. Miles Park United Methodist Church, "100th Anniversary" brochure, 1972.
14. "Methodists Hail 50th Anniversary," *Cleveland Press*, Oct. 1, 1949.
15. *Plain Dealer*, May 9, 1918.
16. "$25,000 Fire Damages Church on Miles Avenue," *Cleveland Press*, Oct. 28, 1949; "Dr. Flynn to Reopen East Side Church," *Cleveland News*, Feb. 25, 1950.

CHAPTER SEVEN
The Near West Side

1. Van Tassel and Grabowski, 736.
2. Ibid., 980, 981.

3. Ibid., 860.

4. Hynes, 73.

5. Ibid., 423.

6. Van Tassel and Grabowski, 857.

7. Doris Millavec, "St. John's Survives Tornado Blitz, Too," *Plain Dealer,* July 9, 1953.

8. "Franklin Circle Christian Will Open Tomorrow," *Plain Dealer,* Oct. 10, 1942.

9. Van Tassel and Grabowski, 420.

10. Papers of St. Patrick parish; Theodore Andrica, "West Siders Built First Irish Catholic Church," *Cleveland Press,* Jan. 1, 1951.

11. "Trinity Church Gets Status as Landmark," *Plain Dealer,* Mar. 31, 1973.

12. Cleveland Landmarks Commission, file 17, Trinity Evangelical Lutheran Church; Schofield, 46.

13. Papers of St. Emeric parish.

14. Ibid.; Eleanor Prech, "Renovated St. Emeric's Marks 70th Anniversary," *Cleveland Press,* Apr. 24, 1974.

15. Van Tassel and Grabowski, 36.

16. Information provided by Greek Orthodox Church of Annunciation officials, June/July 1990.

17. Cleveland Landmarks Commission, file 107, Holy Ghost Byzantine Roman Catholic Church.

18. "Greek Catholics Plan Church," *Plain Dealer,* Jan. 1, 1910.

19. Papers of St. Augustine parish.

20. Don Wilder, "Claims Dividing Line between Varied Protestant Branches Harder to Find," *Cleveland Press,* Aug. 26, 1933; "Confidence in God Is Theme of 85th Anniversary Sermon," *Plain Dealer,* June 19, 1950.

21. "Pilgrim Church to Stage Triple Celebration," *Cleveland News,* Nov. 26, 1949; Van Tassel and Grabowski, 293.

22. "Pilgrim Church to Stage Triple Celebration," *Cleveland News,* Nov. 26, 1949.

23. Johannesen, 51–52.

24. Van Tassel and Grabowski, 39; Victoria George and Drew Rolik, "Tremont's Churches," 6; information provided by St. George Antiochian Church officials, June/July 1990.

25. Information provided by St. George Antiochian Church officials, June/July 1990.

26. Zion United Church of Christ, "100th Anniversary" program, May 12, 1967.

27. Hynes, 317–18.

28. "Our Lady of Mercy Church to Be Dedicated next Sunday," *Plain Dealer,* Oct. 16, 1949.

29. Papers of St. John Cantius parish; "Historical Sketch of St. John Cantius Church," high school dedication brochure, Apr. 16, 1950; "Designed by Potter and Gabriel, Would Seat 1,000 Completed 1925," *Plain Dealer,* Nov. 13, 1926.

30. Saints Peter and Paul Ukrainian Greek Catholic Church, "Diamond Jubilee" brochure, 1985, 33.

31. Ibid., 35, 36.

32. Van Tassel and Grabowski, 863.

33. Ibid.

CHAPTER EIGHT
The West Side South

1. Van Tassel and Grabowski, 129.

2. Ibid., 835.

3. St. Mary Byzantine Catholic Church, "50 Golden Years, 1938–1988" brochure, 1988.

4. Ibid.

5. Hynes, 154, 275.

6. Rose, 190; "Chimes to Ring Centennial of Pearl Road Congregation," *Plain Dealer,* Oct. 10, 1953.

7. Information provided by Archwood United Church of Christ members, June/July 1990.

8. Ibid.

9. "Oldest Methodist Congregation in Cleveland," *Cleveland News,* Nov. 30, 1943; "2 Churches Plan Birthday Services," *Plain Dealer,* Nov. 12, 1932; Rose, 107.

10. "2 Churches Plan Birthday Services," *Plain Dealer,* Nov. 12, 1932; "Brooklyn Church Is 120 Years Old," *Plain Dealer,* Nov. 6, 1938; Van Tassel and Grabowski, 130.

11. Trinity United Church of Christ, "75th Anniversary, Reflections of the Church's History" brochure, 1986, 4; Frank Stewart, "Dedicate $90,000 for Educational Unit," *Cleveland Press*, Feb. 28, 1948.

12. Information provided by Mother of God of Zyrovicy, Byelorussian Autocephalic Orthodox Church officials, June/July 1990; "Byelorussian Church Is Consecrated," *Plain Dealer*, Sept. 5, 1960.

13. Papers of St. Michael parish.

14. Johannesen, 26.

15. Papers of St. Michael parish; Johannesen, 26; Schofield, 48.

16. Rose, 424; "Immanuel Opens Improved Church," *Plain Dealer*, Nov. 13, 1954.

17. "Immanuel Opens Improved Church," *Plain Dealer*, Nov. 13, 1954.

18. "Church Is Dedicated: Bishop Schrembe Officiates at St. Rocco's; 165 Children Confirmed," *Plain Dealer*, Dec. 20, 1926.

19. Papers of St. Rocco parish.

20. WPA, 171; Hynes, 154, 259.

CHAPTER NINE
West Central Cleveland

1. WPA, 125; Hynes, 276.

2. Hynes, 257; "St. Rose's Parish to Have Double Celebration Sunday," *Cleveland News*, June 5, 1940; "St. Rose's Church Is Dedicated," *Plain Dealer*, July 5, 1957.

3. "St. Rose's Church Is Dedicated," *Plain Dealer*, July 5, 1957.

4. Dinwoodie, "Nine Christian Science Churches," *Cleveland News*, May 9, 1942.

5. *Plain Dealer*, June 22, 1926.

6. Hynes, 317; Papers of Our Lady of Mt. Carmel parish.

7. Hynes, 422; Papers of Our Lady of Mt. Carmel parish; "Pastor & Portrait," *The Plain Dealer Magazine*, May 24, 1964.

8. John Mihal, "First Romanian Church in the Nation to Mark Birthday with Party Here," *Cleveland News*, May 21, 1936; Hynes, 319.

9. Van Tassel and Grabowski, 861; Richard Wager, "Romanian Orthodox to Consecrate Church," *Plain Dealer*, Aug. 20, 1960.

10. Carl Romansky, ed., *St. Colman Centennial Celebration, 1880–1980*, 7–8, 10.

11. Papers of St. Stephen parish; Hynes, 154, 259, 276.

CHAPTER TEN
West Park

1. Christ United Methodist Church, "Golden Anniversary" brochure, 1988.

2. Ibid.

3. Rose, 380–81; "St. Mark's Dedication Is Tomorrow," *Plain Dealer*, Sept. 30, 1961.

4. Rose, 488–89.

5. *Plain Dealer*, Aug. 20, 1960; "Faith in Enamel," *The Plain Dealer Magazine*, July 16, 1961.

6. St. Mary Romanian Orthodox Church, dedication brochure, 1960; "A Church Haven for Romanian Art," *The Plain Dealer Magazine*, June 16, 1963; Thomas Andrewjewski, "Guardian Angel to His House of God," *Plain Dealer*, July 13, 1973.

7. WPA, 61; Our Lady of Angels Church, "Golden Jubilee, 1922–1972" brochure, 1922.

8. Papers of Our Lady of Angels parish; Frank Stewart, *Cleveland Press*, Mar. 13, 1944; Our Lady of Angels Church, "Golden Jubilee."

9. West Park United Church of Christ, brochure, 1984; Rose, 295.

10. Frank Stewart, *Cleveland Press*, Sept. 6, 1943.

11. Hynes, 259, 276, 319, 423.

12. Information provided by Riverside Community Church officials, June/July 1991; Parma Presbyterian Church, "A Living Christian Church, 1835–1935," centennial brochure, 1935; Frank Stewart, *Cleveland Press*, Mar. 7, 1955.

Glossary

AISLE. A passageway or walkway parallel to the nave.

AKRON PLAN. An architectural plan that permits the educational unit of the church to be opened to the main sanctuary to accommodate larger groups, so called because the idea was first developed at the First Methodist Church in Akron, Ohio.

APSE. The semicircular form terminating the church sanctuary, first applied to a Roman basilica.

ARCADE. A series of arches and their supporting members.

ARCHITRAVE. The lowest part of the entablature which rests on the capitals of columns. Also the molded frame around a door or window.

ASHLAR. Squared stone laid in regular courses.

BALDACHINO. A canopy supported by columns and generally placed over an altar.

BALUSTRADE. A series of small ornate columns or plain pillars supporting a rail.

BAROQUE. A term applied to design in the late-Renaissance period which was a reaction to the classic forms standardized by Palladio. Often characterized by overelaboration of scrolls, curves, and broken pediments.

BARREL VAULT. An uninterrupted semicircular ceiling vault.

BASE. The lower portion of a structure or architectural feature.

BASILICA. A hall for the administration of justice.

BAS-RELIEF. Decorative sculpture done in low relief.

BATTLEMENT. A fortified parapet composed of alternating solid parts and openings.

BAY. An external or internal rectangular division of a building demarcated by units of vaulting, piers, windows, etc.

BELFRY. The upper room in a bell tower.

BEMA. A raised platform reserved for the clergy in early Christian churches.

BRACKET. A decorative supporting projection.

BUTTRESSES. Masonry or woodwork built against a wall to give it additional support by providing a counterthrust to the arch or vault behind it.

BYZANTINE. Derived from the Byzantine Empire of the fifth and sixth centuries and chiefly characterized by a central dome carried on pendentive arches over a square base, round arches, elaborate columns, richness in decoration and color.

CAMPANILE. A bell tower.

CANOPY. A suspended cover or roof located above the altar.

CAPITAL. The top or head of a column or pilaster.

CASEMENT WINDOW. A window which opens on hinges fastened to the side edges of the frame.

CHANCEL. The space for the clergy and choir. Traditionally separated by a screen from the main body of the church.

CHOIR. Church space where the services are sung. Sometimes located in the eastern arm or in the space between the nave and apse.

CLASSICAL. A style primarily inspired by the ancient Greek or Roman or, secondarily, by the classical trends of the Renaissance.

CLERESTORY. An upper story of the nave which is pierced by windows.

COLONNADE. A range of columns.

COLUMN. A vertical structural support member generally consisting of a base, shaft, and capital.

COMPOSITE. A Roman capital combining the Ionic on the upper and the Corinthian on the lower.

CONSOLE. A scrolled bracket. Also, the desk where the controls of the organ are located and where the organ is played.

CORBEL. Supporting carved or molded projection located on the face of a wall.

CORBEL TABLE. Projecting masonry course which rests on a series of corbels and usually connected by small arches.

CORBIESTEP. The stepped edge of a gable masking a pitched roof.

CORINTHIAN. Generally the most ornate of the three Greek orders and characterized by carved acanthus leaves in its capital.

CORNICE. Any molded projection which crowns the part to which it is attached (door, wall, window, etc.), more specifically, the uppermost element of an entablature.

CRENELATED PARAPET. An indented parapet which has openings called embrasures or crenelles and raised parts called merlons.

CROCKET. Carved projection which decorates the edge of gables, pinnacles, etc.

CROSSING. Space formed by the crossing of the church's nave, chancel, and transepts.

CROWN. The highest point of an arch or vault.

CRUCIFORM PLAN. A church with transepts which project on both sides producing a cross-shaped ground plan.

CUPOLA. A small structure (usually domed) located on top of a roof, dome, or tower which provides interior lighting and/or ornamentation.

DENTILATION. A band of small, rectangular toothlike ornaments which form the lower band of a cornice.

DOME. A hemispherical roof or ceiling.

DORIC. Oldest and simplest of the three Greek orders and characterized by a fluted shaft, lack of a base, and simple capital. Also distinguished by triglyphs and metopes in its frieze.

DORMER. An upright window which projects out from the sloping planes of a roof.

EAVES. Lower edge of the roof hanging over the walls.

ENTABLATURE. Part of the wall resting on the capitals of the columns and supporting the pediment. Made up of the architrave, the frieze, and the cornice.

FAN LIGHT. Semicircular window located above a door.

FINIAL. Ornamental element which caps a pinnacle, spire, gable, pediment, etc.

FLECHE. Thin, wooden spire, occasionally lead-clad, located above the crossing.

FLUTING. Vertical grooves located on the shaft of a column.

FOLIATED TRACERY. Tracery decorated by leafy ornamentation.

FONT. Container used to store water for baptism. Traditionally located at the west end of the church.

FRESCO. Painting done on wet plaster.

FRIEZE. An ornamental band used as a decorative feature often below the cornice of the roof.

GABLE. Triangular wall portion extending from the eaves to the ridge of the roof.

GABLET. A small ornamental gable found on a buttress, over a niche, in woodwork, or in various other locations.

GALLERY. Upper story located above the aisle and arched to the nave. Also called a tribune.

GOTHIC. A medieval style prevalent in Western Europe during the thirteenth to fifteenth centuries and characterized by pointed arches and pointed vaults.

GROINED VAULT. A type of vaulting characterized by the arched diagonals (groins) formed by the intersection of two barrel vaults. Also called a cross vault.

HAMMER BEAM. One of a pair of short horizontal members attached to the foot of a principal rafter in a roof, in place of a tie beam.

HEADER. Brick laid so that the end appears on the wall face.

HIPPED ROOF. A roof with sloping ends and sides.

HOODMOLD. A projecting molding located over a window or other opening designed to throw off rain.

IONIC. One of three Greek orders of architecture. Characterized by the volutes of its capital.

JAMB. An element forming the side of an opening.

JAMB SHAFTS. Decorative features found on jambs.

JERKIN-HEAD ROOF. A roof with a hipped end truncating a gable.

KEYSTONE. A central stone placed at the center of an arch to lock the rest of the stones (voussoirs) into place.

LANCET WINDOW. A tall, narrow window capped with a pointed head.

LINTEL. Horizontal element which spans an opening (usually above a doorway) and carries the load above.

LOUVER. Slatted aperatures with movable fins to control sound or light. Often used in a belfry.

LUNETTE. A semicircular window or panel.

METOPES. The space between the Doric triglyphs.

MOSAIC. Decorative surfaces formed by small cubes of glass and/or stone.

MULLIONS. Narrow strips which divide the panels of glass in a window.

NARTHEX. A long arcaded porch or vestibule forming an entrance into the church.

NAVE. The main body of the church containing the central aisle and generally wider than any side aisles.

NEOCLASSICAL. The style dominant in Europe from about 1760 to 1790 reflecting new eclectic attitudes toward antiquity as a source for modern investigation.

NICHE. A recess (usually semicircular or arched) in a wall, pier, etc., designed to hold a statue or other object.

NORMAN. An English style popular in the eleventh and twelfth centuries roughly synonymous with Romanesque.

OCULUS. Any circular or oval window or opening.

ONION DOME. Dome characterized by its unique shape of a large onion resting on its top. Usually associated with Byzantine architecture.

ORDER. The essential elements by which the classical styles are identified: column, base, shaft, capital, and entablature with architrave, frieze, cornice.

PALLADIAN WINDOW. Named after the Italian architect Andrea Palladio (1508–80). A window characteristic of the neoclassical styles usually with an arched window flanked by narrow, square-headed windows.

PARAPET. A low protective wall usually located at the edge of a roof.

PAVILION. The part of the building which projects from the center or ends of the building.

PEDIMENT. A triangular gable, generally located above an entablature, which acts as a finish to the end of a sloping roof. Also an ornamental feature located above window or door openings.

PENDENTIVE. Designed to serve as the transitional element between a dome and its supporting arches.

PERPENDICULAR STYLE. Derived from English Gothic architecture and characterized by strong vertical lines.

PIER. A support of masonry for sustaining vertical pressure.

PILASTER. An engaged column (often rectangular) which functions as a pier or decorative element.

PINNACLE. Upright ornamental architectural element used to terminate a gable or buttress. Usually capped by a spire.

PODIUM. A raised platform where announcements are made or where the Scripture is read. Also, a continuous pedestal or base on which a building is placed.

PORTAL. A doorway and its surrounding architectural composition.

PORTICO. A structure consisting of a pediment or entablature supported by columns. Usually located at a building's entry.

PRAIRIE SCHOOL. A group of early-twentieth-century architects of the Chicago area who designed buildings emphasizing horizontal lines, responding to the flatness of the Midwestern prairie, in the manner of Frank Lloyd Wright.

PULPIT. A raised platform or table where the sermon is delivered.

PYRAMIDAL ROOF. A roof in the form of a pyramid or a hipped roof which has a relatively short ridge thereby allowing the sloping sides to nearly meet at a point.

QUATRE-FOIL TRACERY. Tracery which has four small arc openings separated by cusps (i.e., points formed by the intersection of foils).

QUOINS. Slightly projecting cornerstones usually laid so faces are alternately large then small.

RENAISSANCE. The term applied to the reintroduction of classic architecture in Europe during the fifteenth and sixteenth centuries.

REREDOS. A decorative screen located behind the altar.

RIB. A projecting band on a ceiling or vault.

ROMANESQUE. A style characterized by the use of the rounded arch and rounded vault.

ROSE WINDOW. A circular window filled with tracery to form a stylized rose or wheel pattern. Also called a wheel window.

ROSETTE. A circular ornament decorated through carving, painting, or molding to resemble a stylized rose.

RUSTICATION. A type of masonry work in which the individual stone blocks have a roughened surface and are emphasized by recessed joints.

SASH. A glazed wooden frame which slides up and down through the use of pulleys.

SCREEN. A partition separating the choir from the nave.

SOFFIT. The underside of any architectural feature, as of an arch, lintel, cornice, overhang, etc.

SPANDREL. The area between two arches.

SPIRE. The tapered termination of a tower.

SPLAY. The diagonal surface created by the cutting away of the window jamb allowing more light to enter.

STEPPED GABLE. A gable whose sides have essentially formed a series of steps following the slope of the roof.

STEEPLE. A tower crowned by a spire.

STRING COURSE. A horizontal band of masonry running along the outside of the building.

TRACERY. Decorative carving (usually of stone) generally found in Gothic-style windows.

TRANSEPT. A transverse arm of a cruciform church which perpendicularly crosses the nave.

TRIGLYPHS. Blocks which form, with vertical channels between, a distinguishing feature in the frieze of the Doric entablature.

TURRET. A small tower usually found at the corners of a larger structure.

TYMPANUM. A triangular surface with sculpture bounded by the sloping and horizontal cornices of a pediment. Also an arched sculptural area located above the doors of a church.

VAULT. An arched covering in stone or brick.

VERNACULAR. A style of architecture exemplifying the most common techniques, decorative features, and materials of a particular period, region, or group of people.

VOLUTES. The scroll or spiral occurring in Ionic, Corinthian, and composite capitals.

WAINSCOT. Term used for wood paneling or, more specifically, the lower few feet of an interior wall when it is finished differently from the rest of the wall.

WATERLINE. An inclined surface located on top of a projection such as a cornice, sill, etc., designed to throw off rainwater. Also called a water table, off-set, or weathering.

Bibliography

Armstrong, Foster. "The Forms of Cleveland's Sacred Structures," in "Special Issue: Cleveland Sacred Landmarks." *Gamut* (1990): 4–15.

Barrett, Timothy H. "Faith, Form, and Function: Ecclesiastical Architecture in Cuyahoga County." In *Sacred Landmarks: A Selected Exhibit of Existing Ecclesiastical Structures in Cuyahoga County,* edited by Cuyahoga County Archives. Cleveland: Cuyahoga County Archives, 1979.

Cigliano, Jan. *Showplace of America: Cleveland's Euclid Avenue, 1850–1910.* Kent, Ohio: Kent State Univ. Press, 1991.

Cleveland Landmarks Commission. Archival Records. Department of City Planning, City Hall, Cleveland.

George, Victoria, and Drew Rolik. "Tremont's Churches." *Habitat,* Feb. 9, 1990, 6.

Hitchcock, Henry Russell. *Architecture: 19th and 20th Centuries.* Baltimore: Penguin Books, 1958.

Hooper, Mary. "These Hallowed Halls." *The Plain Dealer Magazine,* Dec. 22, 1958, 10–11, 14–15.

Hynes, Michael J. *The History of the Diocese of Cleveland: Origin and Growth, 1847–1952.* Cleveland: Catholic Diocese of Cleveland, 1953.

Janson, William C. "The New St. Vitus Church of Cleveland." *Building Arts* 7 (Oct. 1932): 5–7, 15.

Johannesen, Eric. *Cleveland Architecture, 1876–1976.* Cleveland: Western Reserve Historical Society, 1979.

150 Years of Mission to Greater Cleveland, 1832–1982. Cleveland: Cleveland Baptist Association, 1982.

Parish Papers. Archives. Catholic Diocese of Cleveland.

Record of the Founding of St. James Church, August 18, 1857, vol. 1. Office of the County Recorder, Cleveland.

Romansky, Carl, ed. *St. Colman Centennial Celebration, 1880–1980.* Cleveland: Privately published, 1980.

Rose, William G. *Cleveland: The Making of a City.* 1950. Kent, Ohio: Kent State Univ. Press, 1990.

Schofield, Mary Peale. *Landmark Architecture of Cleveland.* Pittsburgh: Ober Park Associates, 1976.

Trinity Cathedral, Cleveland: Historical and Architectural Guide. Cleveland: Altar Society of Trinity Cathedral, 1912.

The Urban Design Center of Northeast Ohio. *Buckeye-Woodland: A Housing Design Portfolio.* Kent, Ohio: Privately published, 1991.

Van Tassel, David D., and John J. Grabowski, eds. *The Encyclopedia of Cleveland History.* Bloomington: Indiana Univ. Press, 1987.

Whitney, James, and Thomas Hallet. "Notable Stained Glass in Cleveland," in "Special Issue: Cleveland Sacred Landmarks." *Gamut* (1990): 35–44.

Wilson, Ella Grant. *Famous Old Euclid Avenue of Cleveland, at One Time Called the Most Beautiful Street in the World.* Cleveland: Evangelical Press, 1932.

Works Progress Administration. *Parishes of the Catholic Diocese of Cleveland, History and Records.* Ohio Historical Records Survey Project, Service Division. Cleveland: Cadillac Press, 1942.

Wyman, John. *Seventy-five Years of Grace: Grace Lutheran Church History.* Cleveland: Privately published, 1973.

Newspapers

The Call and Post 1974
The Catholic Universe Bulletin 1975
Cleveland News 1934–59
Cleveland Plain Dealer 1910–90
Cleveland Press 1926–78
Daily True Democrat 1853

Index

A Guide to Cleveland's Sacred Landmarks
was composed in 10/13 Times with Optima Bold display
on a Xyvision system with Linotronic output
by BookMasters, Inc.;
printed by sheet-fed offset
on 70-pound Warren Lustro Dull acid-free stock,
Smyth sewn with paper covers printed in two colors
on 12-point stock and film laminated
by Thomson-Shore, Inc.;
designed by Will Underwood;
and published by
The Kent State University Press
KENT, OHIO 44242